Faith in Education at the
Skidaway Island Benedictine Mission

Faith in Education

at the Skidaway Island Benedictine Mission

LAURA SEIFERT

The University of Georgia Press

Athens

Most University of Georgia Press titles are
available from popular e-book vendors.

Printed digitally

Library of Congress Control Number: 2024016835
ISBN 9780820367200 (hardback)
ISBN 9780820367217 (paperback)
ISBN 9780820367231 (epub)
ISBN 9780820367224 (pdf)

For Sebastian and all the children in the
Savannah–Chatham County Public School System.
May you finally get the public schools you deserve.

Contents

Illustrations

Acknowledgments

Special thanks and eternal gratitude go to my crew chiefs: undergraduate research assistants Amy Butler, Chase Freeman, and Kaylee Maricle Freeman. I would like to thank Sean Burgess for coordinating fieldwork permissions and paperwork, Mal Welch for her leadership, and Blake Caldwell, Archaeology Committee chair, for her endless enthusiasm, excellent organization, and just being a gracious host. Additional special thanks go to Andy Dyer and his family for the opportunity to do the archaeological fieldwork for this project and for allowing students to participate. The fieldwork for this project would have never happened without all of you.

Every archaeology project is only as good as its crew. The field crew collects your data, so remember to treat them kindly. My field crew included Amy Butler, Sara Reynolds, Reinali Cermeno, Ana Beasley, Aerin Dalman, Will Skinner, Joshua Glossop, J. C. Jones, Pam Imholz, Ethan Marshall, Robert Masters, Maddie Dinges, Victor Richardson, Kaylee Maricle, Ashley Johnston, Chris Lopez, Ayana Brown, Ethan Marshall, Eric Fields, Alice Evans, Vanessa Ilovar, Shane Hoeksema, David Porcile, Chase Freeman, Nicole Wentz, Tim Ellers, Sandra Seifert, Tatyana Callier, Mrs. Callier, Austin Webb, Rebecca Hinely, Gimal Evans, Jenna Ason, Sofia Rodriquez Vincens, Kara Brinson, Destine Burgess, Kelly Westfield, J. Philip Ross, Benjamin Holland, Emanuel Vincent, and Reagan Benton. Benedictine Military School students also volunteered in the field: Michael Dolor, Jimmy Ware, Robby Fenney, Vivan Ragusa, Gavin Lambert, Zachary Tate, and Evan Page. Savannah State University professor Dr. Deborah Johnson-Simon and her students Chelsea Caldwell and Jordan Milton volunteered as well. Lab work was conducted by Tyronne Moss, Morgan Baker, Ananda Shade, Gaolxong Her, Margenta Freeman, Reinali Cermeno, Pam Imholz, Madison Williams, Kelly Marden, Christopher Caster, Johnnae' Stephenson, Angela Nicole de Vega, Jessica Longoria, Maya Snyder, Lauren Boivin, McKenzie Levesque, Jennifer Murphy, Christina Lopez, Nicole Kirby, Logan Corde, Jennifer Yanes, Mabel Vizcama, Ziomara Rivera, Luis Simon, Tiger Thitakham, Mariana Sferelli, J. C. Jones, Nicole Wentz, Farren Smith, Nicole Bennet, Emma York, Allison Manning, and Emanuel Vincent.

Behind every history book is a group of librarians, curators, registrars, and collection managers who helped the author access information and collections. I am indebted to Steven Smith at the Massie Heritage Center, the late Father Andrew Campbell of Saint Vincent Archabbey, Father Ronald Gatman and Father Frank Ziemkiewicz at Benedictine Military School, Mary Davis-Brown and Brenda Taylor at the Savannah-Chatham County Public School System archives, Simon Donoghue at the Belmont Monastery archive, and Stephanie Braddy, director of Archives & Records Management at the Diocese of Savannah. The always cheerful, never failing team at Bull Street Library including the Georgia Room and Interlibrary Loan folks are some of Savannah's treasures. I am grateful to three anonymous reviewers who helped improve this book in several ways. Thanks to Jerome Oetgen for his enormous body of work on Saint Vincent and Abbot Wimmer as well as his clarification on specific details in articles that are decades old!

Thanks to Dr. Lisa Hesse and John Roberson for consulting (aka the free advice). Forsyth Farmers' Market staff graciously allowed me to join their PE sessions. Y'all have helped put more, diverse, thoughtful voices in my head and immeasurably improved my analysis of the mission and its peoples (especially our fearless PE leader Mark Bowen). I am grateful to LaQuandra Bundrage (Miss B) and Dr. Latrisha Chattin for their time and for sharing their expertise with the current Savannah-Chatham County Public School System.

To Barbara Bruno, who admits that she likes to start things and then let other people run them . . . Digging Savannah was your brainstorm that became my first child. I am eternally grateful for that first syllabus that got me started and for the advice, ranting, and support over my years at Armstrong. I never would have made it out alive without your help. I am grateful to Dr. Deborah Johnson-Simon for the encouragement to persist. You are an inspiration when it comes to persistence and getting the project done. Early readers (Sandra Seifert, Jenny Kyle, Jen Donaldson, Kyle Griffith, and Dr. Alena Pirok) were more cheerleader than critique, but were invaluable nonetheless. I am eternally grateful to my parents, who are veteran public school teachers, for the lifelong education in public education and for the support despite my decision to become a teacher. And because the spouse is always last, thanks to Kyle and Sebastian for doing most of the yard work (in August, in Georgia) while I edited this manuscript.

Author's Note

I acknowledge the Indigenous people who occupied Skidaway Island for approximately four thousand years. Guale people left the island around the mid-1400s or early 1500s AD, and no evidence has been found that Indigenous people were living on the island when it was colonized by Europeans (Elliott and Holland, *Archaeological Survey of Priests Landing*, 8–9). This deeper history of the island and the reasons for the Guale's departure are far outside the scope of this book, which is about the people who, willingly or not, colonized Skidaway Island.

In recent years, the horrific truth about many schools for orphaned children and children from lower socioeconomic classes has emerged in the mainstream news. These places include Indigenous boarding schools throughout the United States and Canada, Catholic-run industrial schools in Ireland, and reform schools such as the Arthur G. Dozier School for Boys in Florida. While most of these stories have long been known within their respective communities, the larger world is now becoming aware of the unimaginable abuse that took place and that many children were killed.[1] In researching the Skidaway Island mission, I did not find any evidence of outright abuse or evidence that children were taken from their parents without permission.

I use the terms "freedmen" and "freedwomen," "freedpeople," "Black American," and "African American" mostly interchangeably throughout the book. While I acknowledge that African American is a much more recent term, I use it for several reasons. One, it simply makes for a better, less onerous reading experience to vary terms. It also helps to remind the reader that although freedpeople were now fully American citizens, they were often denied the basic rights of citizenship.

In referring to religious personnel, I use priests' last names (with or without their titles). I preferred to continue this pattern with the lay brothers, but often their last names were not recorded. So for consistency I always use the brothers' first names and apologize to them for using a less respectful form of address.

I have preserved all quotes with spelling mistakes and abbreviations intact. For ease of reading, I moved "[*sic*]" to the end of quotes with multiple errors. In a book about education, I feel it is important to preserve the written language as it was found in the original documents, because this provides important information about individuals' education levels.

Faith in Education at the
Skidaway Island Benedictine Mission

CHAPTER 1

A Brief Sketch of Skidaway Island

October 1, 2016, was typical—gorgeous, sunny, and mild. We are gifted these October days in exchange for Savannah's stormy steam bath that others call July and August. In the speckled shade cast by young trees, two Benedictine Military School students began excavating an archaeological unit (rectangular hole) under the supervision of my undergraduate research assistant. We chose this exact spot based on last semester's survey; the presence of a dislocated, tipsy-looking brick pier; and some educated guesswork about wall locations extrapolated from a nearby tabby-walled basement. As I made my rounds between excavation areas, the students proudly announced they had found a spoon and an arrowhead. Impressed but mildly skeptical, I perused their bag of artifacts and discovered they were right on both accounts. The large tablespoon was relatively modern (early twentieth century) and in good shape. The "arrowhead," or "projectile point" in archaeological terminology, was a beautiful dusty pink chert, broken at the base with a small bit of tabby adhered to one side.

Normally, a projectile point found in topsoil and this far out of stratigraphic context would be fun but mostly uninformative. However, this particular point, dating to the Late Archaic (between twenty-four hundred and forty-two hundred years ago), had a story to tell. When its original Indigenous owners broke the point, they disposed of it in a shell midden, a trash pile filled primarily with mollusk shells discarded from meals. Since stone is a hardy material, the projectile point lay unaltered for thousands of years, only to be exhumed in the later 1700s or early 1800s. Colonists commonly raided shell middens to harvest oyster shells, a raw ingredient for making tabby, a shell-and-sand-based building material similar to concrete. Our intrepid projectile point was swept up with the shells and incorporated into tabby walls; perhaps it was even part of the basement crumbling but still present on site today. Over time, the plantation building decayed and was razed. Benedictine monks acquired the plantation in 1877, reincorporating the old tabby basement into their new wooden monastery and church. Time and the climate again took their toll on the buildings, which were dismantled in 1949, and the now exposed tabby continued to degrade. The projectile point fell into the soil again, this time with traces of its tabby journey still attached, only to be recovered by teenage student "descendants" of the monks. Thus, in one artifact, the broad sketch of the site's history unfolds, much to the delight of the volunteer students who recovered the point.

PROJECT ORIGINS

The St. Benedict's school and monastery site was first archaeologically recorded in 1974 and given the state designation 9CH78 when the Landings residential community was undergoing initial development and completing federally required surveys. Because the site's importance was acknowledged, during the Landings' development phase a 0.62-acre lot was set aside to preserve the archaeological site's core.[1] However, this lot, today bounded on its four sides by the street, residential lots, and a golf course, is a tiny fraction of the whole site, which included a church, monastery, school, barn, other outbuildings, gardens, and plantation fields. Despite its protected status, the Landings staff monitoring the site have noticed bricks and other artifacts being looted since at least 1990.[2] In 2015, residents and staff became concerned when the adjacent undeveloped lot was sold, and the landowner intended to build a house, destroying any archaeological resources in the process. Fortunately, the new landowner, the Dyer family, approached the Landings staff and was willing to preserve or mitigate where possible. The interested parties reached an agreement so that my students and I could conduct archaeology until the landowner was ready to build the new house, and artifacts would be donated to the university for analysis and curation.

Armstrong State University students conducted the archaeological fieldwork and lab work for this project with help from Savannah State University and Benedictine Military School volunteers, under the direction of the author.[3] An all-volunteer crew (except one poorly paid undergraduate research assistant) made for slow work; however, twenty-five shovel test pits and ten 1-by-2-meter test units were dug during the spring and fall semesters of 2016 and 2017.[4] Volunteers gave up part of their weekends (in exchange for class extra credit in many cases). The vast majority of the students had never set foot on an archaeology site before, and the few who had a bit of experience were returning students taking a second class with me. This corps of "regulars" developed and were immensely helpful in orienting and supervising the completely new students. The immediacy of the project plus other institutional constraints meant there was no funding for "extras" such as wet screening or soil samples and little time to apply for grants. The impending construction meant time was short, and our actual time frame was unknown. So our scrappy little group charged forward. Excavations focused entirely on the Dyer property because of the imminent development. Although we could have continued excavating on the Landings' portion of the site after the development, no more excavations were undertaken, because the Landings lot is preserved in perpetuity. Archaeological ethics dictate that the best practice is to leave that lot undisturbed for future excavations.

In a May 2017 interview, Ronald Butchart, University of Georgia professor emeritus, stated of this project: "We're not going to get anything out of this work that scholars would say 'oh, shit, we didn't know that,' But I think, to the extent that anyone pays attention, for the people in that area to say 'oh there was a black school here in 1868? There was a black school here in 1875? Who was attending?'"[5] When the reporter pressed him, he also admitted, "I know of no archeological work done on freedmen's education, none whatsoever."[6] For the record, there have been four other archaeological excavations on nineteenth-century Black schools, all of which predate the American Civil War—the school at New Philadelphia, Illinois; the Old Elliot School in Bermuda; the Abiel Smith School in Boston; and the Parker Academy in Ohio, which was an integrated school.[7]

Archaeologists are familiar with, and mostly tired of, these statements. Archaeological data has been repeatedly proven to be equally valuable when compared with documents. Both data sets have their advantages and disadvantages, "truths" and biases. For this project, we have substantial collections of the monks' letters, newspaper articles, censuses, and other historical records, and even two contemporary photographs of the site. These documents are incredibly valuable for their first-person perspective, but the African American residents created very few of these records. The archaeology allows us equal access to the students, lay brothers, and monks.

By not doing archaeology, we risk losing the reality check that archaeology provides. Archaeology can reveal details that went unwritten, either too ordinary to be considered important at the time or too scandalous to disclose. For a local example, workers at the Central of Georgia Railroad repair shops in downtown Savannah were absolutely forbidden from drinking alcohol at work, for obvious safety reasons. Oral histories and company documents confirm the company's policy that workers caught drinking alcohol were automatically fired. So when preservationists removed the Tender Frame Shop floorboards during a restoration project, they were stunned to discover 655 liquor bottles tucked away (plus a few animal bones and half of a coconut shell). Archaeology revealed the actual human behavior and foibles not recorded in the historical record.

This project's archaeology did not reveal anything quite like that bombshell, but the artifacts and our understanding that comes from their analysis add texture to the story. Does it matter the precise location of the school in relation to the church? Does it matter if the students and monks ate on mismatched plates? Or from bowls? These may not be revelatory details, but these tiny details help form a picture of the people who inhabited this home, church, and school. Artifacts show daily life in all its drudgery and glory much more than a stark list of who was present and when.

The bitter truth is that our limited time and resources combined with the uncertainty of our time line meant that we could not excavate nearly as much as needed, and the historical record dominates in the stories that follow. While these stories are mostly told through the more abundant historical record, archaeological finds are woven throughout. The book draws together the recovered archaeological data and extensive Benedictine archives to reconstruct the intersecting lives of monks, students, lay brothers, and African American neighbors on Skidaway Island, Georgia, to understand the cultural power dynamics underlying this ultimately unsuccessful school. Specific stories emerge not only from the collection as a whole but also from individual artifacts, including architectural materials such as glass from arched church windows, writing slate and slate pencil fragments, a kerosene lamp, and harmonica fragments. When an assemblage lacks variety and many diagnostic artifacts, as this collection does, archaeologists are forced to rely much more heavily than is generally desirable on individual artifacts to tell the story. As Monica L. Smith indicates, "The difficulty in analyzing one-of-a-kind objects usually places them in an anecdotal role; however, they can be used to substantiate interpretations of site function and intrasite variability, and in some cases may provide the only data for certain aspects of site interpretation."[8] Some of these artifacts tell simple stories; others are more complex. For example, few will be surprised that students were using slate writing boards, but the presence of a harmonica and its implications for African American musical traditions are more intricate.

ARCHAEOLOGY OF SCHOOLS

Skidaway Island's Benedictine monastery and school is a singular and highly significant archaeological site, which remained remarkably intact, with distinct, undisturbed soil strata. Little modern material (defined here as roughly post-1950) was found at all. This site is also important because, to date, no other archaeological research on American Benedictine monasteries has been found. Although this site is not a "typical" American school, it helps to understand what has been found on other school sites for comparison. Unfortunately, archaeological research on schoolhouses is scarce, and investigations of African American schoolhouses are even more rare, despite schoolhouses' importance and ubiquity in the American experience. By the late 1800s, schoolhouses were very common public buildings, as typical as churches. Increased state involvement made the schoolhouse a "recognizable architectural form."[9] Our classic image of the one-room schoolhouse was indeed a reality in most every small town in America. Schoolhouses were often the community focal point, hosting religious and social activities in addition to education. The 1890s through the 1930s was a time of school consolidation, and many schools changed from one-room schoolhouses to multiroom buildings with professional teachers.[10]

The few archaeological sites that have been excavated make for valuable comparisons, not just for similarities, but for their differences from the Benedictines' mission site. Most studies looked at one-room schoolhouses from the nineteenth century, although there is a growing body of research on early twentieth-century schoolhouses.[11] Previous archaeological investigations of schools have focused on identifying the schoolhouses and associated outbuildings, understanding their construction and remodeling phases, and exploring issues of lighting, heating, furnishing, and sanitation.[12] Sites often had a low artifact density; therefore archival work is often critical in interpreting schoolhouse sites.[13] Most artifacts were architectural, and few educational artifacts, such as slate pencils and ink bottles, were present. Artifacts were concentrated within and around the schoolhouse foundations. Domestic artifacts recovered are often from the site's dual use as a social center for community gatherings. Jane Eva Baxter theorized that the schoolhouse sites have few artifacts because they were deliberately kept clean, as teachers modeled and practiced cleanliness.[14] Also, teachers limited children's access to material culture during the school day so they could focus on learning. Expensive school supplies were likely conserved and repaired when possible rather than discarded. Toys are common artifacts on school sites, particularly jacks and marbles, which are small, portable, and used in group play. Dolls are rare. Homemade toys, more common in rural areas, are less likely to survive in the archaeological record because they are often made of organic materials (such as yarn dolls).

Few African American schoolhouses have been excavated archaeologically. Researchers at New Philadelphia, Illinois, have tentatively identified the location of the town's African American schoolhouse. Frank McWhorter, a free person of color, established New Philadelphia as an integrated town. Education was a priority, and the "schoolhouse served as an important focus of community life," as there was no public school for African American children in 1850s and 1860s Illinois.[15] Documentary evidence, particularly deeds and oral histories, as well as geophysical evidence, led archaeologists to explore Lots 1 and 2 of Block 8, suspected to contain the 1848 school. Although small amounts of artifacts were found (lamp chimney glass, whiteware, yellow ware, nails, and brick), no features were found. It is likely the architecture was very ephemeral, and therefore little evidence remains of the school. Several nearby features contained slate fragments, adding to the evidence that a school was in the area. However, these school artifacts are only 0.9 percent of the entire assemblage.[16]

Anna Agbe-Davies also excavated the Old Elliot School, which was established by and for Black Bermudians after emancipation. Established in 1848, this school is a powerful symbol, even more so as it is still standing. The school's original trustees were twelve men who bought the land, raised funds, and built the school themselves, as many were craftsmen. Bermuda's government contributed money for annual expenses. The first class had thirty-four boys and girls who learned the basics: spelling, reading, writing, grammar, math, geography, catechism, and sewing.

Two trenches were excavated under the floor in order to understand the building's construction and use. While Trench 2 proved to have modern soils and mixed deposits, Trench 1 contained intact strata and features with fragments of writing slates, slate pencils, pen nibs, shoe fragments, buttons, a glass marble, a scissor fragment, graphite pencil leads, and metal ferrules. The artifact findings conform to the expectations of a school and taken together are a "non-domestic artefact pattern." There are few ceramics or animal bones, and interestingly, the educational artifacts are concentrated in the older layers. Major repairs, including a new roof and raised walls, were identified. The entrance was changed at some point, but the original door on the north wall was Gothic Revival.[17] "In addition to being popular, the Gothic style was thought to be suitable for settings where instruction (spiritual or intellectual) and contemplation were the primary activities."[18]

Boston's Abiel Smith School served Black children from 1835 to 1855 and was adjacent to the African Meeting House, an influential social institution for nineteenth-century free African Americans in Beacon Hill. Both institutions shared missions and goals regarding the abolition movement, educational opportunities, and community activism. Archaeology was conducted at the Smith School between 1991 and 1997 and again in 2005. The 2005 investigations uncovered features including "brick pavements, builder's trenches, a complex drainage and sanitation system (brick drains and privies)," and artifacts such as marbles, slate pencils, and school lunch remains.[19] A fourth school, the Parker Academy, opened in the late 1830s in New Richmond, Ohio. Parker Academy was an integrated school open to anyone regardless of age, gender, or race. It is currently undergoing research, and at the time of this writing, researchers have not yet formally published.[20]

These four schools, while geographically diverse, are similar in that they contained architectural materials and a sprinkling of school-related artifacts but often

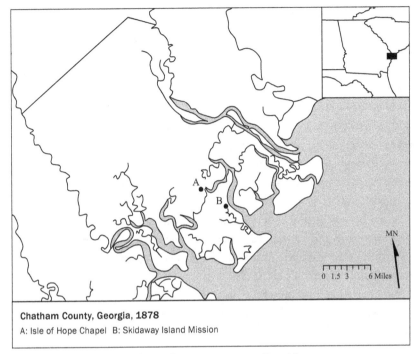

Chatham County, Georgia, 1878
A: Isle of Hope Chapel B: Skidaway Island Mission

MAP 1. Chatham County is the northernmost county on Georgia's coast.

little else. The Skidaway site mostly follows this pattern, although as a monastery and boarding school, more domestic artifacts are present. In addition, the Skidaway site bears traces of its prior residents all the way back to Indigenous occupation.

SKIDAWAY ISLAND AND HAMPTON PLACE PLANTATION

Skidaway Island is typical of Georgia's coastal sea islands, sharing much in common historically and geologically with the surrounding islands (see map 1). Despite persistent, unconfirmed reports of a Spanish mission on Skidaway Island's northeastern edge, no archaeological or documentary evidence has been located so far.[21] Evidence suggests that Indigenous people had left Skidaway Island several hundred years prior to European colonization, so there was little reason for the Spanish to build a mission there. Colonial settlement of Skidaway Island began in 1734, the year after James Oglethorpe established Georgia, the thirteenth English colony, with Savannah as the capital. The colonists' purpose was to guard some of the many water passages into Savannah against Spanish incursion. Tobias Lotter's 1740 map indicates they built two small forts placed at the north and south ends of the island.[22] The early settlement consisted of five families and six single men, each given fifty-acre land grants. None of the settlers were professional farmers or sol-diers, but they were expected to farm the island and do guard shifts. The colonists all left or died by 1740.[23]

The next decade brought political changes to Georgia that resulted in more per-manent colonial settlement. As the trustees gave way to a royal governor, landown-ers were allowed to live off the island, and, more significantly, slavery was legalized in 1750. Between 1745 and 1752, eighteen individuals received Skidaway Island land grants totaling 4,500 acres; from 1754 to 1771, approximately twenty-two people received twenty-nine additional Skidaway Island land grants.[24] One of these grants was given to Henry Yonge Sr., who received 453 acres in 1755. He occasionally lived on this plantation, which he named Orangedale. This plantation would eventually host the Benedictines' school more than 120 years later. By 1762, Yonge owned over 1,000 acres and was the only landowner who continued to grow indigo and silk, while others grew agricultural staples. Orangedale, later called Cedar Grove, stayed in the Yonge family until 1785, when it was sold to Hampton Lillibridge and became part of his Hampton Place plantation.

In 1800, Lillibridge added to his holdings, purchasing Thomas Gibbons's adja-cent tract for $1,500. Hampton Place remained in the family for several generations, passing first to Hampton's daughter Henrietta Lillibridge, who married James Bilbo in 1812. Their eight surviving children inherited the property, collectively selling it to Alvin N. Miller in 1855 for $3,000 to settle their parents' estate and split the inher-itance. But first, John Bilbo had to buy back his brother Hampton's share at sheriff's auction, because in 1852 Hampton mortgaged his share, which was subsequently foreclosed upon. Alvin Miller sold the property to William Wade four years later, apparently swapping the plantation for a lot in Savannah "known as lot number five . . . with the appurtenances and machinery thereon, and for diverse other valuable considerations," all of which were detailed in a separate indenture.[25] At this time, the plantation was extensively developed, and the sale included all additions and contents such as buildings, a stable, yards, gardens, stock, hogs, cows, carts, wagons, boats, "plantation utencils, household and kitchen furniture, corn, fodder, and pro-visions."[26] Three enslaved people (Harry, Hetty, and Maria) were also included in the sale dated May 28, 1859.[27] A few days later, William Wade flipped the property to Bishop John Barry for $9,000.[28] Bishop Barry intended to build an orphanage on the property, but he died in November 1859, halting these plans.[29]

Skidaway Island saw little action and consequently little damage during any of the eighteenth- and nineteenth-century wars. The only notable Revolutionary War conflict was a 1782 skirmish on the island's south side. Although some loyalist landowners had their plantations confiscated after the war, most were passed down through the generations, and the plantations stayed relatively stable. At the height of the plantation era, an estimated two thousand residents, mostly enslaved people, inhabited the island, but by the Civil War approximately a thousand people remained.

The Confederates constructed three batteries on the Wilmington River at Priest's Landing, which is very near the monastery site; however, they were only occupied for a few short and fairly uneventful months. In March 1862, Robert E. Lee decided the Confederate coastal positions were too widespread and could not be successfully defended. Tybee, Wassaw, Green, and Skidaway islands were abandoned, and the troops were pulled back to Savannah with Fort Pulaski and Fort Jackson as the main Savannah River defenses. On March 24, the Union army took Skidaway Island.[30]

Cornelius Redding Hanleiter of the Georgia Light Artillery was stationed on Skidaway Island during this brief period. Hanleiter was a Savannah native and a prominent Atlanta businessman in the printing, telegraph, and publishing industries. He served nearly the whole course of the war, volunteering for Skidaway Island duty on December 15, 1861. His diary has several insights into the state of Hampton Place Plantation. He wrote in January 1862:

> I visited the points of interest near the Forts. From the cupalo [sic] of the old mansion—which is in an unfinished condition except for the first story, and that in a very dilapidated state—I had the finest and widest view since my arrival on the Island. . . . This "Place" is one of the most desirable imaginable for a permanent residence, and I would very much like to occupy it as such were I able to own and improve it properly. The old unfinished Mansion, I learn, has a sad history, however. Two owners, in turn, were broken in their efforts to complete it, and several years ago it was purchased by the Catholic Bishop of Savannah, with a view to establish here, and convert the Mansion into, a Female Asylum (or, I suppose, a Monastery). The death of the good Bishop prevented the carrying into effect his object. The "Place," which embraces some seven or eight hundred acres, is still owned by the Bishop's successor, or the Church, but was rented and occupied during the last year by Mr. George Schley, of Augusta. The Mansion, for some time past, has been occupied as a Hospital for our troops.[31]

Hanleiter also reported on the mansion's fate when the Confederates abandoned the island.

I learned afterward, however, that the cannonading was the work of a party of Yankees, who threw a few shells on Skidaway about our Batteries, and, finding that point unoccupied, landed and raised a Federal Flag on the Red-top House formerly occupied by us as a Hospital and Observatory. This done, they took to their boats and hastened to their ships. A Officer of the Georgia Huzzas, being on duty on the Island at the time, had observed their movements— and as soon as the Vandals had got fairly on their way to their ships, entered the house, hauled down their Flag (which he brought away with him) and set fire to the house![32]

This act of arson caused such a conflagration that it was visible from Fort Pulaski, over ten miles away as the crow flies.[33]

After the war, some newly freed people stayed on the island, while others immigrated to Skidaway under General William Sherman's Special Field Order No. 15, famously referred to as "forty acres and a mule." Field Order No. 15 originated from a meeting held at the Green-Meldrim House with Sherman, Secretary of War Edwin Stanton, and twenty free Black men. At Stanton's request, Sherman invited prominent African American men, mostly preachers, to meet and advise him on "the negro question," meaning what were the best policies to integrate formerly enslaved people into new jobs, housing, and other basic necessities. Garrison Frazier, the elected spokesman, emphasized that land ownership was the most important key for freedom and Black success. Four days later, on January 16, 1865, Sherman issued Special Field Order No. 15 allowing for distribution of coastal land in forty-acre tracts. The land was confiscated Confederate land from Charleston, South Carolina, to the St. Johns River, Florida, and spanned thirty miles inland from the coast. No white people were allowed in the "Sherman Reservation" except military personnel on administrative duties. Sherman's goals were primarily to punish the white Confederate planters for starting the war and to stop Black "refugees" from following the Union army into the Carolinas by providing an alternative, safe space only for African Americans. Sherman never intended these settlements to be a permanent solution.[34] He later wrote, "All that was designed by these special field orders was to make temporary provisions for the freedmen and their families during the rest of the war, or until Congress should take action in the premises."[35]

Informational meetings about Sherman's new policy were held. The first was at Second African Baptist Church in Savannah. The Montmollin building, which held a slave market until several days before Sherman's arrival, hosted another meeting. Here, after prayers and hymns, Union army representatives answered questions, such as, what kind of land title would freedmen receive if they agreed to settle on the confiscated sea islands? Freedmen were reluctant to uproot their families without a guarantee but were told, "You will have the faith and honor of the United States." While some declared they would become settlers, others did not.[36] Their questions proved wise and prescient. By the end of the year, Lincoln was assassinated, and his successor, President Andrew Johnson, had revoked Sherman's Special Field Order No. 15, allowing white owners to reclaim their land.

In the meantime, Union general Rufus Saxton was placed in charge of island settlement. Saxton, per his orders, distributed plots with possessory titles, which gave settlers the right to use the land, but, critically, the new occupants did not own the land. By the standards of the day, Saxton should be considered a Black ally, who advocated for distributing fee simple land titles and was ultimately dismissed from the Freedmen's Bureau for it.[37] "Retired" military mules were also given to settlers as they were available (hence the "forty acres and a mule" moniker). By June 1865, forty thousand people had settled four hundred thousand acres across the Sherman Reservation.[38] Realistically, the land tracts distributed on Skidaway Island were not always forty-acre plots. The allotments ranged from ten to forty acres per family or individual, with 44 percent of the settlers receiving forty acres and the rest getting between ten and thirty acres.[39]

The *Savannah Daily Republican* in June 1865 reported, "upwards of one thousand colored people [are] living on Skidaway Island, nearly all of whom have been transported there since the middle of February by the government . . . several hundred acres of land are in an advanced state of cultivation, on which there is a large quantity of fine corn, a small lot of cotton, an abundance of snapbeans, cucumbers, potatoes, watermelons, and cantaloupes." The author noted "a degree of prosperity that was highly satisfactory, surpassing the expectations of the most sanguine friends of the Freedmen."[40] The Freedmen's Bureau registered ninety-eight individuals or families totaling approximately four hundred people on 2,820 acres of land. Women led several of the families. There were likely more than four hundred settlers, as some did not get registered due to the generalized chaos, and then the program ended abruptly before it ever had a chance to succeed.

Reverend Ulysses Houston was one of the first to assist freedmen in settling the islands. Shortly after General Saxton's February 2, 1865, speech at Second African Baptist Church, Houston and the Skidaway Island colonists laid out a village with forty-acre farm lots. Settlers drew from a lottery to determine which lot they received. Parcels were also set aside for a school and a new church. Before Emancipation, the Sunbury Baptist Association recognized an African American Baptist Church on Skidaway Island, but it is unclear whether this church had an actual building or was a congregation that met wherever possible.[41] A butcher by trade, Houston also brought along five hundred animal hides, with plans to sell them up north. These funds would be used to purchase a portable saw mill so buildings could be constructed. A government was established, with Garrison Frazier elected the first governor. Later Houston would be governor. A sheriff and three inspectors were also elected. By June 1865, they had several hundred acres planted.[42]

Ulysses Houston was an enormously influential and accomplished leader, both during and after the Civil War. He is primarily known as the First Bryan Baptist Church pastor from his ordination in 1861 until his death in 1889. He was also pastor to the Ogeechee Baptist Church, served two terms in the Georgia legislature starting in 1869, served in the Georgia Baptist State Convention and the Zion Baptist Association, helped found the Savannah Education Association, and was a charter member of the freemason's Eureka Lodge No. 1 AF & AM.[43] Houston was born into slavery in 1825 in Beaufort County, South Carolina. As a child, he was hired out to the military hospital in Savannah, where the patients taught him to read. Later he continued to work independently, paying his enslaver fifty dollars per month. Houston traveled extensively to obtain meat and animals for sale in his butcher shop, located in leased ground-floor space near City Market. Two stories above his shop was a slave market. The travel and retail interactions afforded him valuable opportunities to receive and share information among the enslaved and free Black population.[44] His network, literacy, and faith put him in a powerful leadership position at the war's end.

Reverend Houston's group moved back to Savannah within one year because President Lincoln's successor, Andrew Johnson, rescinded Special Field Order No. 15.[45] The September 1865 Circular No. 15 detailed the conditions under which Confederate land would be restored: proof of title and presidential pardon or oath of amnesty. Freedmen with land under cultivation could stay until after the crops were harvested, or they could be adequately compensated for their labor and crops. While most, but not all, confiscated sea island plantations were returned, on Skidaway Island all of the plantations were returned to their white owners.[46]

The sea islands resettlement project had numerous logistical problems beyond President Johnson's death blow. Congress established the Freedmen's Bureau in March 1865, so many received their possessory title and land too late for spring planting, and therefore some needed rations to bridge the gap until fall crops could be planted.[47] Although the Freedmen's Bureau did distribute some rations, most freedmen were self-sufficient. Even when settlers arrived early enough to cultivate spring crops, they often lacked basic resources such as equipment and seeds. Some simply did not want to work the land as they had under slavery, so on the sea islands, locals turned to their other skills to make a living. Fishing, crabbing, logging, hunting deer, and catching wild horses and cattle were all practiced rather than cultivation. Using their other skills allowed for more freedom and a different life. This new, independent lifestyle was precious, and African Americans were determined to protect it. Despite the threat of removal, Black militias and governments formed all along the coast to secure these new settlements.[48]

On Skidaway Island, a different tactic was used. In January 1866, African Americans refused to sign labor contracts with Joseph Waring, whose Sea Side Plantation was directly south of Hampton Place. Instead, the parties strictly leased land plots, so they were independent farmers rather than employees. Over 100 acres were leased to twelve African Americans at $2 per acre.[49] Three of the twelve renters had been given possessory titles by the Freedmen's Bureau and chose to continue their tenancy but at a reduced acreage. Joseph Green and another family member were given 30 acres by the Freedmen's Bureau. Under his new lease, Green rented 10 acres for $20 per year. John Mopson and his "plus one" received 40 acres on June 29, 1865. John Mabson (presumably but not definitely the same person) rented 10 acres and "half of the dwelling house" for $44 per year. Philip Young's five-member family worked 40 acres in 1865. In 1866, he and Saucho Minis shared two leases, one for a "house being the half of what was known as the nursery" and another for 15 acres of land. Their total yearly rent was $54.[50]

For comparison, Ossabaw Island, the next major island south of Skidaway, has a similar history of plantation life and slavery. Many freedmen who left Ossabaw Island bought land within ten years of leaving. Those who stayed were unable to buy land; however, they continued living in their homeplace. They maintained familial connections, knew the land intimately, and passed their culture between generations. Allison Dorsey states, "True, they may not have 'owned' Ossabaw, but they certainly occupied and controlled the cultural space."[51] This was also true on Skidaway. Land ownership remained in the same hands of white owners for decades, but at least several Black families lived for generations on the island, creating an African American homespace.

By 1868, the white Skidaway Island landowners had all successfully petitioned for the return of their land.[52] Despite this, an African American population persisted on the island and, like their Ossabaw neighbors, were determined to maintain their independence and freedom despite pressure. In mid-December 1868, Skidaway landowner Colonel William Symons had "seven of his own hands" working on the Skidaway Road for nine days; however, others refused to work "when called upon."[53] Symons, used to demanding work whenever it suited, was confronted with African American freedom and choice, and Symons was denied the labor he demanded.

Other examples show the residents' persistence and defense of their homespace. Newspaper reports detail conflicts between the island residents and local fishermen over control of the waters surrounding Skidaway. Two white fishermen, Charles Ross and Archibald Griffin, swore an affidavit in late December 1868 about their attempts to sail the waters surrounding Skidaway Island. The newspaper introduced the affidavit using inflammatory, racist language: "Two well-known fishermen, who, while in pursuit of their avocation, were fired upon from Skidaway Island by a mob of riotous negroes, who also announced their purpose to allow no white man to fish in those waters. The affidavit clearly shows the murderous intentions of the vagabonds, who live upon the islands below the city and their conduct is such as to call for immediate interference by the authorities."[54]

The fishermen said they were en route to Little Tybee Creek, passing by Skidaway Island, when a large group of freedmen fired on them from the old Confederate batteries with intent to kill. Further, the fishermen were told that the African Americans "ruled" the water and would not allow any outsiders to fish or collect oysters in these waters. The fishermen stated the attack was unprovoked.[55] A second affidavit was taken and printed the following day. This second statement was from two African American fishermen, Henry Miller and Benjamin Rivers, who had the same experience of being fired upon from the island, despite an earlier report that African Americans were allowed to fish without interference. This time, four Skidaway residents boarded their boat and brought the men to shore. Miller and Rivers were held and questioned about an arrest on Wilmington Island earlier in December. They were finally set free and reported their experience, saying they saw about twenty-seven armed freedmen on the island.[56] The resolution of these incidents is unknown. Since both white and African American fishermen were fired upon, the incidents are not simply about race. The residents were defending their homespace and livelihoods, despite the illegality of their actions.

As property of the Catholic Church, Hampton Place Plantation was not confiscated, so Bishop Gross continued to rent the land to tenants. During this time, the property was casually called "the Bishop's place" and was "occupied by a few negro tenants, who cultivated small fields, raising corn, sweet potatoes, watermelon and a little sea island cotton."[57] The bishop visited the property "for the purpose of inspecting" in 1873 with Father Lewis, Judge D. A. O'Byrne, and Col. William R. Symons, another Skidaway landowner whose land was confiscated, then returned in 1867. The party arrived via boat at William Ziegler's plantation, which was centrally located and bordering the island's eastern side. Then the party traveled overland to Hampton Place. "Passing along through the old settlement which was destroyed by the Confederate forces during the war as a military necessity, they were pleased and surprised at the beautiful and fresh appearance of the crops under the management of the colored farmers in that section."[58]

The men had traveled to Skidaway as part of property and infrastructure development discussions. The Chatham County Commissioners were forever debating whether to build a public road and bridge to Skidaway and how much G. W. DeRenne should be financially compensated for having the road cross his Isle of Hope property. This endless and terribly uninteresting debate was covered extensively in the newspapers for years. Judge O'Byrne was the lawyer for Skidaway landowners (including Bishop Gross) advocating for the road and bridge. The bishop's stated goal of starting a school and orphanage was among the reasons given for building the road. While the bishop offered a feel-good reason, the possibility of development was also a major impetus for the infrastructure. Proponents argued that with better access, more houses would be built, creating a bigger tax base, which would pay for the road.[59]

A bridge was not built at this time, but Bishop Gross would successfully recruit the Benedictines, who built the school and monastery a few years later. The school lasted until about 1900. The island's mostly African American population continued to live as tenants and sharecroppers until Prohibition-era illegal distilling operations made the island more dangerous, and dredging the Skidaway Narrows in 1905 and 1916 made the island more isolated. The local population slowly left, and the land began to return to forest. In 1941, Union Bag and Paper Company bought most of the island's central portion and logged the land for paper production until the mid-1950s. Concurrently, the Roebling family operated Modena Plantation on the north end. In the 1950s and 1960s, the island was used for camping, hunting, and fishing until the late 1960s, when plans were laid for Skidaway Island State Park, Skidaway Institute of Oceanography, and the Landings gated residential community. Development for these three institutions began in the early 1970s, and they remain the major uses of the island today.[60]

Skidaway Island shares a similar broad history with many of Georgia's sea islands—roughly five thousand years of Indigenous occupation that was ended by colonization. Enslaved laborers worked plantations, and then tenant farmers cultivated small farms. In the twentieth century, wealthy individuals built houses as summer retreats and later as full-time homes. The Benedictines' school and monastery is one chapter that differentiates Skidaway Island. The Benedictines' modest school would only leave a slight impression on the island itself, but seeds planted on this island would later bear fruit in Savannah through more schools and churches.

CHAPTER 2

The Radical Act of Education

Throughout the post-emancipation South, demand for African American education was overwhelming. The intense desire for education was seen in the immediate formation of ad hoc classrooms and schools, which were soon crowded or overflowing. African Americans were anxious to benefit from education, which meant steps toward full citizenship, civil rights, and self-determination. Literacy in particular opened many economic, civic, and personal doors. Literate citizens could petition the government, vote (at least the men could), hold governmental office, read the Bible, record family histories, and read contracts, which meant they could more fairly negotiate wages and labor. Education made land ownership more accessible, which was important for avoiding wage labor and building wealth; also, owning land allows for a greater sense of belonging and security in a community. While landowning is perhaps a rather capitalist way to create community, I argue the relative stability of land ownership provides an extra level of belonging, especially for people who experienced slavery and could have been sold away from their family and community at any time.[1] Literacy was valued because it meant self-empowerment, but this struggle "was not merely a fight for access to literacy and education, but one for freedom, citizenship, and a new post war social order."[2] Freedpeople were determined to gain the privileges and rights previously denied to them.[3]

The Black community focused on creating a right to schools, not just access to schools. Freedpeople understood the need to protect their educations; therefore, they struggled over who controlled African American education. Who should be teaching? What textbooks were used? Who would provide funding? In Savannah, this played out as a conflict between the Black Savannah Education Association (SEA) and the white American Missionary Association (AMA), whose members were there to help, but on their own terms. When the AMA representative Reverend S. W. Magill arrived, he assumed control in every sense. First, he assumed that he deserved to control the SEA schools. Second, by controlling the funding, Magill did take control of the schools, making decisions as he saw fit with no regard for the parents' wishes or the goals of the larger African American community.[4] For example, the AMA agreed to fund schools and pay teachers, but their condition was that the AMA administration demoted the African American teachers to assistants and replaced them with white teachers. The racist policies and systems developed after the Civil War formed the basis of our school systems, and these struggles would continue intensively through much of the twentieth century. Many of these structural problems remain even today.

ANTEBELLUM BLACK EDUCATION

The struggle over Black education began in the earliest days of slavery and became increasingly difficult through time. On December 29, 1829, the Georgia legislature passed a law declaring it illegal to teach an enslaved person or free person of color to read. This legislation also outlawed the importation of antislavery or abolitionist written materials. All ships with free Black or enslaved people were quarantined when entering a Georgia port because literacy was another disease, one that could kill slavery. Enslaved people were quarantined to keep medical diseases from spreading, but also to keep enslaved people from interacting with anyone who might teach them to read. Literacy was imagined as a disease that could spread through contact between the literate and illiterate.

After 1829, legislation became even more specific and draconian. An 1833 Georgia law prohibited enslaved persons from conducting business in writing, even on behalf of their enslavers. The City of Savannah had its own anti-literacy laws. Despite this, some enslaved people learned to read, and, more often, free people of color were able to gain literacy.[5] One path to education was a contraband school, and there were several in Savannah.[6] Julien Fromantin, a free Black and Catholic Haitian immigrant to Savannah, operated a school openly from 1819 to 1829, before the new legislation spurred him to operate the school underground until 1844. Catherine Deveaux, a free Black woman, married into the influential Deveaux family and taught for thirty years prior to the Civil War, charging $1 to $2.50 in tuition. James Porter, who was born to free parents in Charleston, South Carolina, had a very good education. In 1856, he moved to Savannah to direct the choir at St. Stephen's Episcopal Church, establishing a music school and teaching violin, piano, organ, and voice. He also participated in the Underground Railroad and taught a contraband school that had a trap door for students to exit if they were about to be discovered by white authorities. Many of these teachers and others opened private schools after emancipation as well, including Catherine Deveaux and her daughter Jane, James Porter, Louis B. Toomer, Mother Mathilda Beasley, and Susie King Taylor.[7]

Despite the laws prohibiting education for people of color, on rare occasions white women taught enslaved children along with their own. Rather than taking these stories as a heartwarming nod to racial justice, readers should view such stories with caution. Enslaved people were sometimes educated to increase their economic value and extract more labor from them. More frequently, enslaved children learned directly or indirectly from the white children in the household. Instances of white people either teaching enslaved children or turning a blind eye to clandestine schools are extremely rare. Take, for example, the story of Ned Purdee, an older African American Methodist pastor, who operated a clandestine school for boys and girls near Augusta, Georgia. Purdee was discovered, jailed, and sentenced to lashes every day for a month. But when he was put in the stocks, Purdee was supposedly told to yell and pretend to be in pain while his punisher hit the stocks, rather than Purdee, who left uninjured.[8] These anecdotes often come from white writers interviewing older African Americans in the Jim Crow South. Interviewees had many reasons to soften their narratives, eliminating the violence and injustice and adding a nostalgic spin to the stories.[9] Were there really that many subversives eager to teach enslaved people, despite the legal implications? Probably not. More typical is the experience of Reverend James Simms, who was publicly whipped in 1861 for teaching enslaved people. When he kept teaching, he was fined $100. He refused to pay, moving to Boston until the war concluded, at which point he returned to Savannah.[10] The vast majority of antebellum Black education was done in secret, by Black people, whether through a clandestine school or informally as when enslaved children listened in other children's lessons.

Savannah's first public school, the Massie Common School, was built well before the Savannah-Chatham County Public School System (SCCPSS) was established. In April 1841, Scottish native and white Glynn County resident Peter Massie willed $5,000 to the City of Savannah "for the education of the poor children."[11] The city had to sue Massie's executors to obtain the bequest, receiving the money in 1845 and investing the funds in railroad and gas companies. A planning committee was appointed in 1849. In late 1852, a second committee finally recommended building the school and investing the remaining money to pay teachers' salaries. Locally notable architect John Norris was hired, and $9,000 was spent building the Massie School in 1855 and 1856. The completed school had six rooms with space for 280 to 300 students in eight grades. The school cost $4,500 annually to run, but only $1,000 in tuition was collected. The mayor and aldermen footed the remaining bill of $3,500 until 1865, when the school was briefly used as a Freedmen School under the orders of federal authorities, after which the school came under the SCCPSS umbrella. The east wing was added in 1872, and the west wing in 1886; architect John Hogg designed both wings. Following a successful run, the school closed in 1974 due to low enrollment but subsequently reopened as Massie Heritage Center, a SCCPSS-operated museum.[12]

By the 1860s, free public education was fairly standard for white students above the Mason-Dixon line. In contrast, poor southern white children did not have a right to an education and received sporadic schooling. Wealthy white children were educated in private schools or tutored at home.[13] Public schools were found occasionally in the South but did not exist in Savannah, with the exception of the Massie School. This lack of widespread educational opportunities complicated African Americans' quest for post-emancipation education both practically and philosophically. In the decades following the war, most southern whites opposed mandatory public schools because it upset their societal order and the planter regime. The South also greatly lacked the infrastructure and funding to build public school systems. As James D. Anderson indicates, "The result was a postwar South that was extremely hostile to the idea of universal education."[14]

POSTBELLUM SCHOOL BOOM

Heedless of the challenges, freedpeople demanded schools immediately upon emancipation. Despite societal pressure and often physical violence, Freedmen's schools were increasingly common in the post–Civil War South. Among African American communities, private schools popped up to answer the call for education. Teachers ranging from those with formal training to those with rudimentary skills would teach what they knew to others, both formally in schools and informally. Often Black soldiers learned while enlisted, then passed along their knowledge after the war, along with new models of self-help and self-determination. Even before the war's end, if the Union army was present, freedmen started schools, often without any outside support, building new schools or renting space and paying the bills and teacher salaries in a cooperative effort.[15] John W. Alvord, inspector of schools and later general superintendent of schools for the Freedmen's Bureau, described these as "native schools" run by African Americans outside of the support and control of the Freedmen's Bureau.[16] In 1865, Black teachers opened at least four hundred schools across the South. More than a hundred students in a classroom was not uncommon. In the five years following the Civil War, the federal government spent $6 million on approximately twenty-five hundred southern schools for 150,000 children. Northern aid societies such as the American Missionary Association (AMA), which was active in Savannah, were also major sources of funding and teachers. Curriculum focused on the basics—reading, writing, and math.[17]

Through student reminiscences and secondary histories, a general picture of emancipation-era schools emerges. Despite our images of the "Yankee schoolmarm," teachers were diverse: men and women, northern and southern, Black and white. The school day was frequently early morning to late afternoon, and students carried their "dinner" (midday meal) in a tin bucket, when walking home for lunch was prohibitively far. While sometimes the local Black community built and financed the local school, more often the schools were in makeshift buildings, including churches. For Athens, Georgia, resident Jefferson Franklin Henry, a school was set up three months after the end of the war and taught by northern, female teachers. He also explained the need for education, which was to stop white Georgians from taking away land once it was purchased by African Americans.[18] Several former students recalled corporal punishment, while only one student said their school was threatened with violence.[19] Modern researchers have shown that violence directed at teachers, students, and their homes and schoolhouses was disturbingly common.[20]

In oral histories, students recalled a "blue-backed speller," which was often their only textbook.[21] Noah Webster first published his blue-backed speller in 1783, at the end of the American Revolution when many Americans were eager to embrace their new country and new American identity. The original title was *A Grammatical Institute of the English Language: Part I*. Part two covered grammar, and part three was a reader. The title was simplified to *The American Spelling Book* in 1786, and later to *The Elementary Spelling Book* (1829). The informal nickname "blue-backed speller" was from the book's cover (obviously blue). The New England–born Webster was a strong Federalist, was a passionate supporter of a unified American culture, and was particularly focused on the intersection of culture and language. Webster wanted a "separation of the American tongue from the English" and created the blue-backed speller to evangelize his version of American English.[22] He was indeed successful at creating and spreading this dialect. He is the reason Americans write "honor," not "honour," and say "zee," not "zed," when referring to the final letter of the alphabet. Webster was much less successful in his goal to eliminate "regional, class, and racial distinctions in accents, dialects, vocabulary, and spelling."[23] Nor did all of his spelling changes take hold. Americans still write "give" (not "giv") and "women" (rather than "wimmen"). The blue-backed speller was more secular than previous textbooks and largely consisted of lists of syllables, words, and American place-names (rather than British ones). The 1790 edition was the first to include "A Federal Catechism," which was a basic lesson on the three branches of American government. The speller influenced because it was ubiquitous, selling ten million copies by 1829. Rough estimates put one hundred million copies sold during the nineteenth century, and it is still in print.[24]

African Americans often used this book to teach themselves, which created a strong emotional connection with the speller.[25] Booker T. Washington wrote about his blue-backed speller in his 1909 *Up from Slavery: An Autobiography*:

Soon after we got settled in some manner in our new cabin in West Virginia, I induced my mother to get hold of a book for me. How or where she got it I do not know, but in some way she procured an old copy of Webster's "blue-back" spelling-book, which contained the alphabet, followed by such meaningless words as "ab," "ba," "ca," "da." I began at once to devour this book, and I think that it was the first one I ever had in my hands. I had learned from somebody that the way to begin to read was to learn the alphabet, so I tried in all the ways I could think of to learn it,—all of course without a teacher, for I could find no one to teach me. At the time there was not a single member of my race anywhere near us who could read, and I was too timid to approach any of the white people. In some way, within a few weeks, I mastered the greater portion of the alphabet.[26]

Despite frequent references to the speller in oral histories, one former student said she was denied a blue-backed speller. Addie Vinson of Athens, Georgia, recalled that it was a long time before schools were set up, and when they were, African American children were not allowed to use the typical blue-backed spellers because whites thought the books taught them too much.[27]

SAVANNAH'S PRIVATE SCHOOLS

Savannah's African American community along with a variety of northern aid organizations, churches, and the Freedmen's Bureau jumped in to fill the gap and start educating Black students in private schools. Although the Georgia Legislature established the City of Savannah Board of Education on March 21, 1866, Savannah's first Black public school would not open until 1872, hence the critical importance of privately operated schools. Louis B. Toomer, James Porter, Hardy Mobley, and Harriet Jacobs's daughter Louisa all taught in Savannah at the war's end.[28] The New York Society of Friends sponsored Louisa Jacobs's school. Lucinda Jackson and K. Saul Thomas taught out of their Savannah homes.[29]

Like Jackson and Thomas, Susie King Taylor brought new meaning to the word "schoolhouse," because for King Taylor, her Savannah home was also her school. She and her younger siblings first learned in Susan Woodhouse's antebellum kitchen. They would walk to and from school with their books wrapped in paper to disguise both the books and their purpose in traveling the streets. Woodhouse had about twenty-five students secretly entering and exiting every day. King Taylor later learned from Mary Beasley until May 1860, then a white playmate named Katie O'Connor, and finally a white landlord's son until mid-1861, when he left with the Savannah Volunteer Guards, a local militia group. Education was obtained wherever and however possible and was often cobbled together from multiple sources.[30]

King Taylor participated in the first all-Black Union army regiment as a nurse and a teacher. During this time, she opened her first school on St. Simon's Island, at the request of a Union officer, Commodore Goldsborough. She taught approximately forty children, plus adults at night. After the war, she founded a private school in her Savannah home on Oglethorpe Avenue, then called South Broad Street, teaching about twenty children during the day and a few older children at night. She charged one dollar per month per child. A combination of factors caused her to close her school after about one year: the Beach Institute opened, and some of her students transferred to the tuition-free school; her husband died on September 16, 1866; and she had an infant to care for. She opened a school in Liberty County in April 1867, teaching for about a year, but did not care for country life, so Mrs. Susie Carrier took over the school. King Taylor would go on to open several more schools throughout her career.[31]

Private school tuition ranged from fifty cents to three dollars per month and was typically one dollar per month per child. Sometimes there was an additional fuel charge for heating the classroom in the winter. Schools run by organizations (such as the SEA or AMA) often did not charge tuition but raised money from the local community or had wider fundraising efforts in the case of the northern missionary societies. No matter the fundraising strategy, most teachers were quite poor. Schools met wherever possible. Most private schools met in old buildings, in churches, at the teacher's house, or on government property. Churches were good options because the rent was free, the buildings were largely empty on weekdays, and the teachers were given freedom. Pews provided seating but lacked desks for writing, which made learning to write difficult. Schools were usually undersupplied, even lacking in simple basics such as fuel for warmth in winter and equipment such as writing slates, blackboards, books, and desks (let alone proper school furniture that was child-sized).[32]

In late December 1864, days after the Union army arrived in Savannah, a group of Black ministers gathered to organize the Savannah Education Association (SEA), which was tasked with creating and supervising schools, establishing policy, and raising money. The group hired fifteen teachers in the first week and developed a "voluntary subscription" system of funding. The SEA paid teacher salaries of fifteen to thirty-five dollars per month, eventually paying thirty-eight teachers in 1865. They typically charged one to two dollars tuition and raised money throughout the African American community, but it was still difficult to cover expenses. Teachers often worked without pay.[33]

The northern benevolent associations were astonished at the SEA's speed and ability to raise money and start schools, and yet the AMA still fought the SEA for each decision and dollar.[34] Reverend S. W. Magill, a local white AMA leader, complained about the SEA's inexperience, calling it a "radically defective organization."[35] He could not understand why African American parents opposed white teachers and wanted to administer their own schools. As the AMA representative, he expected complete authority over freedmen schools and complained when parents wanted to share authority.[36] The more well-meaning white Americans often thought that the schools' goal was to "civilize" African American children and bring them "moral uplift." Northern evangelicals, assuming they knew best, taught northern, white, Protestant values without regard for parents' ideas. At best, white teachers were often patronizing, had low expectations of their students, and were more committed to their evangelical and missionary work than to teaching. At worst, they attempted to retain as many aspects of the pre-emancipation social order as possible, whereas Black teachers were more deeply committed to their students and taught social lessons in addition to scholarly ones.[37] They were much more likely to think highly of their students and created better relationships with their students. They taught political consciousness and economic awareness to make students savvy in their navigation of the larger world. African American teachers often taught holistically, combining academic subjects with citizenship and community issues.[38]

A common solution was to house schools in churches. First Bryan Baptist Church and First African Baptist Church both had freedmen schools in 1865 (see map 2). Reverend Joseph Robert Love started a school in early 1872 on the grounds of St. Stephen's Episcopal Church. The school had 106 registered students with an average daily attendance of 80. Rev. Love left St. Stephen's after eight months and founded St. Augustine's Episcopal Mission in Yamacraw Village at the corner of Bolton and West Broad Street as well as another school.[39]

The SEA's more defiant choice was housing a school in the old Bryan Slave Mart. The Bryan Free School, SEA's first, was on the northwest corner of West St. Julian and Barnard Streets.[40] Slave trader John S. Montmollin had this substantial, three-story brick building built between 1856 and 1857 for $11,500. In June 1859, Montmollin died a gruesome death aboard the Steamer *John G. Lawton* when the ship's boiler exploded. Only Montmollin's "head and upper extremities" were found lodged in the mud.[41] The disaster, which killed several and injured more, made national news. After Montmollin's death, Alexander Bryan leased the third floor as a slave trade and auction facility. Bryan continued to use the building as a "jail and office for the barter and sale of slaves" until several days before Union general William Sherman arrived in Savannah on December 21, 1864.[42]

In early 1865, the building also hosted a meeting to discuss the prospect of freed-

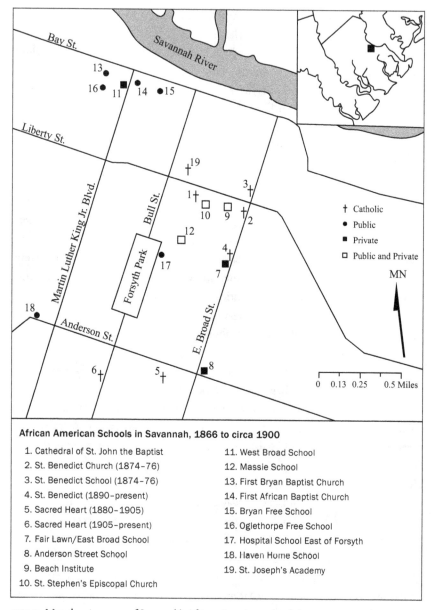

African American Schools in Savannah, 1866 to circa 1900

1. Cathedral of St. John the Baptist
2. St. Benedict Church (1874–76)
3. St. Benedict School (1874–76)
4. St. Benedict (1890–present)
5. Sacred Heart (1880–1905)
6. Sacred Heart (1905–present)
7. Fair Lawn/East Broad School
8. Anderson Street School
9. Beach Institute
10. St. Stephen's Episcopal Church

11. West Broad School
12. Massie School
13. First Bryan Baptist Church
14. First African Baptist Church
15. Bryan Free School
16. Oglethorpe Free School
17. Hospital School East of Forsyth
18. Haven Home School
19. St. Joseph's Academy

MAP 2. Map showing some of Savannah's African American schools between 1865 and 1900.

people settling Georgia's sea islands under Sherman's Special Field Order No. 15. Boston-based journalist Charles Coffin recorded the meeting and the building's details in his 1866 book, *Four Years of Fighting*. Coffin describes walking up to the third floor and envisioning how "thousands of slaves had been dragged, chained in coffle."[43] The eight-foot-square auctioneer's block was still present, as were the iron bars on the windows. "In an anteroom at the right women had been stripped and exposed to the gaze of brutal men."[44] Coffin also records the students attending school the day after the meeting: "I saw a school of one hundred colored children assembled, taught by colored teachers, who sat on the auctioneer's platform, from which had risen voices of despair instead of accents of love, brutal cursing instead of Christian teaching. I listened to the recitations, and heard their songs of jubilee. The slave-mart transformed to a school-house!"[45] Clearly, the irony (and victory) were not lost on him.

By March 1865, Principal James Porter operated the school five hours each day for 450 students ages five to twenty. The school quickly outgrew the space, so it was moved to the Massie School on Calhoun Square. The SEA established their second school, the Oglethorpe Free School, on Fahm Street in the Yamacraw neighborhood on January 15, 1865. The building, alternately called the Styles Building, Stiles House, and the old Oglethorpe Medical College, housed a Confederate hospital during the war and was procured with Freedmen's Bureau help. There were 450 students divided into eight classes, each with its own African American teacher.[46]

The educational role of the Freedmen's Bureau was primarily supporting other institutions such as the aid societies and private schools. When the sub-assistant commissioner for Savannah, Colonel Hiram F. Sickles, requested money for schools, his superior, Davis Tillson, told him to use "available resources, including idle soldiers, to lend the Freedpeople a hand in constructing needed facilities" and wisely warned him to only construct buildings on land controlled by freedmen.[47] Freedmen's Bureau employees had to get creative, moving abandoned buildings to Savannah and using soldier's labor to build additions as necessary. Coordinating with churches and other public buildings and donating former Confederate military buildings now under their control, such as the old Oglethorpe Medical College, were commonly part of the Freedmen's Bureau's toolbox as well. Most of the school resources went to the cities, limiting the impact to Georgia's five largest cities: Atlanta, Augusta, Columbus, Macon, and Savannah. These cities registered almost half of all enrolled students in Georgia, despite only housing 15 percent of the African American population. Between 1865 and 1870, 70 percent of the northern aid teachers went to cities.[48]

Due to lack of funding, all seven of Savannah's African American schools closed for the winter of 1866: the Yonkers School (in the First African Baptist Church basement), the Hospital School east of Forsyth Park, Lamar and Andrew Schools (at Andrews Chapel on New Street), Bethlehem High School (also on New Street), the Bryan Free School, and the Oglethorpe School. Reopening the schools required more funding, which the SEA did not have, so they turned to the AMA. The AMA wanted to demote the African American teachers to assistants and replace them with white teachers. SEA organizers were willing to accept AMA money and white assistant teachers but were unwilling to give up control or allow for African American teachers' displacement. So the AMA denied them funding, began a parallel set of schools, and continued their attempts to insert themselves further into African American education.[49]

Georgia native and white AMA agent S. W. Magill brought northern teachers down to teach in these AMA schools, starting with the Methodist Church on South Broad (today's East Oglethorpe Avenue). In one week, 300 children and 118 women were registered. Other AMA locations included the Methodist Church on New Street, Lamar Hall on Liberty Street, and Sturtevant Hall at Price and Harris Streets.[50] Estimates of student attendance and enrollment can vary quite a bit, but the AMA schools were serving about 250 students by July 1865.[51] Often, there was a rush to register, and attendance was high at first but leveled out as students' labor was needed at home or tuition was unaffordable.

Ultimately, the SEA's donation-based funding was not enough to support the schools and provide free tuition. Freedmen simply did not have enough income to support the SEA school system without help. The Freedmen's Bureau's state superintendent of education gave the available federal funding to Reverend E. A. Cooley, AMA representative and Massachusetts native, rather than giving it directly to the SEA, thereby preventing the SEA parents from having authority over their children's education. In March 1866, the SEA again had to ask the AMA for money, which the AMA would only grant conditionally. Cooley gave the necessary funding but demoted twelve African American teachers to assistant teachers, replacing them with white northerners. Within a year, the AMA had a monopoly on African American education in Savannah, and the struggle for control ended when the AMA "gobbled up" the SEA.[52] The AMA's tactics left parents distrustful and bitter. Any parents who could sent their children to other private schools, leaving the poorest children in the free AMA schools.[53] Savannah was not the only location where the AMA used their power to control schools and replace Black teachers with white ones. Mobile, Alabama, parents experienced similar frustrations, and like many Savannahians, the parents chose to partner with the AMA, using AMA resources as they could while continuing to petition the school board and use every tool to better their schools.[54]

The AMA's move to replace African American teachers with white teachers was explicitly and implicitly about power and controlling the future of all African Americans. The northern benevolent associations wanted to reform, educate, and "civilize" freedpeople, with the goal of creating a labor force that would "cooperate." In the guise of reform and rescue, these societies aimed to create a "tidy, disciplined future of the freed black labor in the South."[55] The reality of this was not pretty—low wage jobs and menial labor, racist structures designed to continue de facto slavery. African Americans, however, wanted real education for their children and for future generations. They wanted to see African American doctors, teachers, lawyers, pastors, and other professionals so they would have less need to patronize white business with all the risks of discrimination and fraud.[56]

Just as education empowered African Americans, it threatened white supremacy and pushed to destabilize the economic and social structure that relied on free, and then cheap, Black labor. The AMA, despite their assertions of good intentions, were complicit in their own agenda to control African American labor and lives. The AMA along with the Freedmen's Bureau sabotaged the SEA despite the SEA's success. The SEA met every funding requirement and successfully operated schools, but because they would not relinquish control and decision-making, they were denied independent funding. As Jacqueline Jones states, "Throughout the South, going to school—or building, supporting, or teaching in a school—became a political act for black people."[57] Creating schools was a way to defy white power and institutionalize Black life (as a positive force by solidifying its existence).[58]

Despite its bias and racist flaws, the AMA did work to provide schools that African American children attended. The AMA's most lasting accomplishment is the Beach Institute, which was built on the razed Sturtevant Hall, an old wooden structure and former Confederate army storage that became United States Army property after the Civil War. The army handed it over to the AMA specifically to build the Beach Institute. *Scientific American* editor Alfred E. Beach gave $13,000 to fund his namesake institute and was joined by additional donations from citizens and the Freedmen's Bureau. Featuring eight classrooms, the new, substantial building was two stories with a raised basement, measuring 55 feet by 60 feet and with two ells measuring 10 feet by 35 feet each. This was a significant investment in African American education, much more than the public schools were offering with their repurposed buildings.[59] The school was well lit and well equipped with standard desks and blackboards. Shortly after the school's opening, a teachers' home was also built on the property, welcoming its first residents on Thanksgiving Day in 1867.

The opening enrollment was 600 African American students, with a mostly white staff of 10 teachers. By early 1868, the enrollment had risen to 711. The Beach Institute charged $1 monthly tuition until becoming a free public school in 1874 after two years of negotiations with the public board of education.[60] The public school system rented the building for $600 per year until a February 20, 1878, fire causing $7,775 in damage temporarily closed the building. The fire was considered suspicious, but no charges were ever brought. The public school moved to Fair Lawn plantation to accommodate the over 300 children currently enrolled. Suspicious fires and arson were not uncommon at Black schools across the South. Hundreds of Black schools burned in the 1860s and 1870s. African American education posed a real threat to white supremacy, and violence against teachers, students, and the school buildings was disturbingly frequent. Arson was often the weapon of choice because it was both destructive physically and emotionally frightening. The American Missionary Association rebuilt and expanded the once-again private school, which now faced Price Street, and reopened the school in 1879 with 183 students taught by Principal Stella Lowe, Laura Lowell, Sarah Lamotte, Isabelle Beachum, and two African American teachers, James H. C. Butler and Alice Miller. A second suspicious fire in 1909 also temporarily suspended the school, which the AMA closed permanently in 1919.[61]

SAVANNAH'S PUBLIC SCHOOL SYSTEM

Savannah did not have a public school system before the Civil War. Once established, the schools were both racially segregated and divided into city schools and rural "county schools," which included the Skidaway Island public school that directly competed with the Benedictines' school. The schools were grouped separately in the school district's annual reports, which often frankly acknowledged the many difficulties of running county schools. The sparse population meant the schools had low attendance. The isolated conditions, poor pay, and challenging teaching loads made it very difficult to attract and retain quality teachers. The schools' poor quality meant that any parent who could send their child to a better, private school would do so. And thus a cycle of school poverty was created, whose racist structures continue today. Few resources are dedicated. Poor quality teaching and a high employee turnover rate result in schools continuing to struggle. Wealthier parents send their children elsewhere, leaving behind the poorest children whose parents are least able to fight structural inequities. Therefore few resources are dedicated, and the cycle continues.

Savannah's public schools for white children began when the Georgia legislature established the City of Savannah Board of Education on March 21, 1866. An amendment on December 18, 1866, extended the board of education's control to all of Chatham County. By 1870, every southern state had constitutional requirements for free public schools with state financing, because the federal government made it a condition of reentry to the United States.[62] The Georgia state legislature ruled in 1870 that public school districts must provide segregated education for all children. Through the early 1870s, Black Savannahians held mass meetings and organized politically. They formed a voting block and refused to vote for any candidate who opposed African American public schools.[63] Still, Savannah's first African American public school, St. Stephen's Church School, did not open until 1872. That year 354 African American students enrolled in public school, while 552 were registered at the still-private Beach Institute.[64] St. Stephen's rectory near the corner of Macon and Lincoln Streets had hosted the private St. Stephen's Church School. Now the board of education rented the property for $300 and renovated the three rooms into four classrooms that could hold only 178 students. Julia Maynard and Elias Yulee taught the girls, and Rev. Samuel Sims and Eliza Pollard taught the boys. This school was short lived, as it was destroyed by fire on November 22, 1873, just shy of its one-year anniversary. With losses estimated at $700, the board of education declined to rebuild, instead opening the West Broad Street School three days after the fire. Today the West Broad Street School is better known as the Ships of the Sea Museum or the William Scarbrough House, a Willian Jay design built in 1819. The house had been occupied intermittently since January 27, 1865, when the nearby powder magazine exploded and the occupants, the O'Byrne family, fled. The Catholic Church had purchased the house, and Sisters of St. Joseph briefly operated a day school for kids and a night school for adults on the property. The building was empty when the board of education leased it for $300 per year in late 1873.[65]

As the only African American public school in Savannah, the school was always full. James Porter was the principal with Eliza Pollard, Emma Simpson, Laura Porter (James's daughter), Elias Yulee, Emma Higgins, Mary Ingliss, and Cornelia Atwell teaching. In 1878, George Wymberley Jones DeRenne purchased the building and donated it to the public school system under certain conditions—that the sccpss would change its charter to include "children of African descent," that the property could only be used for educating African American children, there would be no religious instruction, and the building must be kept in good repair.[66] If these conditions were not met, the property would revert to the DeRenne heirs or, if none remained, the Savannah Hospital Charity. With 452 registered students in

1885, the school needed more space. In 1889, a four-room, $2,000 annex was added so 160 additional children could be accepted. Shortly after, more additions were necessary, and a second floor was put on the annex at a cost of $2,000, bringing the total capacity to 927 students in 1890. An 1896 report was not encouraging. It stated that while the new annex was functioning well, the older home had poor conditions, particularly that it lacked light and ventilation. One room would hold 45 to 50 students but only have one or two windows. In 1914, the school had fourteen classrooms and fourteen teachers for 750 children—that averages to 54 students per classroom. The school remained open until 1962 but was very dilapidated by then and reverted to the DeRenne heirs. Historic Savannah Foundation rehabilitated the building in 1972, and the Ships of the Sea Museum further restored the property in 1997.[67]

The Fair Lawn Public School was initially a stop-gap solution while the Beach Institute was repaired following a suspicious fire. However, the desperate need for school buildings made this a permanent solution. The board of education leased the wooden home for $300 per year, renovated it, and furnished the aging building into a school with eight rooms. The school opened in April 1878, and in February 1879, George W. J. DeRenne bought the property for $2,500 with the intent of donation. His widow finally donated the property in 1882 under the same conditions as the West Broad Street School donation. The delay was caused by a disagreement between DeRenne and the board of education. Located on East Broad Street between Gaston and Hartridge Streets, the school was less than one block from the future location of St. Benedict the Moor Catholic Church. The original wooden home was used for four years; then another school was built on the property and renamed the East Broad Street School. This wooden schoolhouse had a 500-student capacity until 1892, when a six-classroom annex was added for $5,035. On March 22, 1893, the school was the victim of a "supposed incendiary" (likely racially motivated arson). The fire caused heavy damage, which cost the board of education $4,750 to repair. With funds from the Federal Emergency Relief Association, the repairs were completed by October 1893. The school remained open until 1971.[68]

The third and final urban public school that is closely contemporary with the Skidaway Island mission school is the Anderson Street School, which was also on East Broad Street, at the Anderson Street intersection. It was probably named the Anderson Street School to cut down on confusion with the two other Broad Street schools, but this plan was dubious at best, because there already was another Anderson Street School for white students, and there would later be a third school on Anderson Street, built in 1913 and named the Cuyler Street School. This Anderson

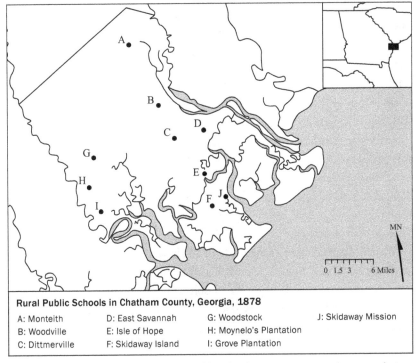

Rural Public Schools in Chatham County, Georgia, 1878

A: Monteith   D: East Savannah   G: Woodstock   J: Skidaway Mission

B: Woodville   E: Isle of Hope   H: Moynelo's Plantation

C: Dittmerville   F: Skidaway Island   I: Grove Plantation

MAP 3. Some of Chatham County's rural public schools extant in 1878 are shown in relation to the Skidaway mission school. Other locations of rural schools are unknown.

Street School, always listed with the designation "colored" to differentiate it, was a rented, dilapidated Longshoreman's Hall that housed grades one through five and operated from 1894 to 1903. The intention was to relieve crowding at East Broad Street School; however, Principal John McIntosh was forced to cram 105 students into four tiny 20-by-20-foot rooms, so it was not much of an improvement. The school was replaced because it was not near the African American neighborhoods, and the children's commute to their school was an "annoyance of the citizens."[69] This pattern of renting buildings and jerry-rigging them into schools continued into the twentieth century until the Cuyler Street School's construction.

CHATHAM COUNTY'S RURAL PUBLIC SCHOOLS

Shortly after the first city public schools opened, rural "county schools" were started as well (see map 3). By the time the Benedictines began the Skidaway mission school, the SCCPSS operated nineteen county schools, including six white schools (Isle of Hope, Gravel Hill, South Newington, Harden's Swamp, Ogeechee, and Cherokee Hill) and thirteen African American schools (Moynelo's Plantation,

Belmont, Skidaway Island, Woodville, Woodstock, Dittsmersville, East Savannah, Monteith, Holiday's Farm, Mount Zion, Grove Plantation, Canal School, and Isle of Hope). Monteith, Isle of Hope, and possibly other county schools had precursors founded directly after the Civil War and were (under)staffed by AMA teachers. For example, Grove Hill School had two teachers for an average attendance of 150 students in November 1865.[70] It is not clear if there is a continuum between these early private schools and the later public county schools. Some of the public county schools, such as Monteith, Mount Zion, Skidaway Island, and Dittsmersville (spelled with varying numbers of *s*'s over time) lasted for decades. Others were more ephemeral. Now well within the city limits, Dittmerville (today's spelling) boasted one of the first county schools. A June 1873 petition from the neighborhood produced a school, which was open until February 1930, when the Florance Street School replaced it.[71]

There is no evidence of a formal school on Skidaway Island prior to 1878.[72] The Skidaway Island county school and Benedictine mission school, both started the same year, appear to be the first two schools on the island. Who exactly was the impetus for the Skidaway county school has been debated. The school board's "Thirteenth Annual Report" neutrally states, "Urgent calls were made for schools at White Bluff, Skidaway, and Ossabaw Islands, which must be responded to."[73] Some researchers, including Jerome Oetgen, believe white mainland protestants "anxious to thwart Catholic influence on the black population" put pressure on the school board to create a public school alternative to the Benedictines' school.[74] Skidaway mission founder Father Oswald Moosmüller certainly thought this was true, writing, "When the white Protestants saw that we establish ourselves on Skidaway & that we would open a School here; they got a Census marshall for the County to take up the names of all children of School-age on Skidaway Island & petitioned to have a Public School established on the said island, as there never had been one before."[75] This was not the first school census, however. Dr. Stephen Dupon, as commissioner for the district, had taken a school census as early as 1871, advertising in the October 7 and 13 *Savannah Daily Advertiser* that he would "be present to receive the names, age, and sex of Children as required by section 37, of White and Colored youth." The ad lists locations, dates, and times for registration throughout southern Chatham County, including Ziegler's plantation on Skidaway Island. This was done "for the purpose of establishing schools in the Districts."[76]

Isabel Mann argues that it was African American residents on Skidaway Island who petitioned the school board. She cites positive newspaper coverage of the Catholic efforts to demonstrate that anti-Catholic sentiment was not that vehement and argues that African American agency is reason enough to believe they were behind the "urgent calls" from several locations.[77] It is possible that both Skidaway's African American residents and white citizens in Savannah were behind the campaign for a school, and their combined appeals were the reason for success. This tangle is relevant because it indirectly speaks to the islanders' desires for their children's education, whether they were receptive to the monks' school, and how the power dynamics were manipulated by each faction.

Regardless of who was responsible, a public school was started concurrently with the Benedictine school. Father Moosmüller, in a brilliant countermove, went to Dr. Read, a Catholic member of the board of education, and requested that Father Siricius, a young African American cleric assigned to the Skidaway mission, be allowed to apply for the public school teacher's position.[78] Originally from Centreville, Virginia, Charles Siricius Palmer had recently graduated from Saint Vincent College in 1876 with a degree in classics. Despite some opposition from a Baptist member of the school board, Palmer took the required exam, "passed the examination tolerably well," and received a teaching certificate.[79] Moosmüller was clear about his real motivation for placing Palmer at the county school: "If Father Siricius is an able teacher, he has a chance to gain the whole islands [sic] population through the children for the Catholic Church."[80] In another letter he stated: "This is to be considered as a very important step in our progress in regard to the conversion of the nigroes [sic]."[81] Late in November 1878, Father Palmer received notification that he was the new Skidaway Island county school teacher. He traveled to Savannah to complete paperwork and receive his certificate.[82]

There was some initial confusion over how much Palmer would be paid. At first, the fathers expected he would receive thirty dollars per month; then Moosmüller reported it would be twenty-five dollars. Once Palmer was working in the position, he did receive thirty dollars per month. It is unclear why this discrepancy occurred, but it was likely because of race. African Americans were paid less than whites, and women less than men, a trend that still somewhat exists today, if no longer institutionally and legally acceptable in the public schools.[83]

Palmer's county school was quickly popular. In January 1879, the school had forty children.[84] In sharp contrast, the monastery school had seven students at the same time (down from twelve after Moosmüller dismissed four and one "ran away").[85] However, the county school was only scheduled to be open five months of the year, so in February, Moosmüller considered extending the public school year by an extra two months "by some kind of subscription."[86] Father Palmer taught at the Skidaway county school in 1878, 1879, and 1880. Then the county school closed for three years, and C. S. Palmer was no longer listed anywhere in

Chatham County as a teacher.[87] It is not entirely clear why Palmer was not replaced immediately, other than the general difficulty of hiring teachers for rural schools. Dr. Read, a Catholic member of the public school board, "expressed his regret with the Bishop that the Benedictines on Skidaway lost or gave up the Public School."[88]

Father Moosmüller later acknowledged Father Reichert and Father Palmers' joint decision to give up the teacher's post, writing, "They foolishly imagined that the Superintendent would not appoint a Protestant teacher as he really did."[89] Moosmüller particularly bemoaned the loss of Catholic influence over the children, rather than the loss of salary. The school had been successful, averaging fifty-five students for its three-year existence.[90] The attendance numbers again speak to the critical need for schools and a great desire for education. Although the monk's boarding school did see a small rise in enrollment after the public school's closure, many students were still left without an education until the public school reopened. Furthermore, while the public school educated boys and girls, the monk's boarding school was only available to boys, so the girls were left without any formal education options at all.

Why did Fathers Palmer and Reichert really give up the teaching post, leaving so many students without education, religious or otherwise? We cannot know their motivations, but Palmer's personal life was likely part of the equation. Father Palmer wrote to the abbot for dispensation from his vows on September 21, 1882. His request was granted in early 1883, and he left the order after only a few years.[91]

From 1884 into the 1920s, the Skidaway Island county school continued with one teacher. However, the teachers changed frequently, often only staying one or two years, until 1895, at which point Issac Jackson stayed for four years. Miss Nona McCrae taught in 1899 and probably again in 1900, but her name was Mrs. Nona Mitchell then. Later teachers included Samuel S. Kelson (1901–3), John Taylor (1904–6), Mrs. Annie Holmes (1907–11), William du Henri Brown (1912–17), and Miss Louise Bing (1918–22).[92]

The county schools were plagued with problems. The schools were uniformly small and badly constructed with inadequate ventilation leading to poor hygiene. The biggest problem was finding and retaining excellent teachers to do a tough job in isolated areas. "Owing to the difficulty in obtaining competent teachers, the quality of instruction imparted in these schools is poor," bluntly stated the 1878 SCCPSS annual report writer.[93] Because the schools had so few students, they were "unclassified," meaning that the students were not separated into grades but were taught as one unit. Attendance was often spotty. Students' labor was needed at home, especially during March, April, and May, which were important months for planting. Transportation to and from the schools was also difficult. Students often had to walk several miles one way, which was particularly difficult in cold or wet weather, when dirt roads turned to mud. County schools' inspection reports have several notations that difficult road conditions caused low attendance on a particular day. White hostility and violence also contributed to low student attendance; however, this was likely less prevalent on Skidaway Island because there were few white inhabitants.[94]

Overall, county school attendance remained "fluctuating, but generally large" for the 1877–78 school year. The eleven Black county schools had seven African American male teachers, two African American female teachers, and two white male teachers for an enrollment of 395 boys and 411 girls. Daily attendance was 74 percent (206 boys and 205 girls attended on an ordinary day). This averages to 73 enrolled students for each teacher, and 37 students for each teacher given a typical attendance day. It is also important to note that girls and boys were attending public school in equal numbers.[95] When the Skidaway Island county school was closed for three years (1881 through 1883), this left girls without any options, as the monks' school was only for boys.

In 1889, the county schools were still described as "grossly neglected."[96] While the county schools were subpar, at least every student who desired could attend. That year "several hundred" African American students in the city proper were denied a seat in public school because there was no space.[97] The next year, no white children were denied admittance, and the school system rented two private homes to accommodate all the white children. Again, several hundred African American students were denied schooling ostensibly due to lack of space but really due to lack of political will to create new schools. By 1892, the public school superintendent estimated the problem had grown to approximately eight hundred African American students who were prevented from attending free public schools due to school shortages.[98] City and county officials were complicit in this shortage because they were unwilling to raise taxes to bring in money that could make more classrooms available. These taxes would have been an anathema to southern whites who resented the federal government and Reconstruction, were more interested in preserving the strict southern social hierarchy, and refused to believe that education for nonelites (Black and white) should be a priority.[99]

The county school buildings could accommodate the numbers of students but were "unfit for school purposes."[100] This was often because buildings were repurposed, or doubly purposed, and often lacked basic equipment such as proper desks, writing materials, and books. To rectify the county schools situation, the SCCPSS appointed Mr. Desverger in 1891 as an inspector to oversee the county schools. "A marked improvement in these schools" was already noted in 1893.[101]

Individual school inspection reports provide particulars. The first record available for Skidaway Island's county school is November 11, 1892, and lists bare details: the teacher is Miss R. E. Harris, six boys and three girls are present, however, twenty-seven students belong to the school. "Visited this day in company with Supt. [Superintendent]. Conditions could be bettered." The next inspection did not occur until March 1893. Eighteen students were examined, "Spelling very good, Reading not very good, Arithmetic backward," noted the observer laconically.[102]

Neighboring Isle of Hope had two segregated county schools. Although the number of students is comparable to Skidaway Island, with generally between ten and twenty attending on a given day, the difference in the conditions between the Black and white schools could not be more stark. The white Isle of Hope school was far superior in both the quality of education and the school's physical structure. When inspected, the white students were "very good" at all of the subjects except arithmetic, which was only "fair." The Black Isle of Hope school was visited more frequently than the Skidaway school (possibly because accessing Skidaway required a boat), but it seemed to suffer from the same problems. "School is in rather bad condition," wrote the inspector on October 14, 1892. The next four visits throughout the fall of 1892 produced similar comments, all indicating the school was "not very promising." Fortunately, the Black Isle of Hope school moved locations and was reorganized, resulting in higher attendance and better results for the students. In 1894 and 1895, the student attendance varied between thirty and forty individuals, and conditions were "very good."[103]

On Skidaway Island, however, the next year did not find much improvement, as the students were late to class, and their "work only fair." The 1894–95 school year had twenty-four students in the fall, but only four students were present in January. The October 24, 1895, visit was typical: "Visited and found present 18 pupils. Condition fair." The Skidaway Island public school was held in a church. This church, while not specifically identified, was 30 by 22 feet, with four windows in two opposite pairs on the north and south sides of the building. Churches had the distinct advantages of being already built, being free on weekdays, and having relatively large open areas for instruction; however, benches or pews are poor replacements for proper desks. When students are learning to write, they need a steady place to rest their books and slates. The summer before (or possibly after) the 1897–98 school year, desks were delivered to nine African American county schools, but Skidaway Island was not one of them. Each lucky school received between three and five desks.

Fall 1896 was Issac Jackson's second year teaching at the Skidaway school; however, the inspector "instructed teacher in methods of instructing pupils of primary class." The follow-up visit in January seemed positive, but in March 1897, Jackson was damned with faint praise: "Children know very little, but teacher seems to be working hard." The 1896–97 and 1897–98 school years boast some of highest student attendance, with twenty-six students present each fall, and thirty-six and forty-six students registered, respectively.[104]

Progress at the Skidaway Island school remained halting in the 1900s. "Pupils very irregular in attendance, and very tardy as a rule, some coming as late as 11 o'clock. Pupils know very little," wrote an inspector in January 1900. The school was better in 1903: "Condition gradually improving." Although the schools had their problems, they were vital to the community, and the annual opening and closing programs were well noted. The 1902–3 school year closed on March 31 with a "very interesting program which was highly enjoyed by all" and an address by James M. Washington.[105] Some more progress was noted in 1904, but the 1905 inspector again "corrected teachers programme [*sic*]." John P. Taylor was the new teacher that year as Samuel Kelson had moved to Excelsior, Georgia. These schools suffered from a catch-22. Poor conditions and poor pay made it difficult to tempt highly qualified white teachers, even if they were able to set aside their own racism.[106] African American teachers had multiple barriers, ranging from the paucity of normal schools that accepted African American students to racist institutional hiring practices. So schools languished with mostly underqualified teachers, who did not have the skills to help students rapidly improve, even when the teachers were highly motivated and enthusiastic.

Into the twentieth century, inspectors continued to visit the island's county school once or twice per year, giving an examination in various subjects. Inspection reports from the 1900s and 1910s become even more terse, often stating only the date, number of students belonging, number of students present, teacher's name, and in what subjects the students were examined. The number of students fluctuated between twenty-eight (January 1906) and seven (February 1912). In 1910, the school was finally divided into grades one, two, and three. Then something drastic appears to have happened between February 1915, when twenty-five students were present (out of fifty-five registered), and November 1915, when the inspector "arrived at school at 1:45 o'clock. No teacher or pupils there." March 1916 was not more productive: "Arrived at school 9:30 a.m. stayed til 10 o'clock. no teacher?" Six students were present.[107] The Skidaway Island county school lasted into the 1920s. Although the school offered education up to the sixth grade, it did not always have students enrolled in the fifth and sixth grades.

Legally, of course, the public schools were required to provide an education for all children. The details, however, created rather large cracks for students to fall through. An 1874 Chatham County school census showed that 1,244 of the 3,066 African American school-age children were registered in the public schools (40.6 percent), with the majority in rural schools, but 2,459 of the 3,853 white school-age children were enrolled (63.8 percent), mostly in city public schools. It is unknown how many of the remainder were enrolled in private schools. A 1908 state education report found 65,000 illiterate African American children in Georgia as well as almost an additional 20,000 illiterate adults. It was not until 1916 that Georgia passed a compulsory education law, meaning every child must attend school. Public school funding came from poll taxes, "sin taxes" (alcohol and entertainment), and half of the net earnings from the state-owned Western and Atlantic Railroad. The state allocated funding to school districts based on the population of all children ages six to eighteen, whether they were in school or not (and regardless of whether there was a seat for them). Once in the school district's pocket, the local boards of education could distribute the money however they saw fit. Chronic underfunding and overcrowding continued well into the twentieth century as the county refused to raise taxes.[108] For the next one hundred years, the Black public schools were radically inadequate in terms of the number of available seats, funding, equipment, and teacher pay. This same story played itself out across the country in every school system, compounded by segregation and racist public policies. These inequities have yet to be erased.

PRIVATE SCHOOLS, 1870–1900

Even though the public school system was established, its capacity remained so limited for so long that private schools continued to have an important role in providing education for African American children. The Catholic Church's first postbellum foray into African American education was when Bishop Verot recruited Sisters of St. Joseph from Le Puy, France (Verot's hometown). They established a school in 1867, which despite initial success, eventually became a white school. Verot saw more success with the school he started in St. Augustine, Florida.[109] Another private, Catholic African American school was the St. Joseph's Academy started in 1877; it only operated for a few years. The Sacred Heart School for Colored Children began in 1880. Father Oswald Moosmüller, Skidaway Island mission founder, also started this church and school. The school was later moved to St. Benedict's Church along East Broad Street.

The Women's Missionary Society of the Northern Methodist Episcopal Church started the school that became Haven Home Industrial School, which was an institution for fifty years in Savannah's Cuyler-Brownsville neighborhood. It began with an outreach program in 1881, and four years later the society purchased a large brick home that occupied the whole block between Henry and Anderson Streets to the north and south, and Burroughs and Cuyler Streets to the east and west. The building was renovated into a two-and-a-half-story boarding school and day school with a cupola and dining room-kitchen addition. A greenhouse was added in the later 1880s, and other outbuildings were added in the 1890s. The school was sold to the public school board in 1912 and merged with the industrial school in Sandfly. The Cuyler Street School was built on this lot in 1913, and the original Haven Home was razed by the 1940s.[110]

Multiple African American schools opened in 1883, including the Sisters of Mercy's school in the cathedral basement. George A. Davidson and Louis B. Toomer opened the Georgia Military Cadet School (also called the Savannah Military College) at the northwest corner of Harris and East Broad Streets. Both of these schools were short lived and only open two years. Martin J. Crawford opened the successful Alma Mater Institute in 1883 as well. Also known as Crawford's Academy, this school was open for more than twenty years. And in 1895, a school was started in Butler Presbyterian Church's basement.[111] There were also "Sabbath schools," or church-sponsored schools. Usually meeting on weekends and evenings, these schools were established with local Black community support and taught by Black teachers, although sometimes they had white churches' support. Because many schools were independent of the Freedmen's Bureau, aid societies, and other institutions, they are not in official histories or official accounts.[112]

As detailed in the following chapters, the Benedictines' school and mission operated concurrently with many of these schools, with mixed results. The Benedictines suffered from many of the same problems (and virtues) as the AMA and other white-led, northern benevolent organizations. The mission school lacked consistent teachers, had too few African American teachers, had staff with racist beliefs of varying magnitudes, and lacked parental oversight and involvement; all sides suffered from cultural misconceptions. Funding and basic school supplies shortages plagued every school, no matter who organized the school. The Benedictines' mission school had some specific challenges. The boarding school accepted African American boys and teenagers, but many parents refused to send their children to boarding school because it meant long family separations. The staff taught a Catholic curriculum on a Protestant island, and the boarding school environment, unlike a day school, meant that students were steeped in Catholic culture. Further, as a manual (or industrial) school, the students were expected to work the farm each day. Many parents felt there were too many work hours and too few academic instructional hours per day, especially when there were fully academic alternatives. These factors all led to low enrollment and high student turnover despite the school's primary advantage: free education.

In the years immediately following the Civil War, schools popped up and disappeared quickly as demand was high, but resources were scarce and diminishing. Other schools, such as the Beach Institute and Haven Home Industrial School, became long-term institutions that served Savannah's African American communities for decades. These early school organizers faced cultural and logistical challenges with which our society still struggles today. Underfunding, racism, white privilege, and segregation all shaped our earliest public and private schools, and, despite progress, those scars have not been erased. The Benedictines plunged into this underfunded, understaffed, and lacking-in-infrastructure mess. They started as bit players and outsiders wading into this always changing, braided stream of public and private, religious and secular education systems, and they had to earn their way toward trust. The need for more schools, teachers, and funding was always enormous, but there were some options for parents to choose. Would they choose the Benedictines' school?

CHAPTER 3

The Benedictines Begin

Catholics have always been a small minority among Savannah's Christian population, even today consisting of less than 3 percent of southern Georgia's population.[1]
A significant portion of Savannah's earliest Catholics arrived from Haiti in the
1790s. These Black and white immigrants fled the Haitian Revolution, and their
arrival caused fears of revolt spreading to Savannah. The Cathedral of St. John the
Baptist's registry contains the recorded baptisms and marriages of these "pioneer
black Catholics."[2] Between 1796 and 1808, approximately one hundred people of
color are listed in the parish registers including forty-two enslaved and free baby
baptisms and two free Black couples and one enslaved couple who were married.[3]
Until the Benedictines' arrival in Savannah, Black and white Catholics were one
congregation, with African Americans worshiping from the church's gallery. Despite legal restrictions, Sister Jane Francis, a white Sister of Mercy, opened a school
for Black children on Habersham Street near Charlton Street, possibly in 1855.[4]
Savannah's Catholic population still remained very small until the twentieth century, with a notable increase from the 1870s into the 1910s.[5] During this time, the
Catholic Church attempted to attract newly freed African Americans. Locally and
elsewhere, the church used schools as a way to introduce freedpeople to Catholicism and promote conversion to the Catholic faith.

FIRST STEPS TOWARD A CATHOLIC EDUCATION

Forty-four Catholic bishops gathered at the October 1866 Second Plenary Council in Baltimore. Among the topics discussed was the church's responsibility toward freedpeople. The bishops concluded that the church should have two goals:
to educate and convert. As Baltimore's Archbishop Martin Spaulding wrote: "Four
million of these unfortunates are thrown in our charity. . . . It is a golden opportunity for reaping a harvest of souls, which neglected may not return."[6] Ultimately,
no cohesive policy was adopted, and each diocese had to reinvent the wheel.

Savannah's Bishop Augustin Verot felt competitive pressure from northern
Protestant denominations who were heavily involved in creating schools, so in
1867, he formed a Catholic school for African American children.[7] Two years previously, Verot had recruited Sisters of St. Joseph from his hometown of Le Puy,
France, for the specific purpose of teaching African American students. The sisters'

first school was in St. Augustine, Florida, a city with a much longer history of Black Catholicism because of its Spanish colonial roots. As more teachers arrived from Le Puy, schools were opened in Savannah (April 1867) and two more in Florida, Jacksonville (1868) and Fernandina (1870). The Savannah school was housed in a frame building on the cathedral grounds and had an enrollment of about fifty students. Two years later, the school had approximately one hundred students and could have accepted more if given more space.

At the Tenth Provincial Council of Baltimore in April 1869, the bishops again discussed their concerns and duties toward African Americans. Bishop Verot suggested a mandate for the dioceses to build schools and churches for freed-people. The proposal passed unanimously. However, the Savannah diocese was split in 1870, and Verot was assigned to St. Augustine, Florida. The Sisters of St. Joseph, who were "trained expressly for African missions," continued their Savannah school without Verot, teaching about sixty students in 1870.[8] By 1879, however, the sisters were teaching more white than Black students. This trend continued, and eventually the school was only for white students.[9]

Verot's successor, Bishop Ignatius Persico, resigned due to ill health after only a few years in Savannah. Bishop William Gross took up the missionary mantle on his arrival in 1873, writing to Right Reverend Raphael Testa, O.S.B., and re-questing Benedictine missionaries who would open schools for African American children. Gross's original plan was to start an orphanage and school for African American boys on the church's Skidaway Island plantation, Hampton Place, but this plan was contingent on the Skidaway road and bridge completion.[10] Georgia's coast is a lacework of barrier islands, some of which are barely islands and are really only separated from the mainland by marsh. A relevant example is Isle of Hope, which is accessible by road and a small bridge. Other islands are more significantly delineated by the numerous winding tidal rivers. Skidaway Island, bounded primarily by the Skidaway and Wilmington Rivers, was only accessible by boat in the 1870s. The Skidaway infrastructure improvements were tied to several development opportunities including the Savannah, Skidaway, and Seaboard Railroad Company, which was incorporated in 1867, and subsequent tourism development ventures including Schutzen Park near Bonaventure Cemetery and proposed summer resorts and homes with frontage on the Skidaway River (advertised in April 1870).[11] The political wrangling and funds needed for the infrastructure were extensively, bureaucratically, and painfully argued as different interest factions fought from 1867 until well into the 1870s, delaying the bridge construction and Bishop Gross's plans.

Although the bridge would not be built for another hundred years, Bishop

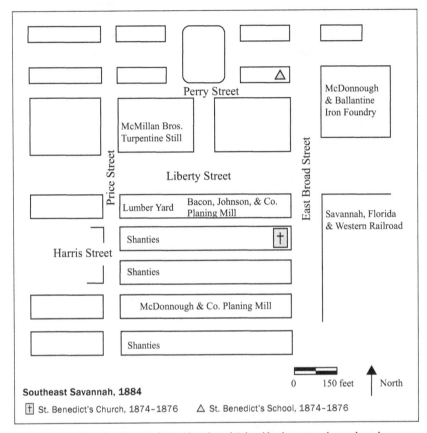

Perry Street

McDonnough
& Ballantine
Iron Foundry

McMillan Bros.
Turpentine Still

Price Street

East Broad Street

Liberty Street

Lumber Yard

Bacon, Johnson, & Co.
Planing Mill

Savannah, Florida
& Western Railroad

Shanties

Harris Street

Shanties

McDonnough & Co. Planing Mill

Shanties

0   150 feet   North

Southeast Savannah, 1884

⊤ St. Benedict's Church, 1874–1876   △ St. Benedict's School, 1874–1876

MAP 4. Map of the first St. Benedict's Church and School built in 1874, located on the east side of Savannah, Georgia. This map is based on the 1884 Sanborn Fire Insurance Map, printed a few years after St. Benedict's closed.

Gross did receive two missionary priests as requested. Rev. Raphael Wissel of Subiaco, Italy, and Rev. Gabriel Bergier of Pierre Qui Vire, France, arrived in Savannah on May 13, 1874, after a brief stop at Saint Vincent Archabbey in Latrobe, Pennsylvania. Their arrival was discussed in a mildly gossipy newspaper column. Gavroche, who wrote from Savannah for the *Augusta Chronicle*, stated the priests were to construct a "college" on Skidaway Island, anticipating the actual school by four years.[12] Despite these indications, it seems the Skidaway plan was tabled at this point because the bridge was delayed. Instead, the two priests quickly established St. Benedict's Parish with a church at Harris and East Broad Streets and a school on nearby Perry Street (see map 4). This area was the eastern edge of the city. The oldest available Sanborn Fire Insurance map for Savannah, 1884, depicts industries and "shanties" in the area. The shanties are interspersed with planing mills, a tur-

pentine still, an iron foundry, and the Savannah, Florida, and Western Railroad
Depot Grounds. This area would have been quite loud at times and certainly had
its fair share of air pollution.

Bishop Gross inaugurated the new church on January 3, 1875. The church was
built at the cost of $1,500, with African Americans donating much of the labor
and money. The church lot was on a five-year lease.[13] Bergier requested teachers
from Saint Vincent Archabbey, and Abbot Boniface Wimmer sent Brother Philip
Cassidy, O.S.B.[14] Initially, the Savannah school was a success, opening in 1875 with
fifty students.[15] Later, Brother Joseph, an African American, taught at the school,
followed by a woman whose name is unknown.[16] Father Bergier also recruited
candidates for priests and lay brothers. Their success is remarkable considering
that Bergier did not speak English well. "The Holy French Benedictine, in spite
of his ignorance of our language on commencing, had already gathered in many
negroes around the convent, had made converts among the whites also," noted
Bishop Gross.[17]

Fathers Wissel and Bergier decided to expand eastward into the islands, spend-
ing $280 on an Isle of Hope property with the aim to build a monastery and no-
vitiate. Dr. Stephen F. Dupon, a Catholic and Isle of Hope native, donated the
adjacent property, which measured 135 by 100 feet and already had a small wooden
building. The building was converted to a church, and a monastery was built, allowing Father Bergier to move in during the summer of 1876 (see figure 1). He was
moderately successful in his ministries. Dr. Dupon estimated that Bergier had "30–
40 'communicants'" during his time on Isle of Hope.[18] Father Bergier had both
Black and white novitiates. Bernard Murphy and John Shea, both white, received
their habits in April 1875. While Father Bergier worked on Isle of Hope, Father
Wissel stayed in Savannah to run the church and open a bookstore.[19]

Unfortunately, this undertaking did not end well, as Wissel "ran away & left
$3,300 or as others say almost $6000 of debts behind."[20] A later accounting of Wissel's debts came to $4,000, which the bishop paid after Wissel left "the diocese in
shame."[21] Despite this incident, Wissel continued his career as a priest. After leaving Savannah, he went to Augusta, Maine. By 1880 he lived in Eastport, on Maine's
northernmost coast at the Canadian border. In 1881, Wissel signed a passport application as a naturalized citizen, swearing that he was born in Bavaria, Germany,
but was the son of a naturalized citizen, having lived his childhood to his majority
with his father in the United States. The passport application gives us an unflat-
tering description of Wissel: forty-three years old, 5 feet 6.5 inches tall with gray
eyes and "iron gray" short hair; a high forehead with small nose, mouth, and chin;
a light complexion and a "large, round, fleshy" face.[22] In early 1885, Wissel traveled

FIGURE 1. The Benedictines founded Our Lady of Good Hope Chapel on Isle of Hope, Georgia, in 1876, pictured here in this undated, vintage photograph. (Courtesy of Saint Vincent Archabbey Archives)

aboard the ship *Yarra* from Marseille, France, to Sydney, New South Wales, in the company of the Bishop of Auckland and several other priests. He lived in New Zealand for several years, until at least 1891, but traveled extensively.[23] The *Baltimore Sun* reported him visiting Baltimore in 1889 on a fundraising trip after a fire destroyed St. Benedict's Church in Auckland and visiting St. James' Church again in 1898.[24]

Wissel's flight to Maine may have saved his life, because in September and October 1876, another yellow fever epidemic struck. Tragically, Father Bergier, Gregory Enright (a clerical novice), and J. McDonald (a brotherhood postulant) were all victims of the disease. Most of the remaining Benedictines went to Atoka, Oklahoma, in early 1877, joining the Benedictine Congregation of the Primitive Observance to work with Indigenous Americans.[25] Bishop Gross put the secular priest Rev. Fridolin Eckert in charge of St. Benedict's Parish in October 1876. Around this time, the new cathedral was completed, so the bishop "gave the old Cathedral to the nigroes [*sic*] and F[ather] Eckert fixed it up very nicely and also cut off a part of the church and built a fine dwelling house into it, furnished it in a rich & splen-did manner."[26] Dedicated in March of 1877, this church replaced St. Benedict's and was named St. Joseph's, located at Drayton and McDonough Streets between Co-lonial Cemetery and Chippewa Square.[27] With Bishop Gross's permission, Eckert sold St. Benedict's Church to the "colored Odd Fellows . . . for a song," or about $250, considerably less than the $1,500 cost of construction.[28] The Odd Fellows also bought the lot and rented the building for events and a dance school.[29]

The white Sisters of Mercy opened a parish school at St. Joseph's Church, which was possibly a continuation of the French Sisters of St. Joseph's cathedral school, started under Bishop Verot. St. Joseph's Church hosted about forty baptisms per year between 1875 and 1879, as well as the funeral of Abraham Beasley, husband of Mathilda Beasley, who is discussed further in chapter 4. Father Eckert was the pas-tor throughout the church's existence.[30] Born in Baden, Germany, in 1839, Father Eckert immigrated to New York City aboard the ship *William Tell* at age twenty. He lived in Savannah until at least 1881, when the diocese closed the church, al-though the school lasted another two years. St. Joseph's was closed because white Savannahians kept going to St. Joseph's rather than attending (and giving offerings to) the new cathedral. St. Joseph's was deeply nostalgic for white citizens who had been baptized or married there, but their presence meant African Americans were relegated to the gallery, negating the purpose of having a church exclusively for African Americans. After the church's closure, the Catholic Library Association took over the building. By 1886, Father Eckert had moved to the Peoria Diocese and remained there until his death on February 26, 1910. He is buried in St. Joseph's Cemetery in Cabery, Illinois.[31]

To continue his missionary work, Bishop Gross requested more help from France (without luck). Next he turned to Abbot Boniface Wimmer, founder of the first American Benedictine monastery, Saint Vincent Archabbey, for help staffing the Isle of Hope mission. Gross wrote that Bergier "died a most holy death" and wished for more monks so "this promising foundation may not per-ish." Gross offered "lands, a monastery, young students, and lay brothers" and "*no debts* whatsoever," promising to hand over the property deeds "most cheerfully."[32] The abbot agreed in January 1877.[33] Bishop Gross gratefully responded to Wim-mer's acceptance with his vision of the Benedictine mission: "I always have been of the opinion that the Benedictines would of all religious be the most eminently adapted for the work of civilizing and educating the immense number of negroes in my diocese. If they could establish a good home in this property and from this home send out evangelical laborers among the countless villages and towns of Georgia, what a great work. Thus to form schools for blacks and whites, instruct and teach the Gospel to these immense multitudes who know nothing of the true religion."[34]

Benedictines have traditionally been dedicated to education, both within their order and as teachers for others. The Rule of St. Benedict requires Benedictine religious to spend part of the day practicing the *Lectio Divina* (Divine Reading), which consists of reading, meditation, prayer, and contemplation, so each monastery had a prized library as texts were critical for daily prayer, study, worship, and schools.[35] Their scholarly traditions made the Benedictines particularly well qualified for developing schools.

RETURN TO ISLE OF HOPE

Father Oswald Moosmüller, recently posted in Kansas but freed from his duties by the election of Abbot Innocent Wolf, arrived in Savannah with Father Maurice Kaeder on March 2, 1877. Moosmüller immediately inspected the Isle of Hope property the next day, describing its daunting state:

> I was advised not to move into the room of Father Bergier yet, as it would not be safe, till it is thoroughly cleaned and aired etc. The rooms & upstairs are neither plastered nor papered nor white washed, only the natural boards; the Chapel consists only of a room 40 x 30 and 11 feet high. . . . The buildings are miserable. The whole ground on which they stand about ½ acre was donated by Dr. Dupont [*sic*], about one acre joining it was bought by Father Wissel for 350 dollars and turned into a garden, along the roads or walks are crap-vines [grape vines]. . . . The chapel has room for 50 persons. . . . But this is no place for a monastery.[36]

Later letters expounded on just how inappropriate the Isle of Hope situation was. The property deed was only promised, but never delivered, so the Benedictines did not own it, and consequently they could lose all investments and improvements to the small property. Most problematic were the neighbors. Next door was a "hotel with a tenpins." Another neighbor was a railroad company, which could build a depot at any time and whose tracks ran about seventy feet from the house. Finally, next to the house was a "public platform for dancing which is used all through the summer by parties white & black coming here on Pic Nics."[37] Bowling, trains, and parties were not conducive to studying, praying, and contemplation.

Within a week, Moosmüller laid out the new plan to Wimmer: Bishop Gross would transfer Hampton Place Plantation to the Benedictines, who would have to start building from scratch. The monks would create a mission on Skidaway Island that included a manual labor school for African American boys and opportunities for training African American lay brothers. Bishop Gross petitioned the court to transfer the property to the Benedictine Order, and the deed was recorded on July 16, 1877. The deed specified the property was for the "advancement of the Roman Catholic Religion in the way of educating Catholic youth."[38]

As a forward-thinking administrator, Moosmüller applied for incorporation under the name "Benedictine Order in Georgia" on March 29, 1877. The corporation, which had a charter for twenty years with possibility for renewal, was confirmed and recorded on May 1, 1877. Their sole reason for incorporation was "the education of youths in the various departments of human knowledge" and to build "schools, colleges, and institutions as may be necessary."[39] The Benedictine Order renewed their corporation for another twenty years when their charter expired in 1897.[40] So while the Benedictines did not specify African American education, their stated reason for existence in Georgia was education and building schools. Their correspondence, however, reveals dual goals: conversion to the Catholic faith and education.[41] Conversion was often considered the primary goal. In acknowledging the challenges of creating the Skidaway mission, Bishop Gross wrote, "The devil will of course do all in his power to root up the work for God's glory and the salvation of souls," but he did not mention educating these souls.[42]

This mission was Moosmüller's first experience in the American South, with the exception of a brief stint in Kentucky in 1858. His letters reveal a quick initiation into southern race relations, starting with his journey to Savannah. He and Father Kaeder stopped en route at the Mary Help mission, near Charlotte, North Carolina. Rev. J. J. O'Connell gave the fathers a tour of his "so called plantation" and the tenant farming system, where African American families worked five- to ten-acre plots rented from the Catholic Church. The advantages for Rev. O'Connell were many, including producing income and "having a control & influence over the nigroes [sic] to convert them."[43]

Once in Georgia, Moosmüller continued to learn. Some of the African American lay brothers gave him advice very directly, including Brother Joseph, their cook, who said, "*It will never do to have white & black brothers mixed together.*"[44] Further he advised, "The negroes prefer a colored teacher to a white man, they have more confidence in him, he knows their ways; they are afraid of a white man."[45] So Brother Joseph offered to teach in the mornings and cook or do housework in the afternoons.[46] Moosmüller had traveled the world, from his native Bavaria, to Canada, Brazil, the Vatican, and many postings throughout the United States, but in Savannah he had a new cultural dynamic to navigate. Moosmüller was lucky to have this teacher who felt comfortable enough to explain racial dynamics. This comfort level may have been because Moosmüller was an outsider, because they were fellow Catholics, because Brother Joseph had a high status as an educated person, or possibly some combination of these reasons.

Brother Joseph, born Francis G. J. Anderson, was one of the first to join the Isle of Hope monastery. Anderson speaks to us through a letter to Dr. Dupon written from Isle of Hope in late June 1877. He shared his vision of a future with multiple Savannah-area Catholic missions and gave advice on racial relations and converting the African American population. He began, "With my experience south among my people I have found that to mix with the whites, that it is bad in the extreme." He repeated this theme throughout the letter, advocating for separation of the races so African Americans feel welcome and comfortable in the church. He explained that many African Americans are "afriad to enter our church, and when they do they are afriad of intruding on the whites [sic]." He wanted to see African American converts, and he advocated for Black priests, calling the lay brotherhood and sisterhood "a beginning." He wished to teach elementary school and recommended that a "reformatory school for Orphans & Vagrants" and a manual labor school be built.[47]

Despite these warnings, African American and white staff did work together throughout the monastery's existence. In November 1879, Moosmüller reported the only known instance of interracial physical violence. "Last week I had to dismiss two Bro's Candidates, one a nigro [sic] from New Orleans and the other a white one from Savannah; they were fighting, using axe and gun."[48] There is no mention of injuries, and the source of the conflict is entirely unknown.

BUILDING ON SKIDAWAY ISLAND

Father Moosmüller quickly lost Father Kaeder's help, because at Bishop Gross's request, Kaeder began work as a missionary, preaching at stops along the three-hundred-mile-long Gulf Railroad. Kaeder was commended for his work, and his superiors noted his public speaking skills, his fluency in German and English, as well as his resilience under adverse conditions. Abbot Wimmer praised him: "As he is a good speaker, he always finds listeners. Lately at a temperature of 105 F. he preached in the court-house of Thomasville to the best people of the town and many asked for catechisms."[49] This was exhausting work, often with so little monetary compensation he could barely cover his traveling expenses. Father Maurice returned to Saint Vincent Abbey at the end of 1877.[50]

To help staff his new Skidaway mission, Moosmüller recruited the three African American lay brothers from Father Bergier's Isle of Hope mission and hoped to keep recruiting. They were to teach school and do domestic work such as cooking, cleaning, and laundry. Moosmüller also asked for Brother Andrew of Atchinson, Kansas, Moosmüller's previous posting, because he believed Andrew would get along well with the African American brothers.[51] Throughout the mission's existence, finding and retaining qualified brothers and monks was a problem—never more so than when Moosmüller was building the church, housing, and stables for the mission and farm in addition to preparing and planting fields, all of which was intense physical labor in rural conditions.

Benedictines had the same class system within their order as Europe had at large. Lay brothers and sisters were essentially working-class religious. They performed manual labor (some skilled, some not), professed only simple vows, and were not required to say full daily prayers. They had no voting rights, had different dress codes, and even lived separately. American Benedictines tweaked the European tradition by recruiting many more lay brothers, particularly because the lay brothers literally built the monasteries and churches from the ground up, as they did at Skidaway. The buildings were often simple, modest structures except for the churches, which were often more elaborate.[52]

Father Moosmüller and his small but growing group of brothers and novitiates lived on the Isle of Hope property for approximately one year while building the Skidaway Island mission. They moved to Skidaway between mid-March and June 16, 1878, when the monastery was dedicated during the blessing of the new buildings ceremony. The frequent commutes between islands would have been challenging. (Isle of Hope and Skidaway Island are adjacent, separated by the Skidaway River.) The exact logistics of this situation are not clear in the documentary evidence, but the process of gathering materials, building the structures, preparing fields, and planting crops to restart the farm took much longer than Moosmüller hoped and anticipated.

When the Benedictines arrived, Skidaway Islanders were recovering from several tough years. In July 1875, drought killed nearly the whole crop for that year, leaving the locals in an "almost destitute condition."[53] Corn fields were expected to produce less than one bushel per acre, compared with ten bushels per acre in previous years. The potatoes and peas had been "abandoned."[54] Disease continued to be a concern, commonly malaria and yellow fever. A particularly scary 1876 headline blared, "Is it Black Tongue?" Two African American men died suddenly within hours of coming down with a fever. Their tongues had turned black, swollen, and spongy.[55] The cause was most likely yellow fever or possibly Dengue fever.[56]

As Moosmüller began his work on Skidaway Island, several African American families were already farming on the property, renting land under a contract with Bishop Gross. The Benedictines continued to rent portions of the property to tenant farmers, thereby providing some income for the fledgling mission. The former main house was destroyed in the Civil War, and consequently this area was devoid of any development. A whole new facility had to be built from scratch. By the end of March, Moosmüller had bought supplies to begin building log houses, and work started on the buildings in the spring of 1877. A stable, monastery, and multipurpose building holding a kitchen, dining room, and boys dormitory were planned. There were practical reasons to place the monastery and school at the same location as the plantation's former main house. While "there was hardly a trace of a building or of any fencing," some infrastructure remained.[57] The monks reused the tabby basement walls as a foundation, and a road provided access to the site. However, by reusing the enslaver's former seat, Moosmüller was, perhaps unconsciously, appropriating at least the slave owners' geographic position if not their social position and power structures as well.

Moosmüller began spring planting with a gifted wagon and mules borrowed from Mr. Moran and Mr. Reilly. The farm needed to produce food for their live-stock (a chicken, a cow, and two mules), food for the mission staff and eventually students, as well as producing crops to sell for cash. Moosmüller's goal was always to make the mission self-sufficient; however, it was reliant on Saint Vincent for money and supplies for several years. Nearly every letter to Wimmer begins with Moosmüller thanking him for sending money, although Moosmüller was thrifty and spent his money wisely. "We live now very poor, we never took a glass of wine nor beer, except once with the Bishop."[58]

Moosmüller started planting in April 1877 with thirty acres "in oats, sweet po-tatoes, corn, rice, sugarcane, beans, cotton, etc." and the hope of planting ten more acres.[59] However, the ground was not well prepared, and they were plowing old fields full of roots and vegetation, which was exhausting labor with little return. Later that summer, he confessed that he could buy the crops cheaper than it cost him to grow, but since he needed the animals to build the house, the loss was not as great.[60] Their animals seemed to suffer too. One cow died, and the other did not produce milk. Their borrowed mules were laboring constantly between working the fields and hauling materials for the new buildings. This must have been ex-tremely difficult physical work. Moosmüller was likely unused to this work, not having a background in farming. He was helped by two hired laborers, paid eight dollars per month plus board, and the lay brothers. Within a few weeks, Moos-müller was worn down. Feeling the full burden of farming, construction, and ad-ministration, he wrote to Wimmer: "This time I have no good news. I must confess that I feel a good deal depressed and discouraged." One of his borrowed mules died, so not only did he lose a work animal, but he had to pay to replace the animal.

Adding to his dilemma, some advised him not to pay "because it is probable that the mule was sick when I got him."[61] Moosmüller was in a bind, practically and ethically. Half of the new house timber was on site, the corn needed cultivating, and mules were essential to this work.

Two days later, the news was worse. The cow's and mule's deaths were not natural. "Some persons told me that the cow was shot and the mule was wounded on one side of the head above the eye, when he died. I dismissed the driver."[62] Moosmüller never revealed his informants or his suspects (beyond the driver). One must wonder if these animals died through accidents or abuse, or were they victims of an effort to push the monks away? After discussing the excellent state of his peas and potatoes, Moosmüller noted, "It will take a good while before the colored people place any confidence in us, and till they believe at all that we intend to work for their temporal and eternal welfare."[63] Moosmüller must have been gaining some trust, because in early June, he had several boys who planned to enter the school once it was completed. Work continued slowly on the buildings including the house, which was intended to be "lathed and plastered inside, and a two story porch on the seaside . . . worth about $1000."[64] He was also making progress on the infrastructure, digging an artesian well eighteen feet deep and approximately one hundred feet west of the house.[65]

July 1877 found Father Moosmüller at perhaps his most stressed and worried. After reporting farm details then writing several hesitant sentences, his letter to Abbot Wimmer switches from English to his native German. He told Wimmer they should cut and run, get as much money back as they could, and abandon the mission: "For we will never accomplish anything with these Negroes; if we stay here any longer, we will lose more; and if yellow fever does not hit, another cause can have the same effect."[66] Their new horse, which was bought for $110 about six weeks prior, had fallen over dead while working the fields. "It had never been sick, was always lively and fresh, about six years old; it is rumored that it was poisoned. It is conjectured that a similar attempt was made eight days ago with the mule."[67] The mule was suddenly ill; its head, neck, and stomach swelled up. Only Moosmüller's quick action saved the mule: "I took him to the tent, fed him bark from the poplar tree as well as sodium sulphate and now he is recovering."[68]

Similar incidents had happened over the years. After the Civil War, several northerners purchased a Skidaway Island plantation and had fifteen mules die in a short period of time. This combined with other mysterious losses forced them to quit. The previous month, two men were jailed for buying strychnine to poison Dr. Dupon's cattle. Moosmüller also notes that many community members, some of whom were employed constructing the mission, held Baptist services on the

Benedictines' land and were "greatly prejudiced against the Catholic religion."[69] The matter was dropped for lack of proof, but Moosmüller had received the unambiguous message that for many residents, he and the monks were not welcome in the community.[70] Much like the fishing boat incidents nearly ten years earlier (see chapter 1), local residents were willing to defend their homespace using violence and threats if necessary to keep unwanted outsiders away. These resistance tactics, honed under slavery, ran from work slowdowns and "accidentally" broken tools to more aggressive strategies such as violence and self-emancipation.

Minor transgressions continued in August. One morning, the monks woke to a broken fence and grapes missing on their Isle of Hope property. "Since that we watched a little during the night and fired a shot occasionally," wrote Moosmüller.[71] The monks later discovered that grapes were taken during the day. The broken fence probably indicates this incident was another act of resistance to dissuade the monks. Alternatively, the grapes may have been a communal resource that for years was available to all, and the tradition was being continued. A similar conflict between private and communal resources is explained in Drew A. Swanson's *Remaking Wormsloe Plantation*.[72] When local individuals harvested oysters along the banks of Wormsloe Plantation, the DeRenne family assisted in prosecuting these perceived trespassers and poachers to protect the family's oyster supply, which was for personal use as well as harvested commercially. Much of the conflict came from a series of increasingly complex laws from 1855 to 1895 that changed which oyster beds were public and which were privately owned.

Another example occurred over fishing rights in 1873. Mr. A. Bonaud, a white man, sued Benjamin Aiken, an African American, for using a seine net to catch fish in the Skidaway River, approximately one mile from Isle of Hope. Justice Dupon's reading of the January 1873 law, which stated that one could not catch fish with a seine net "in certain parts of Chatham County," meant that the defendant was sent to jail and held unless he could post bail.[73] This would have been financially devastating for Mr. Aiken, who likely had no money for bail and would certainly not be making a living in jail. Major Bonaud seems to have been a litigious man. The following spring, he sued the Savannah, Seaboard, and Skidaway Railroad for $100 because the train did not run on schedule, causing him to miss dance class.[74]

The locals' contentious, defensive attitudes exacerbated the religious personnel's feelings of loneliness and isolation, especially in the beginning. Moosmüller wrote to his friend Father James Zilliox back at Saint Vincent Abbey, "I am thankful that you remember your confrater who lives in some way like Robinson Crusoe on the island, at least during the late storm, it was impossible to sail or row across the water from here to the mainland, and most likely it will be the same again on the 22 and 23d of this month at the Equinox."[75] Likely this last reference is to tides, as coastal Georgia has extreme tides with water levels rising or falling up to ten feet every six hours. The "late storm" refers to a hurricane that made landfall in Charleston on September 12, 1878, after sideswiping the Georgia coast.[76]

The African American residents would have perceived the monks as transients, or hoped them to be, although the monks themselves may not have shared this view. Island residents very likely saw the monks as invaders of their homespace, an idea complicated by some families living on the church's, then the Benedictines', land. They may have even thought the monks were using the manual school to create a new plantation system with education as a bribe to re-enslave their children to work in the fields. White landowners used this tactic to maintain a large population of undereducated and marginalized workers. Although the Benedictines did benefit financially by renting their farmland, as outsiders, they had less of a vested interest in maintaining the societal status quo from slavery, which was the social incentive for southern white employers. However, by creating an industrial school, the Benedictines pushed their students toward only working-class options. Abbot Wimmer wrote about the Skidaway mission: "Here the young negros [sic] are instructed in working around the house & in the field & make them get into the habit of doing so & likewise learn fishery—what is their main occupation for livelihood—From an excursion to the bay the abbot [Leo Haid] returned with 200 nice fish—which they had caught in a large net with one draught."[77] Although Wimmer clearly believed in the educational benefits of the "industrial school," as he often called it, from our twenty-first-century perspective, we can see the African American residents did not need instruction in basic housework, fishing, and agriculture. Nor did they need lessons in good work habits.

Despite the locals' resistance, the monks were becoming established. Although the mission continued to receive support from Saint Vincent, in August 1877, the finances were becoming more stable, and the corn crop was harvested to feed the mules and horses. As the men settled into their new life, they took some time to explore the area and relax with an outing to Wassaw Island. Moosmüller, along with Dan Sullivan, a scholastic who was traveling to Saint Vincent, "sent some shells & sponge, which we collected (on the shore of Warsaw [sic] island, next to Skidaway)."[78]

Moosmüller continued his attempts to make inroads with the islanders. "In order to secure the patronage of the most influential negroes on Skidaway, I allowed them to work with our mule on certain days according to special agreement for due compensation."[79] Fortunately for this mule, he was doted on, petted, and treated to as many watermelon rinds as he wanted. Moosmüller also came to an accommodation with a neighbor, Joseph Bacon, so the monks could use Bacon's horse for hauling manure and timber. In exchange, Bacon used the monks' mule the next week. Moosmüller also made slow progress, but progress nonetheless, in recruiting African American lay brothers. In October 1877, he had four new applications, three from Baltimore and one from New Orleans. Some of these recruits were the work of Brother Joseph, who knew two men from Baltimore (his hometown) who were interested in becoming brothers and were capable of teaching.[80]

By September, the plans for the three buildings changed slightly, and the buildings increased in size. The log house was 36 feet by 24 feet. The kitchen, dining room, and boys' dormitory building was 40 feet by 24 feet, and the stable was 30 feet by 13 feet and was anticipated to be completed in a week. Each was "two stories and a garret," and the latter two buildings were wood frame. Moosmüller estimated the houses would be complete in six to eight weeks at a total cost of nearly $1,000.[81] As always, these completion estimates were overzealous. One month later, the house was nowhere near completion. "We, or rather I [Moosmüller] was putting on the plastering laths on the partitions of the second story, but the floor of the first story is yet to be laid and the cellar and stairs etc etc."[82] The stable was complete, however.

FATHER OSWALD MOOSMÜLLER

In addition to farming, constructing the buildings, and his priestly duties, Moosmüller had administrative obligations. One of these was returning the late Father Bergier's belongings to his superior in Oklahoma, Father Isidore Robot, O.S.B. Moosmüller was happy to return any personal property but felt strongly that much of what was left behind had been donated "for the benefit of the Nigro-Mission [*sic*]" and should stay with the mission.[83] Moosmüller had made a complete inventory of all items upon his arrival at Isle of Hope, and he cited Catholic law to the Bishop about what should and should not be sent to Oklahoma—anything other than personal property "will, according to the decree No 187 and several other decrees of the Council of Baltimore, have to remain in this diocese, to be applied for the purpose for which it was given."[84] This was not stinginess. Moosmüller had exacting standards. He was a capable, organized, pious man, who was intent on doing his job correctly. He explained, "As a religious, considering nothing as my own, it shall cause no trouble to me, which way your Lordship [Wimmer] may decide the question or what I have to send to the V. Rev. Father Robot."[85] Moosmüller could be critical of his colleagues, but it was often meant as a constructive criticism. He questioned if the Oklahoma monks would take every last piece of furniture and asked Wimmer, "What do you say to that? Perhaps they will even claim the real estate, this house, lot, and the farm of 121 acres? Please give me some instructions, soon!"[86]

Moosmüller was not a man completely without humor, and his dry wit often comes through in his correspondence. Two days prior, he wrote to Abbot Innocent Wolf at the abbot's request. Moosmüller was at a loss to adequately describe the Skidaway mission and Isle of Hope, writing that if the abbot wanted to know something, he'd better ask some more specific questions. Moosmüller tartly suggested, "I can gather shells on the sea shore for your collection. I can shoot an alligator from 1 to 6 feet in length on our own land & skin him or ketch [sic] a shark with the hook and send you the skin. In a few weeks I will have another boat on the east shore of the island and then I will have a better chance for such sport."[87]

Moosmüller held common, contemporary beliefs and biases, including ideas that were racist, hypocritical, and classist. While navigating the foreign, southern culture, Moosmüller walked a fuzzy line between believing in his mission to educate African Americans and create a Black lay brotherhood while reconciling his own racist, classist beliefs that were counter to that mission. For example, he asked Abbot Wimmer for permission to treat a visiting African American brother differently than the other African American lay brothers. Mr. Willyams had spent seven years studying philosophy and theology at the Propaganda in Rome and was expected to visit the Skidaway mission soon. Moosmüller considered Willyams in a "particular Class of Brothers, distinct from the lay brothers, perhaps as Choir-brothers similar to the Trappists."[88] Willyams was denied ordination because of his race, despite his training in Rome specifically for the priesthood and missionary work in Africa.[89] Moosmüller demonstrated classic exceptionalism, as he both acknowledged Willyams's accomplishments while writing disparagingly about promoting lay brothers to the priesthood within the same letter. "Tow nigro-brother candidates, who are not able to spell a single word correctly, told me that they believe they are called by God to become Priests and to preach. Another one asked our Bishop if this house would not come eventually under the control of the nigroes; the Bishop sent the letter to me to answer it; I told him 'Chi paga, commanda' [Italian for "He who pays the piper calls the tune"]. By this you may see that the nigroes are inclined to make great pretensions [sic]."[90]

Here, Moosmüller exposed his blatant individual racism and ease with institutional racism. He was comfortable working beside and training Black lay brothers, but when asked to share power, let alone give up power, he was completely unwilling. The African American lay brothers were using their newly legislated freedoms to resist racism, to actively lobby for better institutional treatment, and to create a Black space within Catholicism for themselves. Requesting control of the Skidaway Island church and school follows their neighbors' strong attachment to the land and desire to create their own homespace. This struggle is reminiscent of the American Missionary Association fighting the Savannah Education Association for control of Savannah's private schools. The same issues were at stake—self-determination and education as a political force to self-empower future generations of African Americans.

At the end of December 1877, four African American candidates were living at the monastery, and Moosmüller expected several more, including Mr. Willyams, who was teaching high school in Baltimore. Moosmüller describes the candidates respectfully, noting their professions were schoolmasters, cooks, and waiters, but also patronizingly: "They dress and behave themselves like Gentlemen."[91] Yet he enthusiastically writes, "Should there ever be a prospect that colored men will be raised to the priesthood, if they are otherwise qualified; then we could soon have a flourishing College here & plenty of colored Scholastics of all shades, ebony, mahogany, walnut, cherry, etc."[92] These contradictory comments suggest Moosmüller's bigotry is intersectional, rooted in education levels and class distinctions as well as race. By this time, Moosmüller had fully internalized American race relations, and he expressed concern for mixing Black and white brothers. "So far as I can understand our situation here, it seems to me advisable, not to have any other brothers here but colored ones."[93]

Another source of institutional racism came from the American Catholic leadership and hierarchy. Bishop Gross stated at the project's outset, "Taking in the children and bringing them up to habits of industry and gradually accustoming their uncultivated intellects to study, is in my humble opinion the plan for civilising and christianising these poor, black barbarians [sic]." Gross felt older African Americans, "stupified [sic] by slavery, heresy, and all kinds of vice," were not capable of "much improvement."[94] Later that year, Moosmüller wanted to give two lay brothers, Arthur Canonge of New Orleans and Baltimore native James Dorsey, their habit on Christmas Day 1877. Moosmüller requested permission and paperwork from the archbishop weeks prior, "but it seems he will give no answer at all."[95] Dorsey had previously received the habit from Father Bergier, and this ceremony was to reacknowledge him in the monastery and get his paperwork straight.

Not all of the monks who worked at Skidaway were as dedicated as Father Moosmüller. In 1880, Brother Fridolin Stehle wrote a letter to colleagues back at Saint Vincent Archabbey complaining of the conditions and speaking ill of

African Americans. Wimmer's letter rebuking Stehle for complaining about the Skidaway mission and its inhabitants illustrates the duality of paternalistic racism. Wimmer responded:

> You did not go to Skidaway to do *your will* (otherwise you would not be a religious with the sacred vow of obedience), but to do *my* will or that of your immediate superior who rules in my name; whereas *I* also may not follow *my own will*, but do command that which I recognize as the will of God, namely, to found an institution for Negroes whereby many Negroes will retain their Catholic faith or be converted. . . . Even if all were true what you have written, we should make even greater efforts to help these unfortunate Negroes. They are also people and God's children.[96]

Wimmer continued in this manner for some paragraphs.

Moosmüller sought ways to work with his African American neighbors, attempting to build relationships through cooperative labor. For example, the monks' fields needed to be fenced because the locals let their hogs forage on the island, eating crops as they roamed wild. Fencing was expensive ($250 to $300 for this project) and extremely time consuming to construct. Moosmüller decided to flip the problem and proposed that everyone living on the monks' plantation work collectively to build the fence. Moosmüller already had five to six thousand split rails at the field, ready to be installed. The fathers would provide the wood, oxen team, and auger, and each family would build a section of fence. Each family that contributed labor would be allowed to house their hogs in the fenced pasture as long as the family lived there and paid rent.[97] With this plan, Moosmüller hoped the fence would be completed in two months by the end of February 1878. This cooperative manner is a marked change from the monks' animals dying from poison.

In contrast to his defeatist attitude in spring 1877, March 1878 saw Moosmüller's work paying off. He confided to Abbot Innocent Wolf of Kansas, "The prospects for the future are bright."[98] The 36-by-24-foot, two-story log house with an attic was built. This building held the temporary chapel, two school rooms, and bedrooms for the priests. A second wooden frame house, 40 by 26 feet and also two stories with a garret, housed the kitchen, pantry, cellar, dining room, and dormitory.[99] The wood frame, two-story, 30-by-15-foot stable housed two mules, four oxen, and a cow. Farm work had also progressed, and more land was cleared. A one-acre vineyard and an orchard with one hundred peach and fifty apple trees were planted.[100]

SEARCHING FOR THE BUILDINGS

Finding archaeological evidence of these buildings and the people that lived in them was the original mission of this project. Archaeological investigations targeted only a tiny portion of the plantation, specifically a property that was slated for development. An adjacent lot, also a small piece of the plantation's core, is preserved in perpetuity by the Landings Association, the homeowners association that manages communal spaces within the Landings community. Based on the initial archaeological survey, three areas were targeted for more detailed excavations. The first area was a disappointment and only contained cultural deposits that postdated the monastery. The other two areas of interest were more successful, and portions of the church, monastery, and school were identified. Unfortunately, no outbuildings such as privies were found.

The monastery's structures were built from scratch because firebug Confederates withdrawing in 1862 destroyed the 100-by-50-foot plantation main house so completely that by 1878, "not a vestige of its foundations" was visible.[101] The 1880s landscape lacked today's luxuriant tree canopy, as much of the land was cleared for agriculture. Two contemporary photographs show grassy, weedy clearings around the church and monastery (combined in one building) and the school.[102] A newspaper reporter boasted, "The buildings . . . command a full view of [the] Warsaw River and sound as far as the ocean."[103] Today, one can see about half a mile across the golf course and lawns to the Wilmington River (the Warsaw's modern name), but claims to see across Wassaw Island to the ocean stretch the truth unless perhaps the reporter was in the garret or church bell tower.

The mission was developed in stages. After the first three buildings were completed, a church was built, then additions were completed to accommodate up to fifty boys in the school. Unfortunately, time and resources did not allow for large-scale archaeological excavation to definitively map out the landscape; however, we can draw some conclusions about two buildings, the church/monastery and the school.

A historic photograph marked "Skidaway Island, near Savannah, Ga. Chapel and house" shows a three-part clapboard building (see figure 2). On the right side is a section that was painted white (or another light color) and has a slightly different roofline, indicating it was constructed at a different time. It does not appear to rest on brick piers like the church. On the left is a larger portion painted a darker color.[104] The darker-colored section has two parts. In the foreground is the church, distinguished by arched windows and a bell tower. A plain, darker-colored section runs perpendicular to the church, bridging between the church and the

FIGURE 2. Skidaway Island Church and monastery with a priest and brother sitting on the front porch. The decaying log building behind the church was one of the first mission structures built. (Courtesy of Saint Vincent Archabbey Archives and Benedictine Military School)

white section, making an ell. The middle section appears to have angled doors at ground level that allow access to the cellar below. These sections are at least two distinct building phases, probably three, as evidenced by the building's "stratigraphy," which can be seen in the historic photograph, and previous archaeological observations of two different types of brick piers.[105]

At the targeted property's southwestern edge was a small but abrupt slope, a rise of about three feet. Skidaway Island barely averages ten feet above sea level, so any noticeable changes in elevation are significant. A large brick pier sat atop the ridge, which continues west onto the Landings Association's property and envelops the tabby-walled basement. North of the basement is an arc-shaped driveway or road, which remains vegetation free and clearly visible in the landscape without maintenance. These landscape features combined with initial survey data made the slope one of our targets for excavation.

Based on our excavations, the historic photograph, and archaeological observations reported in 1990, the slope and ridge consist of the church and monastery's collapsed remains; the soil layers built up as the building began to fall down and then was demolished in 1949 by Union Bag and Paper Corporation, which owned the property at that time.[106] Our excavation captured the church's northeast corner that is front and center of the historic photograph. The darker-colored clapboard portion of the ell extended over the tabby basement now preserved on the Landings property. This section was built first and was the original kitchen, dining room, and boys dormitory, which had a cellar below. The tabby wall has "mortises for what seem to be floor joists located in the southern wall."[107] The building rested on heavy timber joists, either 8 by 8 inches or 12 by 12 inches, which were, in turn, supported by the tabby basement wall or brick piers (for the church). The slanted cellar door attached to the wall, visible in the photograph, is unusual for Coastal Georgia and may represent a contribution by the German lay brothers.[108] Subsequently the church was added on the eastern side, and the light-colored extension, likely an addition to accommodate more students, was added to the opposite side.

The church and monastery in the photograph is a substantial building that accounts for the amount, type, and diversity of architectural materials encountered, including brick, mortar, plaster, wood, and nails. The layers of collapsed rubble contained enormous amounts of window glass (n=1,049) compared with 106 window glass fragments in soil layers that accumulated when the monastery was active. Some of the window glass sherds have intact corners and curved edges from the arched windows. The church had arched windows in both floors on the building's front facade and at least on the second floor of the eastern wall. Large amounts of plaster were recovered, suggesting a formal, more polished building. Preserved wood, including a few pieces cut in right angles and some with faded green paint, could be from the building's window frames, clapboard siding, or lathing. The wood's survival in Coastal Georgia's hot, humid climate is remarkable. Most likely this was the building that twentieth-century property owners renovated for use as a summer retreat. The longer the building was maintained, the more likely that wood fragments would survive. Smaller amounts of mortar than plaster and the plethora of nails confirm this building was wood frame with brick piers. Large and small fragments of metal roofing tin were found with the largest sheets capping the rubble layer. Some of the larger roofing pieces were over two feet in length.

Generally, American buildings constructed before 1883 were made entirely with cut nails, which have a square or rectangular shaft, although wire nails were used for other applications such as wooden boxes. After 1897, American buildings were made with cheaper wire nails.[109] We would expect the original monastery buildings to be constructed with cut nails, but any repairs, additions, or later buildings could have been built with wire nails. This was exactly the pattern we saw in the strata across the site, as cut nails dominated the nail assemblage, but wire nails, with round shafts, were present and concentrated in the shallower, and therefore more recent, layers.

Evidence of a later modification was also found. After the Benedictines closed the mission, the Floyd family purchased the property in 1906 and renovated the monastery into a country retreat. A trench containing a 1.5-inch diameter iron pipe ran along the outside of the building. The pipe trench contained numerous arti-facts, some redeposited items from the church as well as later artifacts such as a bottle with a distinctive Owens bottling machine scar (in production after 1903) and a bottle neck with a crown cap finish (patented in 1892).[110] This pipe trench was dug as part of the Floyd family's modernizations of the building.

Only a small portion of the church fell on the property to be developed. The great majority of the church and monastery remain preserved on the Landings lot, so our most intensive excavations surrounded a brick and tabby debris pile at the targeted property's southern end. Not surprisingly, a significant amount of brick was recovered, and it appears to come from two central sources: a fallen chimney made of Savannah Gray bricks and a pathway of smaller orange bricks running east to west. There was very little plaster or roofing tin in this area. Window glass was found in highly varying amounts, with levels peaking in the topsoil, but smaller amounts were found in the layers directly postdating the monastery, suggesting this building was significantly simpler in design and construction than the church. Although the exact size of the building will never be known because of the limited archaeological investigation, the fallen chimney and the artifact distribution give us a somewhat hazy picture of a fairly simple wooden building with a Savannah Gray brick chimney.

This building's function can be less definitively identified than the church. As some of the buildings had multiple functions and their functions changed over time, it is likely this building had several purposes. A process of elimination sug-gests this building was the school. Given the artifact content, we know this build-ing was not the stable. The log house, looking rough and run-down, can be seen behind the church in the historic photograph. Based on the location of the church, the log house, which contained the earliest school rooms, must be south of the church, where the golf course is now. With the original kitchen and dormitory sited over the tabby basement, we can conclude the fallen chimney is from the school pictured in the second, mid-1880s historic photograph labeled "St. Bene-dict's Skidaway Island, Sava'h Ga, Negro School" (see figure 3).[111]

The strongest artifactual indication of student usage comes from the twenty-three writing slate fragments found throughout all stratigraphic levels in this area. (Comparatively, one slate fragment and a partial slate pencil with its writing

FIGURE 3. The Skidaway Island school with students and Benedictines posing in front. (Courtesy of Saint Vincent Archabbey Archives and Benedictine Military School)

end intact were found at the church.) The slate fragments were all very thin and smoothed flat on at least one side, usually both. Many pieces were quite small, the largest measuring three-quarters of an inch, and all were unmarked and lacked any diagnostic elements such as incised lines or evidence of hinges or frames. These slate fragments strongly suggest this building was the school. This area will be referred to as the school for ease of reading even though the building may have had multiple functions beyond a schoolhouse.

Slate pencils and writing slates were used until the 1890s, when pulp paper became cheap and available. Slates were used longer in rural areas. A 2004 analysis showed that slate pencils can be used until they are one inch long; then they are discarded as impractical. This is consistent with the slate pencil found on site, which is just a smidge longer than an inch. Unlike chalk, the sound of slate pencils writing on slate is loud and unpleasant. As Jane Eva Baxter indicates, "A classroom full of studious children would have been a cacophony."[112] Knives were used for modifying and maintaining slate equipment. Knives sharpened slate pencils' writing ends and drilled into the opposite ends to create a ring. String threaded through this ring allowed the pencil to be leashed and therefore less likely to be lost. Knives were used to incise lines on writing slates, both parallel lines for text and gridded lines for mapping and graphing. Slates varied in size (small for individuals and large wall-mounted chalkboards for communal classroom use) and varied in function (gridded for math versus parallel lines for writing assignments). Individual sizes were sometimes hinged like a book, allowing for multiple "pages" and more writing space while still a convenient size. Slates were used beyond the classroom and commonly available in mail-order catalogs under both the stationery supplies and the school supplies sections.

The Skidaway site overall had remarkably few artifacts relating to education. Aside from the slate fragments and pencil, no other definitive educational artifacts were identified. Even the monks and brothers who wrote letters would have needed ink and pens, but no ink pots or pen nibs were recovered. Archaeological excavations of contemporary, similarly sized schools have found comparably low artifact densities and few educational artifacts.[113]

The Skidaway Island public "county" school was supplied once yearly each fall. The 1903 list of supplies gives a rough indication of what meager materials schools typically would have: one quart of ink, one box of crayons, one box of slate pencils, one box #2 Faber lead pencils, one box of pens, ten pen holders, one eraser, foolscap (paper), one package of envelopes, and slate tablets. This list is consistent, with small changes such as the addition of a roll book, through the last available handwritten record from 1916.[114] Some of these items would quickly disintegrate in the coastal heat and humidity. Others such as slate pencils and tablets and ink bottles could easily remain in the soil for thousands of years.

Before the students could arrive, Moosmüller needed to complete the initial buildings. With all of the delays and Moosmüller's unrealistic expectations, the Skidaway buildings took longer than anticipated; instead of opening the school by September 1877 as planned, Moosmüller held classes at the Isle of Hope site, living there as well, until the spring of 1878. The final move to the Skidaway Island complex was sometime between March 12 and June 16, 1878, when finally the blessing of the new buildings ceremony took place with great fanfare. The event was advertised in newspapers leading up to the event, extolling the "Grand Excursion to Skidaway Island."[115] An estimated 560 to 600 guests paid fifty cents each to arrive on the boat *City of Bridgeton*, traveling from a River Street dock at the base of Drayton Street. Moosmüller said mass in an oak tree grove; then the Very Reverend E. Cafferty, the cathedral's rector and the diocese's vicar general, blessed the monastery.[116]

Father Moosmüller authored the May 16, 1878, *Savannah Morning News* article on the monastery's dedication. He had promised the Saint Vincent Prior, Father Hintenach, a history of the Savannah-area missions: "I thought it best to give it to you only with the essential points, as I published it in the Savannah dayly [*sic*] news, before the dedication of this house took place."[117] The wording between the news article and the letter are identical, except for the newspaper's last paragraph, which anticipated a May 30 dedication. Moosmüller's authorship explains the very positive tone of the article, as the South was still not very Catholic-friendly.[118]

STAFFING THE SKIDAWAY MISSION

The summer of 1878 was a time of organization and completion to get ready for the school's opening. In August, the Skidaway buildings were still "not finished, not lathed & plastered, nor painted."[119] Moosmüller struggled to retain African American brothers and recruit boys for the school. In July 1878, only two of the five African Americans who attempted to join were still with the mission. Moosmüller relates these wonderfully complex and geographically diverse stories with deadpan stoicism and mild disapproval. His style is terse, but he provides snatches of vivid detail into the men's lives. Unfortunately, without more specific information to research, it has often proved very difficult to track some of these men further.

First, Moosmüller relates Brother Joseph Anderson's background. Brother Joseph had begun his novitiate with Father Bergier and made his simple vows in May 1877. Originally from Baltimore, Anderson was born enslaved and escaped. He "changed his religion 3 or 4 times, was a School-teacher in Canada, a Methodist preacher, a Quaker in London, England, et et et was with the [illegible] the Paulists, N.Y., the Josephites in Baltimore, took the Benedictine habit . . . and finally was dismissed in disgrace."[120] Moosmüller explained his reason for the dismissal: "Yesterday I found myself obliged to raise a row and expel that fellow, after having heard two witnesses in his presence, which proved that he is a Sodomist . . . according to the laws of Georgia there is capital punishment on such crimes; with a nigro [sic] they do not make much ceremony in that matter."[121] It is unclear whether Moosmüller meant that homosexuality was rarely tried and punished when African Americans were involved or that an African American accused of homosexuality would simply be lynched without a trial. In the 1870s, the State of Georgia's legal definition of sodomy was rather vague, but the punishment was not: "imprisonment at labor in the penitentiary for and during the natural life of the person."[122] Moosmüller was correct that sodomy laws were rarely enforced, but he still expelled Brother Joseph with little further mention.[123] Of course, as a lay brother who had taken vows, Brother Joseph should not have been engaged in any sexual activity; however, one suspects he would have gotten a less severe punishment had he been caught with a woman.

The next two brothers left of their own accord. Brother Diego was born enslaved in Cuba and ran away at the age of twenty-three. He "was 2 years with the bandittes [*sic*] in Cuba," meaning he lived within a maroon community and likely one without a permanent settlement.[124] In approximately 1865, Diego left Cuba by stowing away in a hogshead on a French man-of-war ship bound for New Orleans. After arriving, he "joined the Redemptorists on their large plantation in Mississippi and finely [*sic*] took the Benedictine habit under J Bergier. When we first got mules he was afraid of the work and ran away."[125] Brother Diego was about thirty-seven years old in early April 1877.[126] Should we believe Brother Diego was courageous enough to escape slavery and stowed away in a large cask to leave Cuba but apparently could not handle mules? This seems to be a contradiction. Mules have a deserved reputation; however, it seems likely there was another underlying cause to Diego's departure other than fear of mules or fear of hard work. Either he did not want to lead a religious life or was otherwise unhappy on Skidaway Island.

"Benedict, James Dorsey of Baltimore, his father was a slave, he took the Benedictine habit twice under J Bergier and through myself, left."[127] Little else has been found on this man except that Brother James was well educated and came and went several times from the Savannah-area monasteries. He started under Father Bergier, left, then returned from Baltimore via the steamer *Saragossa* in April of 1877.[128] By June of that year, he was back in Baltimore but was expected to return once he recovered from a hospitalization due to a "sore eye."[129] It is unknown if he did return.

In a community of men, who does the "women's work" as it was understood and defined in the late 1800s? Lay brothers like Brother James trained in all of the skills needed to run an institution—from domestic work to minor medical care to skilled trades—and were the support team that enabled the priests to teach, study, and minister. At the Skidaway mission, the cooking and housework as well as some of the farm work, such as managing livestock, fell to the African American lay brothers. White lay brothers, who were frequently German American or German born, were often sent to Skidaway for their building trades, especially in the early years, when the monastery was under construction. This was not a strict division of labor, as some African American lay brothers taught school, and as in most small institutions, mission staff would have worn many hats and worked on tasks as needed.

Elizabeth Kryder-Reid excavated a Redemptorist monastery in Annapolis, Maryland, that housed a novitiate during the second half of the nineteenth century. She examined the site's exclusively male inhabitants from the perspective of gender and class; noting that the monastery's internal hierarchy "reinforced and naturalized" the lay brothers' roles as domestic workers by assigning feminine roles and attributes to the brothers, specifically the Cult of True Womanhood's four primary virtues of piety, purity, submissiveness, and domesticity. This was in contrast to the priests, who were often of a higher socioeconomic class and received only academic training. She wrote, "The argument postulated here is that the lay brothers' association with female qualities was one means of maintaining their docile acceptance of menial tasks and their position on the lowest rung of the congregation's hierarchy."[130] While for the Redemptorists, class and education levels reinforced the hierarchical and vocational differences between priests and lay brothers, at the Skidaway Island monastery, race was a more divisive factor. The African American brothers were often as educated as the white brothers, and sometimes more so, although they were most often relegated to the lowest-status domestic work.

Brother Rhabanus, born Arthur Paul Canonge, lived almost his entire adult life as a Benedictine monk. Born January 5, 1848, in New Orleans, to a French father and an enslaved mother, he began his religious career with Madame Gantheret in Mandeville, Louisiana, a small town on the north shore of Lake Pontchartrain, opposite New Orleans.[131] Brother Rhabanus, also known as Brother Boniface, was a trained, "excellent" cook. In addition to cooking at the Skidaway mission, Rhabanus did the washing "but not as the Bros at St. Vincents; he washes irons & starches as fine as any woman can do it."[132] After working with Moosmüller for several years, he requested a transfer in February 1879, shortly after professing his simple vows on February 2. Brother Rhabanus wished to go to St. Mary Help Priory (later Belmont Abbey) in North Carolina, to be with "F[ather] Herman with whom he got acquainted here last summer."[133] Moosmüller suggested swapping Brother Rhabanus for the St. Mary Help cook, as it would be cheap and easy travel.

Rhabanus had several reasons for leaving. He did not get along with Brother Alphonse, and he also "dislikes the colored boys and is afraid to go into a boat and thinks this climate does not agree with his health."[134] These reasons are unexpected for an African American from New Orleans, and, as with Brother Diego, there may be more to this story. Brother Rhabanus was caught between two worlds with few allies. He was light skinned, highly educated, and talented. Reflecting his Louisiana roots, he inflected his letters with French. He did not identify with Skidaway's African American residents, most of whom were Gullah Geechee. Yet he faced discrimination from the white religious men who were supposedly his community. He hoped to find better colleagues at St. Mary Help as he had "great confidence in P. Herman that he would care for him."[135] Brother Rhabanus had Father Moosmüller's respect and blessing for the transfer, but he was still on Skidaway nearly two years later.[136]

Father Siricius Palmer, who taught the county public school, was in a similar position as a well-educated African American, although Palmer was born free. In the fall of 1882, he decided to leave the order and asked Abbot Wimmer for dispensation of his vows. Palmer was worn out physically and emotionally from the toxic environment. "I was totally disappointed in my expectations . . . the loss of my vital strength of mind and body (although now regained to a great extent is in danger of relapsing) . . . I cannot agree to live in peace with the abused, arrogant and undisciplined (according to the statutes) religious, and last of all, I cannot love except a generous and noble heart and without love I cannot live; first the love of God and his Holy Church; second, the love of those who constitute my atmosphere."[137] Father Reichert was aware of tension and racial problems in the house. He asked Wimmer to remove some of the worst offenders, Brother Fridolin, who was present for his farming expertise, and Dan Sullivan, were "going in company. . . . The sooner they leave the better."[138] Although Palmer's solution was leaving the Benedictine order, rather than transferring, he still offered parting advice and commentary on the fathers' relationships with the Skidaway islanders. "Father Melchior should continue with his medicine and other trifling favors which they [African American islanders] appreciate beyond expression and is an antidote for their hatred of whites."[139] Brother Rhabanus also addressed racial relations, believing that racism would end the mission. He wrote to Wimmer, "I know that this House will never succeed. I told you these words in North Carolina and I want to see them verified." There was a "confusion of tongues" among the brothers "which we could compare to another Baliel."[140] Rhabanus reiterated his desire to profess solemn vows and requested a transfer, this time to Oklahoma.[141]

Brother Rhabanus was eventually transferred away from Skidaway, but by 1900, he was back with Moosmüller and living at the new Cluny Monastery in Illinois. In 1892, Moosmüller began the Cluny monastery as an experiment in returning to medieval-style monasticism focused on prayer rather than missionary or parish work. Moosmüller published a monthly magazine, *Die Legende*, to support the monastery and college.[142] Cluny was small and struggled through most of its existence. In 1900, there were only sixteen men living there. Brother Rhabanus was an exception in many ways to the others. He was one of three who were American born, and the other two were first-generation Americans. The only African American, Brother Rhabanus was the only person in the community without German or Irish roots.[143] At age fifty-three, Brother Rhabanus was listed as a "pupil" among the teenage and twentysomething men but likely continued his work as a cook and possibly did other housework. Whether Rhabanus strictly acted as a lay brother serving the monastery or was participating as a student, his presence at Moosmüller's utopian experiment shows Brother Rhabanus's piety and devotion as well as Moosmüller's respect for him. Father Moosmüller died January 10, 1901. After-

FIGURE 4. Aloysius Mason wearing civilian clothes but holding a cross. A second photograph in the Saint Vincent archives has Mason depicted in his habit. (Courtesy of Saint Vincent Archabbey Archives)

ward, the remaining monks decided to transfer the priory to Humboldt, Saskatchewan, Canada, in 1903. Rhabanus moved with his conferes, helping to found the new community and continuing his work as a cook. He died there on January 25, 1920, and is buried in St. Peter's Abbey Cemetery.[144]

Lastly, Brother Aloysius, born Arthur Francis Mason of Baltimore, was tasked with washing, milking the cows, and other household duties.[145] Brother Aloysius, an experienced cook and washer, had entered Saint Vincent in 1878 (possibly as Brother Albert) but left shortly afterward for the Skidaway mission (see figure 4). He departed Skidaway at the end of 1878 to spend three months in New York earning money to pay debts before returning to Skidaway. Moosmüller thought he was "rather a Dandy like fellow with high and vain notion" but also thought Mason had a good heart and was a talented worker.[146] Through Brother Aloysius's eyes, we get one of our rare African American voices inside the monastery. He received his habit from Reichert in the summer of 1880, and four months later, Aloysius wrote to Abbot Wimmer requesting permission to be professed.[147] Several days later, he wrote again to Wimmer, addressing him as "my very Dear and venerable Farther Abbot." He confirmed that Brother Rhabanus was unhappy, unhealthy, and still eager for his transfer. When Brother Rhabanus left, the cooking would fall to Aloysius, who contradicted Moosmüller by claiming he was a poor cook: "brother Phillip tould you that I was not fit for the kitcen [*sic*]."[148] Unlike Brother Joseph, who was educated and could teach, Aloysius's education was more basic. For example, he wrote, "I am houseceeping the refectory the wasing sowing and tow cows."[149] Meaning, he was housekeeping, serving in the refectory (dining hall), doing the washing and sewing, and milking two cows.

Brother Aloysius is not complimentary of Moosmüller, believing he was eager to leave Skidaway for the new Sacred Heart Parish in Savannah. "Prior Oswald plade his game well he is glad to get away and leve the burden full on farther Melchior [*sic*]."[150] Father Melchior Reichert, Moosmüller's replacement, was praised in the letter. Aloysius believed he learned more from Reichert in a few months than his previous three years with Moosmüller. In contrast to Moosmüller's later assessments of Reichert's lax management style, Aloysius believed "farther melchior wroks like a slave from morning untel night [*sic*]."[151] Perhaps it was exactly Reichert's more relaxed personality that appealed to Aloysius. The reference to working like a slave is also interesting. Brother Aloysius, born in Charles County, Maryland, in 1854, was about twenty-six years old when he wrote this letter. It is unknown whether he was born free. His choice of the word "slave" is surprising to modern ears, and it certainly is an exaggeration in order to press his point. Father Reichert returned the young man's regard, noting that Aloysius was "received into the third Order of St. Benedict," meaning he was a regular oblate. Reichert did not heap him with praise, but he acknowledged the brother was doing "well" in his duties.[152]

Brother Aloysius boldly requested that the abbot send him $100 if he did not send additional brothers to help with housework, and because "I need so meny [*sic*] things for the house."[153] He intended to spend $65 on a sewing machine but did not specify his other costs except for a vague mention of clothing needs. He reassured the abbot that Reichert would see the money was spent wisely. This was an extraordinary amount of money and a very brazen request, which Aloysius acknowledged, "Indeed I could use more but I dea [*sic*] not ask any more."[154] This request would have been dismissed as inappropriate at best. The prior managed the monastery's finances, and the monks and brothers were provided for. A lay brother's request for this huge sum would have been considered improper and ignored.[155] More interesting is Aloysius's perception of Abbot Wimmer—a benevolent father, a white authority figure without compassion, or something in between? His words, taken at face value, indicate he saw the abbot as a benevolent father figure of his religious family and community. However, in the context of 1880 America, the question must be asked whether Aloysius truly trusted the white Catholic leadership to support and provide for him or was he strategically using the few resources available to him as an African American? As a literate young man from Baltimore, Aloysius likely had other prospects and options. His choice to isolate himself on a barrier island monastery suggests he was committed to Catholicism as a true believer who wished to make his profession in the church, as he declared in his letter.

Although Brother Aloysius was a committed Catholic, he had difficulty settling into a religious community, frequently moving and even changing names from Albert to Aloysius. Brother Aloysius left Skidaway Island in 1881 to return to Saint Vincent, again becoming a novice and making his first profession in 1882. No reason was given for his departure, but Moosmüller's reference to him as "Mason alias Albert (he is in Richmond Va), or what other names he may have adopted yet" suggests it was not under positive circumstances from Moosmüller's perspective, again indicating tension between the two.[156] Although Aloysius did not stay long at Saint Vincent, he remained a practicing Catholic, became a lay leader, and attended the first Black Catholic lay congress in 1889 in Washington, D.C.[157]

Brother Aloysius's commitment to Catholicism was sincere, so why did he not find a place in the Benedictine's community? Racist attitudes among the Skidaway staff were partially (and perhaps mostly) to blame. Reichert wrote: "In my opinion and judging from what I have seen and heard from P. Oswald and from Rev. Bergier's accounts, the colored people are not easily to be permitted to make professions. Rev. P. Bergier had a community of colored Brothers. One left after the other. Rev. P. Oswald had about 6 or 8—where are they?"[158] Reichert assumed the African American brothers left because of personal failure or weakness, rather than because of a structural problem or the toxic environment described by several of the African American brothers. These same patronizing and racist attitudes were prevalent throughout the Catholic Church and defined the status and occupations available to African Americans. In 1884, Wimmer discussed personnel problems, namely, not having enough men to staff the missions. He wrote: "My only hope is that the dear Lord will send me Negro brothers as a reward for the many sacrifices we have made on their behalf, for their conversion. We already have three such brothers. They are born cooks, servants, etc. We have converted many on Skidaway Island."[159] Wimmer believed that African Americans were inherently suited to low-paying service jobs that required little education, which only fed his interest in the manual labor school.

THE KITCHEN TABLE

So Brothers Aloysius and Rhabanus toiled in the kitchen and served at the monastery's refectory table. Plates and bowls recovered archaeologically show their table was quaintly eclectic and set with mismatched, old-fashioned dishes. Some ceramic sherds that were found are contemporary with the monastery (such as white granite, a plain white pottery). These and other undecorated whitewares and yellow wares could pre- or postdate the monastery's occupation as they were made for over one hundred years, but the rest, which dominate the ceramic assemblage, substantially predate the monastery by decades. These ceramic types include hand-painted wares, colorful dipped and mocha wares, and intricate transfer printed wares, all dating from the late 1700s to the mid-1800s. Even if we consider the time lag between ceramics being manufactured and purchased and then their eventual breakage and deposition in the archaeology site, the monastery-era ceramics are old-fashioned and include styles that are fifty years old on average.[160]

This pattern holds into the 1890s and early 1900s, when there was an even greater diversity of ceramics present, adding lusterwares, edged wares, and sherds with brown Rockingham glaze into the mix. The ceramics present are still forty years old on average.[161] Tablewares, and kitchen artifacts in general, were more prevalent at the school than the church before 1890, again suggesting a multipurpose building. At the church, tablewares, especially expensive porcelain, increased substantially after 1900, likely relating to the building's change in function to a residence after the mission's closure.

Surprisingly few utilitarian ceramic sherds such as large bowls and storage vessels were found archaeologically, considering that all meals for a substantial number of people were prepared on site. Utilitarian glass bottle sherds were found in relative abundance throughout the site. Tracking with the growth of American consumerism, bottle fragments became increasingly common in the more shallow, and therefore more recent, soil layers. Few of these fragments were diagnostic enough to be identified specifically, but the diversity of bottles, recognized through different manufacturing techniques, bottle closures, shapes, and colors, show that a diversity of foodstuffs was present, especially bottled drinks and condiments. In contrast to the old-fashioned pottery at the table, most of the diagnostic bottle glass is contemporary. The age of the ceramics speaks to the socioeconomic status of the monks, who might have purchased outdated (and therefore cheaper) materials or accepted donations and hand-me-downs, whereas the bottles would be acquired along with newly purchased foodstuffs or medicines and discarded more rapidly. Unlike previous centuries, glass bottles became disposable goods in the late 1800s as changes to the bottle and transportation industries made single-use bottles economically practical.[162]

Excepting architectural materials, which comprise nearly two-thirds of the artifacts, most of the site's artifacts relate to food and drink. Although some of the mission's food was produced at the farm or gathered nearby, other food and farm supplies were shipped from Saint Vincent Archabbey, including meat, flour, sunflower seeds, and osage-orange seeds. Additional supplies were purchased in Savannah.[163] Moosmüller wrote frankly about food and life on the island: "You ought to animate some good novices for this mission, but you must not forget to tell them that here on Skidaway we have no beer, no wine, no fresh beef, nor many other luxuries of that kind; nevertheless we enjoy good health and like the place very well."[164] Instead of eating beef, the students harvested oysters for Wednesday, Friday, and Saturday meals. Faunal artifacts bear out these statements. Shell, particularly oyster shell, was found throughout the site and is by far the most numerous food-related artifact in every soil layer. Shell heavily outnumbers animal bone, in ratios of hundreds to a few dozen, indicating the monks were eating what was easily available and cheap. Fish may have been eaten but were not represented in the archaeological record.[165] Reichert would go fishing "when I can get away from the Boys."[166] However, some, if not all, of these fish were sold in the Savannah markets to raise money, rather than landing on the monastery table.[167]

Farm labor was ever present in the monks' and students' lives. Their produce partially sustained the monastery's people and livestock, and selling crops was supposed to fully support the mission financially. The fall 1878 harvest included sugar cane, which the monks processed into molasses and sugar, and 150 bushels of sweet potatoes. These amounts were expected to last a full year. Of the three newly purchased cows, only one had a calf, and she produced only two pints of milk each day. Somehow, Palmer was the only person capable of milking; "at least he tries to milk," wrote Moosmüller.[168]

The monks were less successful with their corn harvest. Although twenty acres were planted, they only harvested a scant one hundred bushels. Weather does not appear to be the problem, however, as "the corn grew up high & nice, but it gave nothing."[169] Moosmüller was not a farmer and had little experience in growing crops. While he had an admirable vision of elevating the farming profession, he also found himself asking for help from the very people he was supposed to be teaching. As Mann states, "This particular situation shows the irony at the heart of the Benedictine's schooling endeavor. Although they established this school to improve their students' agricultural skills, the brothers lacked the very skills and knowledge they aimed to teach."[170] The previous fall, Moosmüller admitted that had they simply bought the supplies they harvested, rather than growing the food themselves, they would have saved money. In short, the expense of seed, work animals, and labor was more than the cost of goods. Moosmüller further acknowledged his ignorance: "Still once we must commence and in a strange climate & country like this we have to pay first for learning how to get along."[171] A year later, the situation remained much the same. The African American families were harvesting corn, cotton, rice, and more, but the monks had not planted their corn in time. Moosmüller again admitted the brothers were still unfamiliar with the land and climate and so had to depend on local African Americans to teach them.[172]

THE CURRICULUM

The summer before classes started on Skidaway, Moosmüller began planning his curriculum around farming skills and a basic elementary education. He sent Wimmer a brochure and a four-page prospectus about the school, suggesting that five hundred copies be printed (after proofreading) and distributed widely throughout the South to advertise the school.[173] The boarding school, located on "an extensive plantation in a delightful and healthy situation," would serve students who wanted a "business education" and those who would be farmers, focusing on management and cultivation methods along with agricultural science.[174] Religion would form the base of the academic education, with elementary basics provided: "reading, writing, arithmetic and singing."[175] "It will be also a special object of the managers to counteract the increasing disinclination towards manual labor, and to vindicate its dignity by showing that it is compatible with intellectual culture and social refinement."[176] In response to African Americans criticizing the manual school concept, Moosmüller designed a curriculum with two tracks, one academic and the other industrial. However, both "classes of students" were going to receive instruction in farming and a general education, with little truly distinguishable difference between the tracks.[177] Bishop Gross cited the "demand for skilful [sic] farmers and the cheapness of land throughout Georgia" as reasons for maintaining an industrial school with its strong emphasis on manual labor and farming.[178]

Students as young as nine years old could apply, and all would be expected to do uncompensated manual work three hours daily to learn "the various operations of the farm, garden, nursery, silk-culture etc."[179] Report cards were sent to "his parent or guardian" after each term, which ran from the last Monday in September to the last Monday in June. The superior could inspect any letters, books, or other documents, and books and paper could be purchased "at current prices."[180] Few behavioral rules were listed, except tobacco use was "positively prohibited."[181] Since it was a boarding school, students were required to bring a fairly large array of specific clothing items as well as student-provided linens (blanket, pillow, towels, napkins, sheets) and other personal items including "combs and brushes; knife and fork, tea and table spoon, and a metal cup."[182] Yearly board, lodging, and tuition were $80, plus there were fees: a one-time $5 entrance fee, $15 for washing, and $3 for using the circulating library, totaling $103 for the first year, an exorbitant amount when private day schools typically charged $1 per month.[183] A few months later, Moosmüller was asking $25 for tuition and board, but rarely did students pay anything. In November 1878, Moosmüller had nine boys who had not paid, and he was not optimistic about the tenth.[184]

Less than one week after sending the prospectus to Wimmer, Moosmüller admitted his plan had problems. "In Savannah I was told that my plan with the Manual labor School for colored boys will not please the nigroes [sic] in general. 1, because they have a horror against working in the field. 2, they want their boys to get such an education that they would not need to do manual labor, they rather would be clerks, bookkeepers, or anything else than a farmer."[185] Moosmüller was advised to offer a traditional education, but he did not have the buildings or teachers to do so, and he needed the farm's crops to fund the school.

THE FIRST DAY OF SCHOOL

When classes began in September 1878, there were perhaps several hundred people, mostly African American, living on Skidaway Island. Except for the mission staff, none were Catholic. Moosmüller estimated the population at two hundred, but noted that twelve years earlier, the population was five hundred people.[186] Out of the several hundred residents, there were approximately eighty school-age children.[187] Of these children, more than half attended the county public school, whose average attendance was fifty-five students in its early years.[188] On September 30, 1878, Moosmüller listed the monastery's residents including the first students (his spellings are retained):

1. P. Oswald
2. F. Siritius Palmer
3. Bro Philip
4. Bro Alphons
5. Bro Boniface [Rhabanus] (col)
6. Thom. Taaffe, Aspirant
7. Dan Donnelly, white, Scholastic
8. Anthony Johnston, mulatto, 20 years old
9. Abraham Jackson, black, 16 years old
10. Charles Franklin, 12 years, mulatto
11. James Franklin, 11 years, mulatto
12. Robert Rolain, 12 years, mulatto

13. John Speare, 15 years, mulatto
14. Charles Hopkins, 13 years, black
15. Henry Cook, 12 years, black[189]

Of the eight students, only three (Charles and James Franklin and Henry Cook) were still present two years later. Five additional students were living in the household at that time: Robert Burksteiner, Robert Davis, Henry Clending, John Hayes, and Richard Allen. None of the students appear to be from Skidaway Island or have parents living on Skidaway in 1880.[190]

The students are extraordinarily difficult to track in the historical record, because so little is known to start with. An Abraham Jackson of the right age and race is listed in the 1870 Census living in Savannah with his parents, Jack and Laura, and his four older siblings (Cora, Anne, Oscar, and Hanne), but there is no evidence to concretely link these two. Similarly, a matching Abraham Jackson died on May 17, 1908, in Savannah, but we cannot conclusively determine if these records represent the same man.[191]

Charles and James Franklin's family may have been living on Reynolds Street in Savannah in 1880. Julia Franklin, a 39-year-old widow employed as a wash woman, had six children: Charles (13), James (10), Martin (8), Adam (6), Willie (3), and Lucie (2 months). The first two boys were listed "at school." Charles was able to read and write, while James could only read.[192] If these are the same students as at the monastery, they were listed twice in the federal census, which is not entirely uncommon. Julia Franklin, widowed and bereft of education, would have struggled to raise six children without her husband. One empathizes immensely with a difficult decision to send her young children away to a free boarding school. Given the structural barriers she faced, the word "decision" is inadequate because it assumes Mrs. Franklin had real choices available to her. Extreme poverty meant that parents were forced to choose between buying food and paying for school. Sometimes children did not attend school because they lacked shoes or their clothing was so ragged it was unacceptable according to school rules.[193]

Moosmüller ran the school according to his "Prospectus." The school taught practical basics—reading, writing, and arithmetic, with religion as the educational "groundwork," because most of the boys were not baptized. Each student worked daily in the fields, gardens, or workshops. With Wimmer's encouragement, Moosmüller maintained that the school should be an industrial school: "All should have been convinced theoretically and practically of the necessity and usefulness of farming."[194] Wimmer believed in small, family farms as the basis for a healthy nation and believed that training farmers was good for the students and the nation

as a whole. However, in creating an industrial school, the priests were contributing to a larger trend in postbellum education, where African American children
were prepared for low-wage, manual labor to intentionally retain as much of the
antebellum social order as possible. This debate would continue for decades, most
famously (and more constructively) played out as the debate between Booker T.
Washington and W. E. B. Du Bois. It is unclear how much the Benedictines truly
believed in vindicating the dignity of manual labor and how consciously complicit
they were in maintaining a social order that devalued Black lives.

TOYS AND LEISURE

Perhaps it is this focus on work and industry that explains why archaeologists
failed to find any toys, despite the fact that children as young as eleven lived on
this site. Although toys are common finds on sites, they are often forgotten in
archaeological analyses. On this site, it is easy to get lost in the archival weeds
of farm details and church building and forget that educating children was the
one of the two primary motives for creating the mission. The priests' stated the
purpose for coming to Savannah and building schools was education, yet they
rarely mentioned the students in correspondence or other historical documents.
One exception was Father Moosmüller's 1878 comment that "though they [the
students] are poor and can pay nothing at all, nevertheless I think they bring the
blessing of God into the house."[195]

While some of the boys were teenagers, others were younger, and one hopes
they would have all found time for games and leisure, but the artifacts suggest otherwise. Nearly twelve thousand artifacts were recovered, but none were formal toys,
which is very unusual, as toys are typically a common denominator for schools.[196]
Does the lack of toys show us the lack of childhood as we define it today? Unlike
today's eleven-year-olds, the students were expected to work. Was there simply no
time for leisure? If there was some time for play, there are several possibilities that
explain why we did not find toys on site. One is that toys were highly valued, therefore highly curated, and were not discarded. Another explanation is our limited
excavations simply did not find the discarded or lost toys and that we did not dig
in the "right" place. For example, the school at Amache, a Japanese internment
camp in Colorado, did not have any toys either. However, researchers suggested
their finding was because of regimented work/play spaces, rather than a real lack
of toys. School was work time when toys were not allowed, and play time was conducted elsewhere.[197] The Wea View Schoolhouse No. 8 in Indiana is a more typical
example. Marbles and jacks, which are small, portable, and used in group play, were

found.[198] Similarly, a marble was found mixed among the writing slate and pencil fragments at the Old Elliot School in Bermuda.[199] Dolls are rare, except at boarding schools.[200]

If the mission boys did not have access to manufactured toys (balls, metal trucks, marbles), they may have constructed toys from materials available. For example, the boys could have played makeshift games such as stick ball or used nuts as marbles. Organic materials from makeshift toys would have deteriorated quickly. Other materials may have been repurposed through imagination but without physically transforming them, and therefore without leaving archaeological traces of their secondary use. Of course, these site formation processes are not mutually exclusive, and several factors probably contributed to the lack of toys recovered. Regardless of these explanations, the students clearly had few, if any, frivolous items, as toys are nearly always found on sites with children.

CULTURE SHOCK AND COMMUNICATION CHALLENGES

Despite Moosmüller's misgivings about the mission's viability, the school gathered enough students that he had to buy more beds because some boys were sleeping on the floor. But by November, they were down to seven boys.[201] Moosmüller wrote: "It seems to me that I should not *receive any boys that are older than 12* or 13 years, because they are so lazy and unruly that nothing can be done with them. I had to dismiss three such fellows."[202] Much of Moosmüller's frustration was due to cultural differences and serious social misunderstandings between himself and the students. Students were expected to follow a schedule similar to the lay brothers' daily routine, but the students were up at "only" 5:00 a.m. for mass and meditation and then had to work for four hours, attend school for two hours, and say the rosary three times per day with the brothers.[203] This schedule was more appropriate for religious students and candidates, not an elementary school, and left little time for leisure or personal time. The balance of religious observance and manual work versus academic schooling is not what most African American parents wanted for their children. Most other schools had much more instructional time, without the burden of farm work and pressure to convert to Catholicism.

The monks were using a Euro-American classroom model. These pedagogies, which were "hierarchical, unidirectional, competitive, rationalized, and individualistic," were very different from a Black culture that "valued mutuality, community, and active engagement."[204] There was simply a disconnect between the cultural values of each group. Jerome Oetgen observes, "A stern disciplinarian and a Teuton, Fr. Oswald had not taken into consideration the temperament of a naturally easygoing and demure people who lived in a climate which demanded slow motion and ease."[205] Moosmüller was also trying to instill discipline and the value of hard work in the students and novices, although this was not necessary because the students were long familiar with hard work. What Moosmüller perceived as laziness was the students questioning the type of work required and whether this work would give them the economic and social benefits they wanted. Additionally, some students had never entered a classroom before and had not been exposed to "school culture," including basic classroom behavior such as sitting still for long periods of time and raising their hands before speaking.[206]

Although it was nearly December, the log house where the monks slept still did not have a stove or chimney. "I will see how it will do," Moosmüller remarked offhandedly.[207] December temperatures in coastal Georgia can vary wildly from highs in the seventies to lows in the thirties, and frequently do so in the same week. The frame house, where the students slept, also housed the kitchen and was hopefully warmer. These accommodations again illustrate the discrepancy between the monks' expectations and the students' needs and wants. Were the students truly "lazy and unruly"? Or were they legitimately cold and reluctant to leave their beds? Did they view Moosmüller's strict discipline and control over the plantation as simply a new form of slavery? Without genuine conversion and a true commitment to Catholicism, students did leave. Moosmüller used the word "left" but also used the phrase "ran away" to describe students who departed. "Leaving" implies a much more deliberate, decisive action, while "ran away" has connotations of either cowardice or escapism, depending on the perspective. The ability to leave without negative consequences or pursuit would have important meaning to the African American students and lay brothers. Deliberately leaving an unsatisfactory situation is a level of self-determination and self-empowerment that was rare prior to 1865 for most African Americans.

In January 1879, the school had only seven students, three of whom were paying twenty-five dollars per year to attend. Moosmüller continued to complain about the students' laziness. Over the months, he dismissed four and another ran away; however, the students who stayed were committed, and the priests began to convert some students. Moosmüller commented, "Three of them I baptized after a long instruction of several months; now we have two more who are not yet baptized."[208]

Language differences also hindered the students' progress. Dialect and cultural challenges that hindered teaching and learning were not uncommon between northern teachers and southern students throughout the postbellum South.[209] Many of the monks, including Moosmüller, were native German speakers. Moosmüller was a talented linguist, speaking and writing German, English, Italian,

Latin, and possibly Portuguese from his year in Brazil. However, it is unlikely Moosmüller would have recognized the Geechee dialect spoken on the Georgia sea islands as a new language to be learned and spoken. Instead, he would have expected the students to adapt to his dialect or standard English. Likewise, Moosmüller's German accent, depending on its strength, may have been difficult for the students to understand at first.

One clue relates to the monks' attempts to understand the Geechee dialect and culture. "Negro Dialogue" is a two-page, handwritten document of dialogue, written like a short play. The "plot" concerns one man (Tom) trying to trick another man (Bob) into believing his girlfriend (Jenny) is using him for food and money without actually returning Bob's affection. The author is unknown, and the handwriting is not Moosmüller's or Reichert's, but one of the monastery's white residents almost certainly wrote the document. The dialogue is not written in actual Gullah Geechee dialect, and the sentences lack consistent grammar and African grammatical attributes.[210] The most charitable interpretation is that the document was the monks' attempt to understand the Gullah Geechee dialect. The dialogue, lacking in literary value, might have been used as a training tool, to give those assigned to Skidaway a sense of the dialect prior to their arrival. Alternatively, one of the monks may have recorded the dialogue to share on a personal level (like a souvenir) or simply wrote it down for posterity.

The brothers coming from Pennsylvania also had to make cultural adjustments. Many of the Saint Vincent brothers and monks were German immigrants or first-generation Americans born of German parents. Brother Philip, who arrived in early September 1878, did not speak English. Now he was thrust into an entirely English-language environment. Assigned to the Skidaway mission for his carpentry skills, Brother Philip was from Carrolltown, Pennsylvania, a small town northeast of Saint Vincent Archabbey. He also had to adjust to a new diet. At Carrolltown, he was used to meat at every meal, "milk, butter, cider in abundance, and beer on Sundays."[211] Four months into his stay, Brother Philip still "does not understand any English at all," Moosmüller commented.[212] This caused logistical difficulties for Moosmüller, who was forced to conduct their retreat twice, once in English and once in German.

Saint Vincent Brother Ignatius Ackerman arrived in January 1879, staying the night with Father Eckert in Savannah and the next night with Dr. Dupon on Isle of Hope before making his way to Skidaway Island. "Next week we will get his trunk etc out from Savannah," commented Moosmüller, making one appreciate the conveniences of modern travel.[213] Jerome Berchtold, another Saint Vincent brother, arrived within the month.[214] Neither would last long. Brother Alphonse Schoene, who had been at the Skidaway mission almost from the beginning, highly recommended Ignatius, believing he would be a good fit and find Skidaway Island "first rate."[215] In September, Reichert reported, "Brother Ignatius is almost continuously sick. He has not worked one day for the last week."[216] By November, Moosmüller requested Brother Ignatius's reassignment "because the Doctor told him he cannot get well again here as his system is filled with Malaria, which consists in little animals that pass from the Atmosphere into the blood and regenerate and propagate themselves in the blood, and which can be killed only by Quinine, or a preparation of Peruvian bark."[217] However, quinine is not effective for everyone. Poor Brother Ignatius had been "sick continually since June" and hospitalized repeatedly. Moosmüller regretted losing him and wrote very highly of the modest, pious man who was the best carpenter on Skidaway.[218] Brother Ignatius was transferred back to his native Pennsylvania before year's end and spent the rest of his career working throughout western Pennsylvania including Pittsburg in the 1890s and Mount Pleasant, a small town near Saint Vincent Archabbey, around 1900. Brother Ignatius died in 1914 at the age of sixty-two and was buried in the Saint Vincent cemetery.

Before Brother Ignatius got sick, early in February 1879, the monks prepared to build the church. The bishop allowed Moosmüller to take as much sawn lumber from the cathedral's yard as he wanted, so Moosmüller helped himself to five thousand board feet, which then needed to be cut to size at a sawmill. The bishop's generosity was in exchange for Moosmüller's help in recruiting a "good Spanish Benedictine, who could be the Confessor of the Carmelite Nuns, who came here from Guatemala."[219] Later in the month, Moosmüller requested dispensation from fasting during Lent. They had much physical labor to accomplish, including "cultivate this half wild & neglected soil" and build the church, which would be even more difficult to do while fasting. The new settlers' challenges were many: they still lacked a vegetable garden, had not erected a sufficient fence, and continued to struggle with "briars and roots" in the cultivation fields.[220] Although the oysters were plentiful, the boys were "too lazy" to shuck them without help, and no one was yet a competent fisherman. Brother Jerome was unable to eat oysters altogether, likely an allergy.[221]

GROWING THE MISSION

In July 1879, Father Moosmüller, overwhelmed as the only Benedictine priest in the Savannah area, lobbied Wimmer to send an additional priest. White Franciscan sisters from Minnesota had settled in Augusta, Georgia, starting a wildly successful school with 120 African American children enrolled and were beginning to convert the mostly Protestant students. Next they opened a convent on Isle of Hope. Unfortunately for Moosmüller, this made for very long workdays. For example, on Sundays, he would preach at Skidaway at 5:30 a.m., Isle of Hope at 9 a.m., and then back to Skidaway for "the Rosary at 2 1/2, Sing the Litany & give devotion & Culpa etc."[222] Travel by boat between Skidaway Island and Isle of Hope was relatively easy if moving with the tides, but Saturdays were even more hectic. Mass on Skidaway started at 4:30 a.m., then Isle of Hope mass at 8 a.m., so he could get to Savannah for confession.[223] To travel between Skidaway Island and Savannah, they had three options: sail seven miles to Thunderbolt (a small town southeast of Savannah) and go the last four miles by horse cart; put their horse and wagon on a flat boat, sail three miles to Isle of Hope, and drive eight miles into town; or sail directly to Savannah, an eighteen-mile journey over three or four hours, given favorable tides and winds.[224] Today, this trip can be accomplished with a thirty-minute car ride. Moosmüller thought the bishop should establish a new African American parish in Savannah and move the Franciscan sisters' house there as well.[225] Within the same letter requesting expansion, Moosmüller also addressed the rumor that the Skidaway mission was closing, speculating that Wimmer's failure to send the promised extra personnel prompted the rumor.[226]

Wimmer remained devoted to the many missions he started, despite resistance from many at Saint Vincent Archabbey. There was a general philosophical divide at Saint Vincent (and other monasteries) whether missionary and outreach work was important, or whether a more contemplative, studious interior life was most critical. Wimmer never waived from his concentration on missionary work and regularly visited his missions throughout the United States. He visited Skidaway four times between its founding and his 1887 death, writing in December 1882, "The Negro mission is very close to my heart."[227] When asked about his motivations for the Skidaway mission, he quoted Matthew 25:40, "I tell you solemnly, in so far as you did this to one of the least of these brothers of mine, you did it to me."[228] Although Wimmer acknowledged the particular importance of a school for those who had been historically denied schooling, the Georgia mission was daunting to many Saint Vincent men. "Our Patres [sic] of St. Vincents fear to come here," wrote Moosmüller.[229] Specific reasons for the resistance were rarely stated outright, but tropical diseases, heat, insects, and racism were the most common reasons why staffing the Savannah-area missions remained difficult. Moosmüller remained optimistic and saw his time in Georgia as long-term, possibly his final posting. He pressed Abbot Wimmer to let him train scholastics specifically for the Georgia mission, "in order to acclimatize them & make them consider this place as their home and love it as such."[230]

During Wimmer's visit in August 1879, the Benedictines, in consultation with Bishop Gross, decided to follow Moosmüller's recommendation and create a new Black parish, with a new church, Sacred Heart, on Habersham Street. To raise money for this new venture, Moosmüller published a monthly German-language historical magazine, *Der Geschichtsfreund* (literally translated, "History Friend"). The magazine was profitable from 1880 to 1883, when interest waned, but it was successful in raising a significant amount of money for the new parish. In 1884, Moosmüller signed a contract with Rev. Joseph Buch to print and publish *Der Geschichtsfreund* as well as increase the number of subscribers. Moosmüller would continue to write and edit the magazine, receiving fifty dollars for each edition.[231] The Franciscan sisters in Augusta may have inspired Moosmüller. The sisters published the *Franciscan Annals* in-house and sold it throughout the United States to fund their school. The publication was quite successful with fifteen hundred subscribers. Moosmüller suggested a similar publication, the "Benedictine Annals," to Abbot Wimmer, hoping the newsletter would function as advertising for the Benedictine Order in general and Saint Vincent College in particular, would raise several thousand dollars per year, and "would improve literary taste amongst ourselves."[232]

This was not the first time Moosmüller's scholarship had helped fund the Georgia missions. Two years prior to *Der Geschichtsfreund*, Moosmüller sold a substantial "historical treatise of about 223 pages" titled *Europäer in Amerika vor Columbus* for two hundred gold mark, and he donated the money to the Skidaway Island mission.[233] The title, which translates to "Europeans in America before Columbus," is still in print today. The book was about European exploration, specifically twelfth-century Scandinavian explorers, and contained research material Moosmüller found while studying at the Vatican.[234] The publisher, George Joseph Manz, was from Ratisbonne, Germany, today's Regensburg, in Moosmüller's native Bavaria. Moosmüller received twenty free copies, which he used wisely and with political tact to gift his book to influential men. His sister had the books bound and sent to "Cardinal De Luca, Cardinal Hohenlohe, Your Grace [Wimmer], Archbishop of Salzburg, and other Gentlemen with whom I have the honor of being acquainted."[235]

LAMPS AND LIGHT

Father Moosmüller's scholarship, maintained despite his long work days, and the students' schooling required a good light source for study and reading. Physical evidence of this need was found archaeologically throughout the site in the form of lamp glass. Primarily, these sherds were very thin, colorless glass fragments from kerosene lamp chimneys. At the church, a nearly complete kerosene lamp font was found broken into twenty-six sherds but still loosely articulated. The colorless glass font was made with pressed glass. Reconstructing the lamp revealed a very simple, faceted design, reflecting the monk's simple needs and lifestyle.[236] The font is top-heavy, suggesting it sat on a metal or ceramic base or perhaps was a hanging lamp that fitted into a metal support. The font is somewhat unusual because it has two holes in the top—one for the number 2 burner, which held the wick, and another, smaller hole for filling the font, which would have had a cap. Although no exact match has been found for this lamp, a similar design was patented in 1868.[237]

Prior to kerosene lamps, the primary forms of lighting at night were firelight, tallow or wax candles, and oil lamps fueled by animal and vegetable oils, including whale oil. In the nineteenth century, there were three revolutions in lighting technology: gas, kerosene, and electricity. Beginning in the early 1800s, coal gas, produced through coal distillation and a by-product of making coke for the steel industry, was harnessed, producing brighter light at 25 percent of the cost of oil light. Gas lightning quickly became popular in urban areas for lighting homes, workplaces, and the streetscape. London had gas streetlights by 1807. The obvious downside to gas lighting was that it required substantial infrastructure to pipe the gas where needed. Dr. Abraham Gesner, a Canadian geologist, solved this problem in the mid-1800s by developing kerosene, which he patented in 1854. Kerosene lamps were a major improvement in light quality and intensity and produced less smoke and soot than both oil and candles. By the end of 1859, approximately 1.8 million kerosene lamps had been sold.[238] Kerosene proved to be so low cost and versatile that it coexisted with electricity for decades in the United States. Electric lights had similar infrastructure demands as gas and were not practical until the filament incandescent lamp was developed in the 1880s.[239]

For Skidaway Island residents, gas and electrical infrastructure was completely inaccessible, so kerosene lamps would have been essential. Kerosene lamps had numerous advantages over their predecessors—brighter light, less smoke and smell, less maintenance, lower costs, portability, and a safer flame enclosed in the chimney. As whales neared extinction, Dr. Gesner could be reasonably credited with helping to truly "save the whales" by inventing a popular substitute to whale oil. Today, of course, the numerous, horrific disadvantages of fossil fuels have been made clear.

The social implications of kerosene lights were also numerous. It is hard for the modern reader to understand how dark a moonless, rural night used to be. Before modern lighting, work and travel were organized around the daylight. For the students who needed bright light for writing, kerosene lamps allowed the day's work to be extended into night. Brother Aloysius Mason in his letter to Abbot Wimmer mentioned he was writing at ten o'clock at night while the rest were in bed.[240] He certainly would have been writing by a similar lamp, if not the lamp we found. Even during the day, rooms could be better lit for scholarly work. Southern students had an advantage over their northern colleagues, as southern buildings had large windows for cooling the building during the warmer months and therefore were better lit. Northern buildings often had small windows for retaining heat and short winter days, making it difficult to read and write without supplemental light. For Moosmüller, this meant he could write his monthly historical magazine, *Der Geschichtsfreund*, at night and travel or do farm work or teach during the day. The monks also rose hours before sunrise for prayer and mass, and a portable light meant safely traversing dark hallways and outdoor walkways. These lamps made rural life safer and more productive than when candles with open flames were in use. The lamps simply allowed more to be accomplished each day, with the caveat that they allowed more to be accomplished each day, leading the way toward today's culture of unrelieved busyness and overwork. Kerosene was the dominant lighting method in much of the rural United States until the 1930s and rural Canada until the 1940s.[241]

BUILDING SACRED HEART PARISH

Three years into the Skidaway school, the mission housed two priests, six lay brothers, and twenty-five students, plus Siricius Palmer, the cleric teaching the county school. Palmer taught fifty-six students, more than twice the fathers' school.[242] With this modest but propitious start, the Benedictines moved forward with their expansion plans. Father Moosmüller's new church campus in Savannah was located across fourteen lots along Habersham Street between St. James and St. Paul Streets, which at the time was considered the outskirts of the growing city (see map 5). The modern address is 31st and Habersham Streets. (The names "St. James" and "St. Paul" are no longer used.) The Benedictine Order in Georgia purchased the lots from John Moore, bishop of St. Augustine, Florida, in September 1880 for $500.[243] Construction started the next month. The buildings cost $3,177, which Moosmüller funded via *Der Geschichtsfreund* and a few donations from Captain Blun ($50), Rev. Richard O'Brien ($50 and a bell), Col. Haynes ($58.41), the Sisters of Mercy ($10), Conference of the Third Order of St. Francis ($15), and Mother Mathilda Beasley ($350). Moosmüller mortgaged the remainder. Dr. Read and Mr. McDonough donated furniture for the priest's residence, a modestly sized, 36-by-12-foot building facing Price Street. Other elements came from the congregation, including donations to buy the pews, altar, and pulpit.[244] The church, dedicated

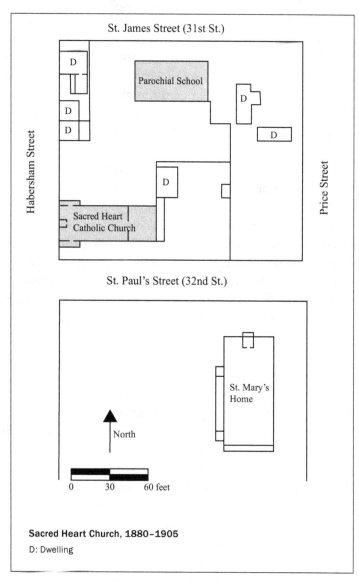

St. James Street (31st St.)

D

Parochial School

D

D

D

D

D

Habersham Street

Price Street

D

Sacred Heart
Catholic Church

St. Paul's Street (32nd St.)

St. Mary's
Home

North

0   30   60 feet

Sacred Heart Church, 1880–1905

D: Dwelling

MAP 5. Map of Savannah's original Sacred Heart Church and School, located on Habersham Street. This map is based on the 1898 Sanborn Fire Insurance Map.

FIGURE 5. The original Sacred Heart Church and Parish School on Habersham Street in Savannah, Georgia. (Courtesy of Saint Vincent Archabbey Archives)

on December 12, 1880, was 60 by 40 feet in size, painted green, and topped with a gilded cross (see figure 5).[245]

Wimmer described the completed development in 1883: "P[rior] Oswald had bought and paid for an entire city block, with the exception of two corner lots, on which are a neat frame church and dwelling for two priests and a large school building with assembly hall, and the entire property to be used for white and negroes. . . . The income of this property however provides only a scant living for one priest, but there is considerable construction going on in the neighborhood."[246]

Building Sacred Heart Church and School was a major investment in Savannah, but one can see missteps if the main intent was truly to serve the African American population. First, this location was a largely white neighborhood. Second is the surprisingly naive idea that Blacks and whites would use the church together. Wimmer even reiterated in a second letter, "P. Oswald has a pretty little church with a schoolhouse etc and is making all effort possible in taking care of the White & Black ones. Namely he has a mixed congregation."[247] In reality, there were two schools on site, one for each race.

By the end of 1881, there were 50 African American children enrolled in the school, which was held in the lower floor of a two-story annex. A separate schoolhouse was built starting in March 1882. Moosmüller paid about $4,000 for this school, mostly with money earned from *Der Geschichtsfreund*.[248] In October 1882, the Sisters of Mercy took over the schools, sitting boys and girls in separate classrooms. Enrollment had increased to 125 students. White and black students were taught separately, with the white students expected to pay tuition.[249] It is a tribute to Moosmüller's administrative skills and the quality of his history-themed, monthly magazine *Der Geschichtsfreund* that by June 1883, Sacred Heart was getting on solid financial ground. The next year, the Sisters of Mercy moved their orphanage and free school to the block south of Sacred Heart. This orphanage, soon after called St. Mary's Home for Female Orphans, was for white girls and housed between 35 and 37 girls until the later 1890s, when the numbers jumped to 60 girls.[250]

In April 1885, the parish infrastructure consisting of the church, schools, and orphanage were debt-free and financially self-sustaining.[251] However, the "mixed congregation" was ultimately unsustainable, and "by 1886 the parish was for all practical purposes a white parish."[252] Sacred Heart was within city limits by September 1885, and residences grew quickly around the church.[253] Without a separate church, Savannah's Catholic African American worshippers mostly attended the segregated cathedral or St. Patrick's if they lived on the west side of Savannah.[254] By 1886, the parochial school for white children had 40 students and occupied the same building where Moosmüller lived. Another, larger schoolhouse was the African American school, which had 160 students registered and 130 in average attendance. The white Sisters of Mercy taught the school in three regular classrooms, with a fourth classroom outfitted as a sewing room. African American girls were "kept only two hours after the elementary school is closed" to further their skills.[255]

Founding Sacred Heart Parish marks a transition for Moosmüller. While he remained the superior over the Benedictines' Skidaway Island mission, he lived in town starting in late January 1881 and handed over the daily Skidaway mission responsibilities to a young priest, Rev. Melchior Reichert, who had been ordained in 1875 and was at Saint Vincent before being assigned to Skidaway Island in 1879. Moosmüller had built a strong foundation for the Benedictines' work in Georgia. He was pleased with the mission's expansion, but he would simultaneously struggle to delegate responsibility and relinquish control over Skidaway while serving in the new Sacred Heart Parish.

CHAPTER 4
Expanding the Benedictine Mission

While Moosmüller managed the new parish, Rev. Melchior Reichert, who had traveled from Saint Vincent with Wimmer, took the lead on Skidaway Island. Father Reichert moved to Skidaway in the late summer of 1879. He was pleased with everything except the water, the food, the lack of musical instruments, and boating to the island, which took all day, made him sick, and ruined his clothes and shoes. "Bad water" was a frequent complaint of the new recruits. They likely referred to the water's lightly sulfurous smell and taste, rather than actually tainted or dangerous water. Since Skidaway was a newly established and always impecunious mission, there was not always an alternate drink such as beer or wine, which the brothers were used to drinking elsewhere.[1] Reichert also noted the lack of progress on the buildings. At least one needed a roof, possibly the church. Years later, Reichert recalled his arrival, "I found Father Moosmüller, several brothers, and some boys there, all living in a log house."[2] Although the mission finally had a musician in Reichert, apparently mice had destroyed the melodeon, and although there was a violin, it lacked strings. Wimmer sent a replacement melodeon in November, and Reichert began teaching the boys to sing. "If only they could read then we would soon be able to sing a High mass," grumbled Moosmüller.[3]

HARMONICAS AND MUSIC

No archaeological evidence of the violin or melodeon were uncovered, but three harmonica fragments were found. Portable and versatile, harmonicas have been found in phenomenally diverse archaeological contexts including a privy at a Chinatown gambling establishment in San Bernardino, California, and the homes of rural Patagonian Indigenous people living beyond the Argentinian reservations. Both of these sites were contemporary with the monastery site.[4] Harmonica fragments were also found on early nineteenth-century domestic sites in Missouri's Ozark Mountains and a 1930s Civilian Conservation Corps camp in Bandelier National Monument, New Mexico.[5]

Although the modern harmonica is about two hundred years old, it is based on the Chinese sheng, invented around 3000 B.C. These two instruments are both freestanding reed instruments, with the reed only attached at one end, and both are uniquely played by blowing and drawing breath to play single notes.[6] Today's harmonica dates to circa 1825, when a man named Richter invented the first twenty-note, ten-hole, blow-draw, free reed mouth organ in Bohemia, Germany. A few years later, German clockmaker Christian Messner was building harmonicas with his cousin, Christian Weiss. By 1829, W. Thei was mass-producing the harmonica, known as the *mundharmonika* or *mundaeoline*, in Vienna. A popular novelty, the harmonica was also controversial. There are "contemporary accounts of raids on music stores by bands of vigilantes who seized concertinas and harmonicas and tossed them in huge bonfires."[7]

German clockmaker Matthias Hohner visited Messner and Weiss's harmonica factory, learning enough from Weiss before Messner wisely ejected him from the premises. Shortly after, the twenty-four-year-old Hohner began manufacturing harmonicas in his kitchen with his family and one or two staff. In 1862 he began exporting them to the United States, quickly gaining a near monopoly. Five years later, he was making twenty-two hundred per year. General stores usually sold them for ten cents, but some were as cheap as five cents until 1900, and harmonicas became popular gifts. By 1887, Hohner's company was making one million harmonicas per year. The 1893 American economic depression forced Hohner to export to additional countries, but his production numbers continued to soar: three million per year in 1897 and eight million in 1911.

Popular and cheap, the harmonica became important to many styles of American music. In the 1880s, the cross harp technique was developed. The musician put the accent on the draw (as opposed to blow) notes, "bending" the notes' pitch and tone. This technique, particularly good for creating effects such as train horns and animal imitations, was used in proto-blues and other African American musical styles. African storytellers used a "quill," a hand-held mouth instrument, to produce a similar tone, so African American musicians were familiar with these notes, using the harmonica as an extension of this deeper history and musical tradition. The 1920s is considered the "golden era of the harmonica," when the instrument was used in blues and country music, jug bands, and vaudeville. The popularity continued throughout the 1930s when harmonicas were taught in public schools, and harmonica bands were in the movies. Hohner's production peaked in 1930 with thirty million harmonicas made.[8] As an easily accessible instrument, the harmonica did not require a specially trained teacher. Many musicians were taught by their mothers, sometimes by their fathers.[9]

Both sacred and secular music were enjoyed at the monastery. Of course, music was part of the Catholic Mass, but students and islanders also had their own musical traditions, even if the monks did not recognize the traditions as such. In late December 1878, Moosmüller requested funding for musical instruments and an instructor: "If we could establish a *brassband* for the nigroes on this island, not only the whole population of this but also those of the neighbouring islands would come to us. Of course, in church at Divine Service, I would have nothing else but Gregorian Chant, but before and after Service, they might play their brassband etc. The nigroes got a big drum and a small drum, 2 pipes, 6 muskets, and a sword, on Christmas day and on other festivals they hang around our place all day and make an awful noise [*sic*]."[10]

Moosmüller's motivation was to "gain the Nigroes [*sic*] by means of Music as the Jesuits did once with the Indians of Paraguay."[11] The bishop supported the idea, but Moosmüller was denied. Although Wimmer initially agreed to send instruments and an instructor, the monks at Saint Vincent protested. They were against this mission to start with and resented more money being sent there. Two Christmases later, Wimmer directed Reichert to buy the boys a drum and two fifes. One drum can be seen in the historic photograph taken of the school (see figure 3).[12] More importantly, this anecdote illustrates the passion for music among the students and African American neighbors, including traditional drumming. Moosmüller misunderstood the cultural context of drumming. Was there truly an "awful noise"? Or were they practicing African American drumming and ring shouts similar to those documented in the WPA project *Drums and Shadows*? Gullah Geechee people continue the practice of ring shouts at festivals and celebrations today.

The three harmonica fragments were found in a soil layer dating to the 1890s, which was when an African American teacher rather than a white priest was teaching the school and managing the property. Therefore, the harmonica's owner was either a student, the teacher, or a member of the teacher's family. In any case, the harmonica shows African American musical traditions being practiced on site, which was a critical means for maintaining cultural and storytelling traditions. Black musicians, called "musicianers," were the antebellum "folk elite," similar to preachers.[13] Prior to the Civil War, musicians used their skills like any other skilled slave, negotiating for more freedom of movement and income, as well as playing for Black community gatherings, including "frolics" on Sundays after church, which earned them status within the Black community. At frolics, the musician's role was a facilitator. While on the sometimes literal but always symbolic stage, musicians wore bright, fancy costumes to attract attention. Communities gave rewards or special privileges to talented musicians. Also as folklorists and teachers, musicians played an important role in cultural continuity, teaching new generations to play violins, quills, and cane pan's pipes.

That cultural and social role continued in the postbellum era. Unlike preachers, musicians usually did not get involved in politics. Slave trickster stories evolved into other trickster tropes including Br'er Rabbit, who was often portrayed as a fiddler, and these evolved into legends of the twentieth-century bluesman.[14] As Paul A. Cimbala writes, "Musicianers could be considered subversive in that they actively nurtured resistance to the white domination of the black soul."[15] After emancipation, politics changed, but musicianers were still traditional carriers of culture and a "lightning rod of community identity."[16] They continued to teach the next generation of musicians into the twentieth century. Musicianers worked for whites to earn wages, while playing to African American audiences free of charge, albeit gaining status and celebrity. Some big social events meant returning to plantations for all-day, all-night reunions that maintained social and family ties, especially after people began to migrate north and west. Musicians were also important communicators of news and politics, when few could read and civil rights were virtually nonexistent for African Americans.[17] It is significant that these harmonica fragments are associated with the time when an African American teacher was present at the Skidaway mission. At a minimum, she would have encouraged traditional musical practices, or she may have been teaching musical skills and storytelling to the next generation.

FINANCIAL CHALLENGES

Despite the priests' creative attempts to attract students through music, the school's attendance remained low in the first few years, and the school continued to struggle financially throughout the 1880s. The Benedictines received about $100 per year from the ten families that were tenants on their Skidaway Island plantation.[18] The monks found various ways to make money beyond their tenants and church funds. Moosmüller reported in 1881, "F. Melchior sent yesterday some fish to the market by a nigro [sic] for which he got $12."[19] This nugget is tucked into more pressing business about building and financing Sacred Heart Church in Savannah but clearly warranted a mention. Reichert traveled throughout Georgia asking for donations. The Benedictines often gathered and sold palms for Palm Sunday. The palms were sent as far as Canada as well as to several American cities. In 1884, they sold approximately ten thousand palms.[20] Although parents often simply did not pay tuition, alternative, nonmonetary arrangements were also made. For example, Mr. O'Byrne "paid" for his son's education with groceries at least during one school year, and Reichert asked permission to let him pay by barter again.[21]

By mid-1885, Sacred Heart Parish was financially self-supporting. The Skidaway mission was not, by admission of both Fathers Moosmüller and Reichert. Moosmüller blamed Reichert; however, comparing the two institutions is beyond apples and oranges.[22] A white institution in Savannah could marshal much greater

resources from its congregation than an African American mission on the sea islands—the number of congregants, their families' wealth, and their religious motivations were all completely different.

BROTHER ALPHONSE AND MEDICAL TREATMENTS

Staffing the monastery was another ongoing administrative chore. Many brothers
and priests worked at the mission over its brief existence. Some only stayed a few
months, often because they were miserable, especially during the difficult summer
months, which brought oppressive heat and humidity, clouds of biting sand gnats,
and disease-carrying mosquitoes. Very few remained for long, toughing out illnesses and isolation. Brother Alphonse Schoene, who was a white policeman in Savannah prior to taking the habit, first became a Benedictine under Father Bergier
at Isle of Hope. He lived at the Skidaway monastery for nearly ten years and often
suffered from illness.[23] In August 1878, Father Moosmüller administered the last
sacrament to Brother Alphonse. Although he did recover, Moosmüller acknowledged, "but still he will never be strong."[24] A month later, "Poor Bro Alphons is at
the hospital again in Savannah, he has dispepsy [sic] in a high degree, these many
years already; and the fever besides."[25] Brother Alphonse's stomach trouble (the
dyspepsia) was attributed to his childhood but not further explained. The fever
was likely malaria, which became a frequent complaint among the monks. Despite
his frequent absences due to illness, Moosmüller held him in high regard, noting
that both Brother Alphonse and Father Siricius "take the greatest interest in the
welfare of this house."[26] Brother Alphonse, a German native, was the "Boat Man."
He caught fish for either home consumption or sale in Savannah and piloted and
maintained the boat that was their transportation on and off the island.[27] In August 1887, Brother Alphonse was still fishing, although he remained in poor health
and was plagued by headaches. Abbot Haid allowed him six weeks at Belmont
Abbey in North Carolina for rest and retreat.[28] He returned to Skidaway in mid-
October 1887.[29] Brother Alphonse was transferred to Belmont Abbey (probably in
the later 1880s) and was eventually buried there.[30]

Retaining staff was a frequent challenge at the Skidaway mission. Many that
came to Skidaway left shortly after, often because of disease. It was not uncommon
for a priest or brother to arrive and leave within a year, then continue on to a successful and healthy life once he left the island. Malaria, yellow fever, sand gnats, and
the high-humidity heat were a constant drain on the staff and the islands' residents.
Early in his tenure on Skidaway, Moosmüller began several programs to improve
living conditions for everyone on the island. Using the example of Trappist monks
in Italy, Moosmüller got eucalyptus seeds to plant trees and dug canals to drain the

marsh. The eucalyptus scent deters the mosquitoes much like citronella and is used in "natural" mosquito repellent products today. There is no record of whether the eucalyptus grew successfully or not.[31] Although many island inhabitants suffered from malaria, the white lay brothers were perceived as being more susceptible and had to be "replaced" when they fell ill.[32]

Given the frequency of diseases noted, it is surprising that so few glass pharmaceutical bottles were found on site—only one deposited in the 1880s and one in the 1890s. In the twentieth-century layers that postdate the monastery, at least nine glass bottle fragments are pharmaceutical. The 1880s bottle fragment found near the school has few diagnostic attributes. However, a whole bottle dating between 1880 and 1895 and manufactured by Whitall Tatum & Co. was found near the church. This company was owned by two Quaker families who refused to manufacture alcohol bottles on religious grounds, so they made small bottles and vials for holding prescription drugs for individual sale as well as "shop furniture," meaning larger bottles for holding druggists' supplies. The company specialized in making bottles embossed with individual company names by using inset lettered plates. This innovation proved popular compared with much more costly individual molds.[33] Another Whitall Tatum bottle in a post-1900 layer is embossed with "SAVANNAH GA," but unfortunately lacks a company name on the opposite side. A twentieth-century fragmentary bottle was embossed with "LOMONS & CO./ . . . RUGGISTS/ . . . ANNAH GA." This bottle was purchased at Solomon's Drug Store. Abraham Solomons opened his drug store in 1845 and expanded to several locations throughout Savannah. It was passed down through several generations of Solomons before it closed in 1981.[34]

Medicines, as today, were available in two broad types—those obtained by prescription from a physician and proprietary medicines, which were similar to over-the-counter medicines. Unlike today's highly regulated drug market, nineteenth-century proprietary medicines were a minefield. Frequently a combination of alcohol, sugar, and water, at best they were relatively harmless, at worst they contained powerful narcotics. Narcotics, such as opium, had two advantages: they really did relieve pain (if temporarily), and the subsequent addictions meant more sales. The common term "patent medicine" is misleading, as these medicines were usually not patented, because that would require proof of innovation and effectiveness as well as revealing the ingredients and formulas in the application. More often, these drugs were protected through trademarks and copyrights, or patents on bottle designs, neatly sidestepping any oversight or consumer protections. Without any federal drug control, people took advantage. Between 1850 and

1900 is considered the peak of pharmaceutical fraud, when much money was made from the vulnerable public. Journalist Samuel Hopkins Adams's ten-article exposé, "The Great American Fraud," combined with the advocacy of Dr. Harvey Washington Wiley, the USDA's chief of the Bureau of Chemistry, led to the Pure Food and Drugs Act of 1906, which regulated the contents of proprietary medicines and improved labeling. This legislation was still limited and enforcement was challenging, so many amendments and subsequent legislation have been passed. Given the dangers these "medicines" posed, Brother Alphonse may have been better off without proprietary medicines, despite his serious health issues.

FATHER MELCHIOR REICHERT

Father Reichert led the boys' school and priory with a lighter touch than Moosmüller. He was not comfortable in leadership positions, especially as the Skidaway community was so small. He wrote: "I am well, Thank God, and willing to live and die for the Negroes, but if possible Dear Father Abbot, please, as soon as you can, take away from me the Superiorship. According to our Rule it is wrong to call a person Prior unless there are three or more fathers at the place."[35] Reichert did not, however, shy away from his duties. He continued to require diligent studying including meditation, spiritual reading, and examinations for all the community members. When Brother Fridolin attempted to evade his studious responsibilities, Reichert "went for him the other day and now he seems to give in."[36]

Exact numbers of students and staff varied over time. Typically, 2 to 3 priests, 5 to 10 lay brothers, and 15 to 25 students lived at the mission at any given time, although there may have been as many as 50 boys at the school during its peak in the later 1880s and early 1890s.[37] Under Father Reichert's leadership, the school grew from 12 students in April 1881 to 20 students by 1883.[38] In June 1883, the little community had "two Patres, one candidate & one cook, different carpenters in woodwork, masons (bricklayers), fishermen, gardeners, and twenty little boys only on lack of room but we are kept busy with erecting more buildings [sic]."[39] Reichert was highly invested in Skidaway and felt positive about its growth. Abbot Wimmer had invested at least $1,000 into the Skidaway mission, was committed to its further growth, and arranged for additions "at considerable cost to accomodate [sic] fifty boys and also afford convenient living quarters for a small community."[40] This was a major investment in the property with high expectations of recruiting more students. Not all of the boys were locals. In September 1883, Reichert traveled to New York, Richmond, and Baltimore, recruiting and returning with three boys for the school from Baltimore along with many presents for the boys and the church.[41]

BROTHER BRUNO HUEBNER

In anticipation of more students, additional staff arrived from Saint Vincent Archabbey. Brother Bruno Huebner (1851–1931) joined the Saint Vincent monastery
in 1869, four years after immigrating to the United States probably from Gdańsk
(Danzig in German), Poland. Over the course of his eighty years, his nation of ori-
gin changed names from Prussia to Germany with the shifting political situations.
He became a naturalized U.S. citizen in 1872. Brother Bruno spent his early years as
a religious in Chicago at a small church with several priests and only two lay brothers. In 1880, he was living at Saint Vincent Archabbey and working as a laborer but
left shortly after to spend four years at the Skidaway mission. While working at
Skidaway, Brother Bruno received a metal crucifix with an inscription on the back,
"I received this cross 1883 at Skidaway Island for my name day Br Bruno."[42]

After his time at the Skidaway mission, Brother Bruno briefly worked in the
Belmont Abbey kitchen starting in 1885. Bruno hated the kitchen and wanted
to be reassigned to the garden partially because of the racial conflicts present in
the kitchen. Brother Cornelius picked fights with a Black candidate, John. When
"corrected," Cornelius stated that African Americans "have no business here."[43]
Abbot Haid threatened to dismiss him if he did not improve. Two weeks later,
the kitchen situation had settled, but Haid was still fearful of accepting African
American brothers. White brothers *do not like Colored* Brothers—at least some
of them. I am afraid they would be displeased should one be admitted."[44] This
harassment and abuse is exactly why several African American lay brothers urged
Moosmüller to accept only Black candidates and lay brothers. They were trying
to prevent abuse while creating a supportive environment for Black religious to
succeed. Instead, both locations accepted Black and white candidates. Few African
American lay brothers succeeded in the long term at either Belmont Abbey or the
Skidaway monastery, whose mission specifically included training African American lay brothers.

Brother Bruno did not have to suffer long in the Belmont kitchen, as he returned to Saint Vincent in early 1886 when two African American "boys from
Skidaway" arrived to replace him in the kitchen and refectory.[45] The monastery
could "now get along if Br. Cornelius behaves."[46] It is unclear if the people from
Skidaway were students under the age of eighteen or were adult novices pursuing
the lay brotherhood, who were called "boys" because they were African American.
Either way, these individuals were pursuing further religious education after their
initial schooling at Skidaway Island. They were not named, so it is impossible to
follow their educational journey or determine if they professed vows.

Brother Bruno Huebner, relieved of his kitchen duties, was back in Chicago by

1900, but this time at a priory with one superior and eight brothers. He returned to Saint Vincent Archabbey and was a nurse in the infirmary in 1910. An oral historian in 1927 described him as a "small, roundish man, pleasant and jolly with a fairly good command of English."[47] He remained at Saint Vincent for the rest of his life.[48]

SAINT MARY'S COLLEGE

St. Mary Help Priory, the future Belmont Abbey, had also started a school in 1878, Saint Mary's College, but there were significant differences between this school and the Skidaway Island school. Saint Mary's College, which would eventually become Belmont Abbey College, was for white male students who took advanced classes. The school trained young men for the priesthood as well as trained those who pursued professions. Despite the disparities between the schools, several Belmont faculty members taught at both schools or were priests in the Savannah area. The frequent crossover between institutions meant there was a certain sense of community shared within the larger South. Brother Philip Cassidy, who had taught at Bergier's Savannah school in 1874, went to St. Mary Help to teach in the school's formative years, serving as the first prefect of studies. Brother Philip was a lay brother in Ireland before immigrating to the United States and becoming a Benedictine. He took simple vows January 1, 1873, and professed solemn vows on February 2, 1876.[49]

Rev. Joseph Keller arrived in 1877 from Richmond, Virginia, and was "in charge of the spiritual affairs of the [St. Mary Help] community." With so few monks, Keller also found time to work on the buildings, including an 18-by-30-foot chapel.[50] Father Cyprian Moncton Creagh was fondly remembered as a "born teacher." He taught commercial law and accounting in the early 1880s at Belmont. At forty-eight years of age in 1880, Creagh was "bearded and gray" and inspired loyalty in his students.[51] Despite the students' enthusiasm, the school remained small in its earliest years. Like the Skidaway posting, "faculty looked upon North Carolina as a land of exile," away from the community and physical comforts of St. Vincent Abbey, as St. Mary Help was literally being built up around them.

From 1879 to 1882, Swiss native Daniel Hefti taught algebra, trigonometry, and surveying "practically, in the field" as well as German and general science before being sent to the Skidaway school.[52] Rev. Irwin, one of Hefti's Belmont students, remembered his "splendid abilities." Hefti immigrated in May 1871 on the ship *Silesia*. Immigration documents list him as a farmer, which, if true, better qualified him than most of the Skidaway staff to teach both scholarly and practical skills.[53] Hefti was educated at Saint Vincent College and was frequently listed among the top students in the 1876 and 1877 school catalogs, along with Alexius Grass, who arrived at Skidaway after him.[54] Rev. Hefti was thirty years old when he arrived at Skidaway in 1883 to take over as superior. Reichert was glad for his company. "Father Daniel is well and a first rate companion; he has two bee hives and is able to furnish us with honey."[55]

Hefti had only lived on the island for several months when there was a tragic accident. Reichert was away in Savannah assisting Moosmüller, who was suffering from a medical problem with his eyes. Reichert relayed the bad news to Wimmer: "Last night Father Daniel was to rid us of several strange dogs which were frequenting our place, annoying us and preventing us from sleep. He had a fair chance to shoot, but, it seemed, wished to spare them once more, and inflicted a good blow with the butt of his gun; but alas, he missed the dogs and struck a log, causing his gun to go off. He shot himself in the intestines and Dr. Dupon says that he cannot live."[56] Dr. Dupon stayed with Father Hefti until he died the next day, December 8, 1883. He was initially buried in a cemetery adjacent to the monastery but was later reinterred at Belmont Abbey Cemetery.[57] Abbot Wimmer eulogized: "He was a very zealous and good priest who had already converted many Negros. His death was edifying—but so unnecessary."[58]

GUN VIOLENCE

In June 1877, Wimmer gifted agricultural implements and a gun to the Skidaway mission. Moosmüller was grateful and described both as "really needed & will be most welcome."[59] They used the gun that August to scare away grape thieves from their Isle of Hope property by randomly firing shots into the night.[60] The other known incident of gun violence was when two lay brothers were fighting using an axe and a gun. These brothers were dismissed because of their altercation.[61] Despite knowing about these serious incidents, field researchers still were surprised by the number and variety of armaments found on site. The majority of the weaponry recovered archaeologically were brass cartridges; most were for .22 caliber bullets, with some .32, and one each of .33, .45, and .45–70 caliber. Five pistol percussion caps and two rifle percussion caps were found. Three partial shotgun shells and two rifle bullets complete the assemblage. The objects are evenly distributed through the occupation phases, though there is a slight increase over time. Smaller arms predominate, with more .22 caliber cartridges than .32, and only a few larger cartridges. Likewise, pistol percussion caps outnumber rifle percussion caps.

Since the majority of the gun evidence is post-1890, we can interpret at least some of these artifacts as belonging to African American residents— the students, the Mirault family who taught and were caretakers in the 1890s, or neighboring tenants. While hunting is a probable explanation for some of the arms found, self-protection is another, not mutually exclusive, explanation. Violence against African Americans was, and still is, disturbingly common, often perpetrated by several white men in disguise. For most occurrences, the injured party knew their attackers' identity and knew them personally, because the goal was intimidation in addition to physical harm. During Reconstruction, it was common for freedpeople to have guns in their houses and carry them in the fields and on the streets. African American men also formed militias up and down the Georgia coast to block violence and intimidation. As Paul A. Cimbala writes: "The patterns of justice, or rather injustice, remained the same. In the process, those patterns revealed the impossibility of bringing to justice criminals who were implementing the wishes of their [white] communities."[62] The Freedmen's Bureau had little enforcement power. While they used the military when possible, there simply was not enough manpower to cover the number of atrocities committed. Local law enforcement and courts would bond out offenders and rarely found them guilty.[63] These patterns continue today.

Annelise Morris has interpreted firearms evidence as a complex combination of hunting practices and the social practices of recreation and protection.[64] Hunting provided both food and a social activity that bonded men and provided new neighbors an entrance into society. At Morris's sites, a group of nineteenth- and twentieth-century farmsteads, target practice from the front porch was a social activity that also demonstrated the presence of guns and the competence of their users. "At the same time these items (and the skilled use of them, demonstrated in this "friendly" way) were indexing the means and skills of defense. . . . I would argue that these artifacts represent a skillful negotiation of social practices that at once underscores Black masculinity by opening previously restricted social networks and showcasing the ability to provide for a family, while at the same time subtly indicating the willingness to defend this same family."[65]

DIFFERENCES IN LEADERSHIP

Father Hefti's death meant Father Reichert was again the superior at the Skidaway mission. Reichert was not comfortable in leadership positions, and this was magnified by his contentious relationship with Moosmüller. In the mid-1880s, Moosmüller began to struggle somewhat with poor health and his charges. He suffered from malaria and its complications, including problems with his eyes, which was especially difficult for a scholar of Moosmüller's capability. He also has trouble understanding and relating to Father Reichert, writing, "P. Melchior is a queer man."[66] Reichert had let a young African American man stay alone in Moosmüller's room for more than a week while Moosmüller was away. This "notorious thief" had previously stolen $50 from Reichert, but Reichert had recovered most of it. Moosmüller returned to find his desk broken into and money missing including "$15 belonging to the Altar society, a bankers draft from St. Louis Mo. of the Agent of the *Geschichtsfreund* for $76.50 and some $5 silver out of my pocketbook."[67] Between sick calls and confession duties, Moosmüller could not immediately travel to Skidaway, so he wrote to Reichert informing him of the situation. Moosmüller's frustration is understandable. Was Reichert simply naive and gullible? Or were Reichert's motives rooted in trust and belief in the goodness of others? Perhaps the accused young man was not guilty. Unfortunately, Reichert's response and the resolution to the problem are lost to us.

Reichert was very reluctant to be in a leadership position. In the same letter reporting Father Hefti's death, Reichert immediately asked for another superior.[68] He did not get his wish and repeated his request in 1886, asking for Father Moosmüller to return as superior.[69] Despite his resistance to the leadership position, Reichert continued to recruit and train brothers. At the beginning of 1884, he invested two African American candidates and one white candidate.[70] Even as Sacred Heart was becoming more segregated and losing its African American worshippers, and against the earlier advice of several African American brothers, Reichert had both African American and white brothers and candidates living together. Perhaps this is further evidence of Reichert's innate optimism.

Moosmüller reacted to Reichert's leadership (or lack thereof) by suggesting to Wimmer that he might help with some needed repairs on Skidaway. With *Der Geschichtsfreund* publishing responsibilities contracted out and the anticipated arrival of Father Alexius Grass, he would have more time. While Grass presided at Sacred Heart, Moosmüller could "do something to fix up the place & house on Skidaway . . . build a stable, a kitchen etc."[71] He obliquely referenced that it was not his job to help, but he cited his continuing interest in seeing the Skidaway mission succeed, and now he had the time to be involved. Reichert was clearly not a detail-oriented manager, but it is unclear if this was an unnecessary intrusion, or if Moosmüller's intervention was truly needed.

A month later, Moosmüller continued to push "help" on Reichert through Wimmer. This time he suggested that Father James Zilliox, who was sick at Saint Vincent, be sent to cover Sacred Heart for several months, so he could build a stable on Skidaway. His critique of Reichert continued with the subject of school enrollment. Moosmüller found a benefactor who would pay the tuition for African American boys attending the Skidaway mission school. Moosmüller had six boys in mind, but "the impediment is that I could not speak an earnest word or learn a proper answer from P Melchior whether he will take them or not."[72] Moosmüller directly criticized Reichert, stating this had been an ongoing problem for two years. The school could have had more boys but did not because of Reichert's unresponsiveness.[73] Reichert retorted in a letter to Wimmer, "What Rev. P. Oswald, OSB, says about those boys is—I am sorry to say—not *true*. He can send them today if he chooses. True our dormitory is full and [we have] several applications from Florida and Alabama."[74] Reichert's answer speaks to a large part of their problem; instead of Reichert and Moosmüller communicating with each other, the abbot was forced to act as intermediary.

Moosmüller's exasperation with Reichert's administration continued into the spring. Moosmüller begged Wimmer to visit, or at least threaten to visit, "for the sole & only reason that they may sweep or scrub their house & clean up the place."[75] Some of the students and brothers had lice. Clothing, shoes, and tools were scattered between the house, yard, garden, and fields. Clothing was infrequently washed and worn by whomever picked it up. "Even Rev P Melchior himself came into town with shoes on his feet that belonged to one of the colored boys."[76] Personal hygiene was seriously lacking. "Since the weather is getting warm the new school-house, outside the fence on the corner of the cross road, smells like a water closet at a good distance, because the beds are in the first floor & some boys water them frequently."[77] Brother Aloysius, who had been keeping house, left, and no one took his place. Moosmüller blamed Reichert for his lack of administrative organization and discipline. Reichert could not or would not assign each brother to particular tasks, making sure that everything was completed. Work was chaotically assigned throughout the day, with any person potentially assigned to any task. The lack of consistency resulted in no one taking responsibility or pride in their work. Tools were left strewn everywhere and were subsequently lost or damaged.

At the end of May 1884, Moosmüller delineated a plan to "help" at Skidaway, if given Wimmer's blessing. Moosmüller would travel to Skidaway once a week to teach the brothers the Holy Rule and give confession. Moosmüller divided up and assigned work, suggesting that "a practical brother who could be 'Decan' [*sic*]" was needed to supervise all farm and garden work.[78] Moosmüller perceived a serious lack of discipline and maturity among the students, which he attributed to inconsistent teaching and attention. Some of the students who had attended the brothers' school for five years "are boys yet in spite of the habit."[79] The students constantly needed to be prompted what tasks to do and how to do them. The poor mules seemed to bear the brunt of the boys' ineptitude. The students left the harness exposed to the elements, which consequently damaged the mules' skin. The fields did not fare much better when one boy left the harnessed mule standing in the field and took off for a drink of water. The mule wandered around, ripping up about 100 watermelon plants with the plow as it went. A second boy did something similar, and a plow was broken in the process.[80]

In 1884, Reverend Joseph Keller, O.S.B., and Reverend Alexius Grass, O.S.B., came from Saint Vincent to help; neither stayed long.[81] Reverend Grass was born Michael Grass in 1860 in Chicago. He was the oldest of Mathias and Margaret Grass's ten children. The Grass family, like many families with sons at Saint Vincent, was composed of immigrants and first-generation Americans. Margaret Grass is alternately listed as being born in Prussia (same as her husband), New York, "Atlantic Ocean," and "at sea."[82] Averaging these answers together creates a powerful image of motherhood, immigration, and courage. By 1880, Grass was in school at Saint Vincent alongside Daniel Hefti, who also served on Skidaway. After his brief, unremarkable stint on Skidaway, Father Grass returned to his native Illinois to teach at St. Bede's College in Bureau County, over one hundred miles from Chicago, and later he was sent to a Benedictine college in Colorado. His next assignment was Fourteen Holy Martyrs Catholic Church in Baltimore, starting in September 1909. Father Grass seemed to thrive in this assignment, making the newspaper several times with feature stories about weddings he performed and his distinguished guests such as Abbot Dom Francis Gasquet, head of the English Benedictines and chairman of Pope Pius's 1907 commission to revise the Latin Bible.[83] Father Grass died rather young, at fifty-eight, at St. Francis Hospital in Pittsburgh. His death certificate lists arteriosclerosis, or heart disease, as his cause of death, but he died in October 1918 during the Spanish flu epidemic, so heart disease may have been a contributing factor, or it may have been coincidence that he died during the flu epidemic. He was buried at Saint Vincent.[84]

Father Keller had a more memorable stint on Skidaway Island. "A very saintly priest, Father Joseph Keller, had sunstroke there [on Skidaway], but he did not die. No one likes to go there because of the malaria and the terrible heat," wrote Wimmer bluntly.[85] Keller, a German native who immigrated in 1867 at age twenty, was never happy at Skidaway, and the boys were unhappy with him. Reichert recommended that Reverend Keller return to Saint Vincent in August 1885.[86] Later that month, Keller left for Alabama.[87] He eventually returned north and continued his work at Saint Vincent.[88]

The year 1884 brought a celebration to the Skidaway mission when Bishop William Gross held a vespers service there in July. Savannah priest Father McNally and some African American members of the Catholic Knights of America traveled with the bishop via the City and Suburban Railway to Isle of Hope and then boarded small boats to complete the journey. A "large number" of locals joined

Father Reichert and the brothers in greeting the bishop and his entourage. Bishop Gross confirmed twenty African American islanders, the majority of whom were adults, and gave the sermon. "The children of the Sunday school were present in the chapel, where the brothers have a fine cabinet organ, and rendered the music of the service very acceptably."[89]

It is critical to note that the bishop was confirming, not baptizing, the islanders. Confirmation is a deeper commitment to the Catholic Church than baptism, requiring more time, education, and religious duty. This strongly suggests Fathers Reichert and Moosmüller were not only gaining converts but getting sincere converts, not those looking for short-term gain. However, the decision to join the Catholic Church did not come without consequences for some. When one African American woman in her eighties joined the church, her family banished her from their house. She came to live on the Benedictines' land.[90]

POOR CLARE NUNS

Right before he left for a new assignment in Oregon, Bishop Gross invited a group of Poor Clare nuns to build a boarding school and orphanage for girls as a complement to the Benedictine's school. This missionary invitation was one of many Gross extended during his tenure, but it would prove to be the most troublesome and controversial. Although Mother Dominick O'Neill may have been a legitimate nun and member of the Poor Clares from York, England, it is doubtful whether she had permission to be in Georgia from her superiors. Her three companions lacked formal religious credentials. During her short time in Georgia, Mother Dominick, a rather daring, spirited, and possibly shady woman, drove the collective male Catholic leadership crazy.[91]

This small group of white nuns arrived in Savannah in late 1884, and initially the women lived with the Sisters of Mercy at Sacred Heart and worked in Father Moosmüller's schoolhouse. Mother Dominick tried to persuade Bishop Gross to allow her to start in Savannah, but the bishop was unmoved. He wanted a girls' boarding school on Skidaway Island, so off they went sometime after January 1885.[92] The Benedictines helped build structures on their plantation for the nuns' use. The Poor Clare school, much like the Benedictine's start, remained small and generated very little revenue. It is unlikely the school reached more than a handful of girls during its brief time. The women left behind twelve bedsteads and fourteen mattresses. However, they also abandoned twenty-four double-seat school desks, twenty-one single-seat school desks, a blackboard, and a table. The women were better equipped for teaching than housing students and may have gotten a few local students, although by this time the county public school had reopened. The public school offered education for girls and boys, unlike the single-sex Benedictine and Poor Clare schools.

The nuns had no source of income, and their attempts to raise money in unconventional ways raised the ire of Catholic leaders. The women supposedly rowed out to ships in Savannah's port and visited the taverns along the riverfront to ask for donations.[93] They also took begging trips out of state. The recently installed Bishop Becker, "an old style southern gentleman with a strict sense of propriety," was mortified by their irregular behavior. The women also faced the same problems of excessive heat, rural and rough conditions, and mosquito-borne diseases as the Benedictines. Ultimately Bishop Becker officially dismissed the women in mid-1887, because "they failed notoriously in their insane attempt" both to maintain discipline and finance their operations.[94] They did leave behind heavy debts, but Becker was most aggrieved because the abbess, whose title was dubious, did not establish a proper religious community with discipline and order.

After the women left, the newly minted Abbot Leo Haid locked the house and gave Father Lester the keys, absolutely refusing to pay their debts. Instead, he allowed the sheriff to auction the buildings and their contents to recover some money.[95] Many of the debts were typical costs from starting a new institution and constructing buildings. For example, they owed a lumber merchant, Mr. McDonough, $300. The sisters owed Mr. Hanley another $300 for painting services, doors, locks, windows, sash and blinds, and other items.[96] The buildings, wharfs, fences, and loose construction materials were valued at $500, and the buildings' contents were appraised at $255.20 for a total of $755.20.[97]

Abbot Haid correctly predicted the women would sue for damages, called the whole situation a "bad mistake," and promised that "no Sister will be permitted to live on the island" as long as he was superior.[98] The women did appeal to the Vatican, asking for compensation for their services and the loss of their property. The appeal was investigated, but Bishop Becker made several strong arguments, including the women's lack of title to the property, "irreligious conduct," and their disastrous finances, even implying the women left town with donations that should have been used to pay their debts. In fact, Becker argued, if anyone was owed, it was the diocese, which had to cover the remaining debts. The dismissal was sustained, the women were barred from returning, and the incident was closed in 1890.[99]

Although Bishop Becker had legitimate reasons to deny the Poor Clares' compensation claims, including letters from the abbess's superiors in York, his ranting also betrayed his biases. A significant portion of Becker's anger stems from racism, pity, and rage at those who would spend money and effort to provide educational opportunities for African Americans. Bishop Becker was uninterested in the women's educational mission because he did not believe an academic education for African Americans was worthwhile.[100] He wrote: "The colored people need to be taught less in schools, and a great deal more in individual work. They have a notion that the sovereign panacea for all their woes is to be able to read and write a little, and learn something of figures. They believe that such knowledge would somehow keep them from being obliged to work."[101] He did not believe the Benedictines' Skidaway work was worthwhile either: "The O.S.B. simply sunk, spent, swamped, from $10,000 [to] $12,000 hard cash in trying a dreamy experiment, viz: to found an 'Industrial School' on the Island of Skidaway."[102] He claimed the island was unhealthy, especially for white people, and the monks would never be successful, "not to say a word about women unacquainted with and incapable of governing the blacks."[103] Ultimately, Becker felt he owed the women nothing, and it was the Poor Clares "who owe us much for our trouble on account of their irreligious conduct & indecorous methods of procedure."[104] Were the women truly bawdy or even indecent? Or did the women just offend Bishop Becker's patriarchal sensibilities and threaten his sense of white privilege and societal order?

The women, with the exception of Mother Dominick, were not legitimate members of the Poor Clares and were not legal owners of their land on Skidaway, which was borrowed from the Benedictines. Although the women were certainly flawed, it is unclear if they were corrupt, as Bishop Becker and other male Catholic leaders continually implied. To modern eyes, the women seem resourceful and driven. Haid wrote, "The poor Bishop is heartily sick of the trouble and annoyance these Sisters caused him."[105] The women were not able to build a successful school, but they lacked the necessary support and funding from higher-level Catholic leadership. Bishop Becker, rightly or wrongly, refused them help when they could not produce the proper paperwork proving their status as official Poor Clare nuns. Abbot Haid refused to receive Abbess Dominick when she traveled to meet with him.[106] Therefore, they were forced to beg for money in ways considered unacceptable, making them even bigger pariahs in the eyes of the Catholic leaders. The women were in an untenable situation partially of their own making, but the school's failure was also the result of many barriers erected by male Catholic leadership.

ABBOT LEO HAID AND THE NEW ABBEY

Abbot Wimmer finalized the elevation of St. Mary Help Priory to an abbey in late 1885. St. Mary Help (later Belmont Abbey), near Charlotte, North Carolina, now presided over the southern missions including Richmond and Savannah. This administrative reorientation had been a year in the making and would impose major changes on Savannah's religious personnel. Father Leo Haid was elected the first abbot of Mary Help, but only after Moosmüller was elected and rejected the appointment, seriously aggravating Wimmer in the process.[107] Moosmüller responded to his election via telegram, "Thanks for the honor; I cannot accept," a few hours after receiving Wimmer's telegram. Wimmer "became very angry" and wrote the second election "took all my thoughts, my fingers, and pen."[108] Wimmer decided to ask for volunteers to transfer their vows to Belmont, and only those volunteers (Melchior Reichert, Willibald Baumgartener, Anastatius William Mayer, Julius Pohl, Felix Hintemeyer, George Lester, Patrick Donlon, and Walter Leahy) were allowed to elect the new abbot. On July 14, 1885, these eight monks elected Leo Haid, and the group left Saint Vincent on July 20.[109] Shortly after the election, Wimmer admitted that Haid was an excellent choice: "A man like P. Leo belongs to this place. He is a good English speaker and scholar. Oswald would not fit so well."[110]

Abbot Haid was much less of a missionary than Wimmer and more interested in a contemplative life.[111] Nevertheless, Haid would carry on the missions Wimmer began. They visited the southern missions, starting with Savannah, to get Haid oriented and familiar with each mission and diocese. Not all of the administrative tasks were worked out in these few days. There remained problems with staffing. Abbot Haid did not have enough priests to cover the geographic span of Savannah, Isle of Hope, and Skidaway Island, and Haid was grateful for Wimmer's aid and personnel: "I am glad you take such an interest in Savannah. I know nothing of affairs there & leave all to your goodness & wisdom."[112] Over the next few years, Haid took an increasing role in managing the Savannah missions, as Father Moosmüller did not transfer his vows to the new abbey but remained with Saint Vincent.

Moosmüller continued to preside at Sacred Heart but asked Wimmer for a transfer for several reasons, primarily his health. Malaria was taking its toll after many years. He was sick for much of June 1885 and traveled to Richmond to recover with Reichert's assurances that he would cover Sacred Heart services. When Moosmüller got word that Reichert did not personally preach, but sent secular priests, Moosmüller hastened back sooner than he wanted. There were also administrative reasons to leave. Moosmüller chose to remain with Saint Vincent, rather than transferring his vows to the new abbey, and he wished to be transferred somewhere under Saint Vincent's purview. Further, Moosmüller requested an Irish priest to replace him, because that was Sacred Heart Church's majority ethnicity.[113]

As requested, Father Creagh arrived in late August 1885 to take charge of Sacred Heart Church and the small, white parochial school. He had offered as early as

April 1884 to help Moosmüller in Savannah.[114] Father Cyprian Moncton Creagh was chosen partially because he was a native of Ballyduff, Ireland, in the diocese of Kerry, and this area of Savannah was increasingly white, and particularly Irish American. Father Creagh was a postulant and novice from 1861 to 1865 with the Congregation of the Holy Redeemer. He immigrated to the United States in 1871 with the intention of joining Franciscan brothers in Brooklyn; however, family obligations and other jobs (including bookkeeping) took him to New York City and Charleston. He was about to return to Ireland to help his brother with his business when he discovered the Benedictines' work in North Carolina. He became "almost certain that this is the goal which I have been seeking." So he applied to Herman Wolf and headed to St. Mary Help, taking simple vows September 8, 1879, and professing solemn vows on September 8, 1882, at the age of forty-seven.[115]

The Sisters of Mercy ran Sacred Heart's larger African American school, which was "in good order."[116] The church was fully outfitted for mass, and the finances were in good standing, enough so the parish priest could help the Skidaway mission.[117] The Skidaway mission remained messy in all aspects including finances and scholarly discipline. Moosmüller again offered his services to set Skidaway straight once Father Creagh was settled. He felt Skidaway could be successful with "the application of certain ways & means—not in the far future—but right now."[118] Without naming names, Moosmüller and others "acquainted with the affairs of Skidaway, consider as absolutely necessary . . . the *change of one or two persons* (*not* pecuniary assistance)."[119] Once these particular personnel changes happened, Moosmüller, Wimmer's "most prominent troubleshooter," would step in as he had so many times before in his career.[120]

A month later, Moosmüller was still adrift. Father Creagh was ready to take the reins at Sacred Heart, leaving Moosmüller without much to do. However, Father Creagh did not remain in Savannah long. He was not very healthy and in August 1886 was sent to Dade City, Florida. Wimmer continued to restrain Moosmüller in his zeal to "fix" the Skidaway mission, because it belonged to the new abbey, and Reichert had transferred his vows to this abbey. Moosmüller reluctantly wrote to Wimmer that Reichert was "getting along well enough, it *will be better to leave things there as they are*."[121] Moosmüller again requested a transfer because he felt "only in the way here."[122] A week later, Moosmüller tried one last time, without much hope, suggesting Reichert go to North Carolina and a priest from St. Mary Help Abbey be sent to Skidaway. Moosmüller could orient the new priest, right the ship, and then be sent on a new assignment.[123] Thus continued the struggle for control of the larger Savannah-area mission. Moosmüller understandably had proprietary feelings for the Savannah-area churches and priory, as he had quite literally helped build them from the ground up. Yet he did not have authority to administer them as he saw fit after they were transferred to St. Mary Help, despite the fact that many of Wimmer's staff remained in place.

Father Moosmüller was popular in Savannah but continued to clash with Reichert, even reporting to Abbot Haid in the summer of 1886 that Reichert was drinking too heavily. Reichert was recalled to Mary Help, where it was discovered he was suffering from exhaustion, not overindulgence in alcohol.[124] While visiting Mary Help, Reichert was "well pleased and happy. He has not touched anything since [arriving]."[125] Haid wanted to reassign Reichert either for a year or permanently, but it was not possible. Reichert was needed on Skidaway. A month later, Father George Lester was sent to live with Reichert during the week and help in Savannah on Sundays. "I'm glad the affair with F. Oswald is settled," wrote Haid.[126] Unfortunately, the affair was not settled. The next summer, Moosmüller again accused Reichert of excessive drinking, and Reichert was ordered to return to Mary Help Abbey, where he lived "more like a saint than a bad man as he was described."[127]

Haid traveled to Savannah for a conference with Bishop Becker in which he presented the following proposal: Haid would assign one priest to each location (Sacred Heart, Skidaway, and the proposed new St. Benedict's). The three priests would live together in Savannah, with the Skidaway priest commuting each Sunday and a few weekdays. The aim was to "not expose anyone to the dangers of living alone; at the same time they can encourage and help each other."[128] Haid requested that Wimmer finally reassign Moosmüller. Haid had enough of Moosmüller's meddling and recognized his work would always be hampered unless Moosmüller was removed. "I appreciate his labors—at least his good intentions—but that is no reason why we should bear the burden."[129] This solution allowed the Belmont monks to live peacefully in community. It was also the end of Moosmüller's time in Savannah.

In late July 1887, Haid instituted the new living arrangement plan with Bishop Becker's blessing. Brother Matthias, the new cook who arrived at the beginning of the year, would remain on Skidaway with Father George Lester. Abbot Haid also hired an African American man previously employed by the Poor Clares, who had all left the island, "deserted by the Abbess."[130] Father Reichert would oversee the new St. Benedict's, which had not even broken ground yet.[131] In August 1887, Moosmüller left for a brief stint in Alabama, where Andrew Hintenach was superior. In February 1888, Hintenach was elected Saint Vincent Archabbot to replace Archabbot Wimmer, who died on December 8, 1887. Hintenach brought Father Moosmüller with him to Saint Vincent to serve as prior.[132]

BAPTISMS AND CONVERSION

The Benedictines had two goals for the mission. First, and most important, was convincing African Americans to convert, and second was educating African American children. Wimmer makes this clear from the very beginning: "In Savannah, P. Oswald has undertaken the establishment of an institution for the conversion of negros. He had many difficulties to overcome, because the negros on the island, where he planned to erect this institution, were mostly bigoted, ignorant Methodist and Baptist. . . . I take great pleasure in this institution for the negros. It is, of course, now only a small building, but with God's blessing will accomplish much good [sic]."[133] It can be hard for twenty-first-century people to reconcile the monks' beliefs that they were doing important work "helping" African Americans on Skidaway while simultaneously ignoring the actual words and wishes of those who did not wish to convert. Despite this contradiction, the priests did baptize islanders.

Catholic baptisms were recorded on Skidaway Island as early as 1883.[134] In April 1885, Wimmer estimated the island had 50 families, "yet some thirty are already converts and their children go to our school."[135] A subsequent letter clarifies that 30 families rather than 30 people had converted. While visiting Skidaway early the next year, Wimmer saw "114 catholic baptisms entered in the official book."[136] This is a considerable number, even as tracking accurate population counts is very difficult. Skidaway Island population estimates range from the probably exaggerated 1873 newspaper account of "nearly 1000 persons" to Moosmüller's report of 500 in 1866 and his possible undercount of 200 people in 1878.[137] In 1900, the federal census lists 217 people on the island. The population did fall considerably after the postwar surge from Sherman's Special Field Order No. 15. Even a conservative judgment puts the 1880s population at several hundred, and 114 baptisms is a considerable percentage of 200, 300, or even 400 people since the mission was less than ten years old.

Considering the strong resistance the fathers initially faced, why were islanders willing to convert? Were they really converting or just appeasing the priests? Researchers at the San Gabriel mission in Southern California have identified many different Indigenous strategies to navigate missionization: "accommodation, apparent conversion, persistence, passive resistance, withdrawal from the mission, and even active resistance through violent rebellion," all while creating and reinforcing new communities within the mission using their traditional culture.[138] There are significant differences between the earlier Spanish missionaries and the Benedictines. The Skidaway monks had much less overt power than Spanish colonial monks, who were backed by the Spanish military and government. The

Saint Vincent monks were not interested in compelling the local adults to work at the mission, nor did they need Indigenous labor to support an increasing colonial population. The Benedictines used the carrot of education rather than a stick, but they were still very much a colonizing force. African Americans living on Skidaway did not need Catholicism, as the protestant churches were deeply ingrained in the African American culture and were woven into the religious, economic, social, and educational fabric of African American society. Most protestant churches had mutual benevolent associations, military companies, brass bands, congregational singing, and associated schools.[139] Skidaway Islanders did not need a free private school either, as there was a public county school, lacking as it was.

So why agree to baptisms and convert at all? Was it true conversion? In the case of one family, we see several strategies for navigating missionization including sincere conversion, apparent conversion, and persistence. By 1887, there were twelve families living as tenants on the Benedictines' plantation. Most built their own houses. Some had come at the invitation of Dr. Dupon acting on behalf of Bishop Gross, others through Father Moosmüller's and Father Reichert's encouragement.[140] Likely these families had a closer relationship with the Benedictines and were more likely converted. Sister Mary Anthony Rosa Lucas, who eventually became a Third Order Franciscan nun, belonged to one of these African American families. She lived on Skidaway Island as a very young child, and her brothers attended the Benedictines' school. Sister Rose's family were tenant farmers on the Benedictine plantation but seemed to work collaboratively with the Benedictines and were better off financially because of the connection. Either Sister Rose's family members were exceptions to the general resentment toward the mission, or they chose accommodation and persistence in order to work the system better, because when Sister Rose's family left Skidaway for Midway, Georgia, they were able to buy property with a four-room house and keep livestock including several cows, horses, mules, pigs, and chickens. Although the Benedictine fathers baptized her whole family, not all the family remained Catholic after leaving the island.

There was no Catholic religious instruction in Midway, so her mother sent Rose and her sisters to Mother Beasley's St. Francis Home on East Broad Street. The girls were not orphans; they were sent to the school for religious and secular instruction, living there for several years. Sister Rose moved to New York City for work and joined the Third Order while in New York, later returning to Savannah to care for her mother. When her mother died, Rose remained in Savannah with the Franciscan sisters.[141] While Rose and her mother remained lifelong members of the Catholic Church, the rest of the family did not, which saddened her, but this shows that not all conversions were sincere.

ST. BENEDICT'S CHURCH: TAKE TWO

As early as the summer of 1886, Moosmüller asked permission to revive Bergier and Wissel's St. Benedict's Church on Savannah's east side as part of these continuing efforts to convert African Americans.[142] Unlike Sacred Heart, the new parish was situated in an African American community, or as Moosmüller wrote, "This new church is to be a mission in partibus infidelium, right in the midst of protestant infidel negroes, out of them the new congregation is to be recruited."[143] By Christmas, the bishop was interested in creating an African American parish, with his office supplying much of the funding, and the Benedictines providing the priest.[144]

In 1888, Reichert moved to Savannah to lead this new church, and Rev. George Lester took over as the priest at Skidaway. Father Lester was born John Densea Lester to Andrew and Elizabeth Lester in Mobile, Alabama, and was baptized at Saint Vincent Church on March 24, 1861. Father Lester took his simple vows in July 1881 and his solemn vows on July 16, 1884.[145]

Reichert held mass at the Sacred Heart school chapel until the new St. Benedict's Church was completed.[146] In July 1888, Bishop Becker had occasion to preach to the congregation. While apparently attempting to instill morals, Becker declared that "mulattos," being biracial, were not worthy of regard, and he only had respect for Black men. As the congregation's majority identified as mulatto, Becker's sermon insulted the parishioners who "have been very irate over the matter ever since." When the congregation members were asked if they would consider that his intent was to impress upon them the importance of morality and being good representatives of their race, members responded that this interpretation was "a severe strain on the charitable side of their nature to do so."[147]

Despite Bishop Becker's bizarrely specific racism, the church and school, which cost $10,655, was a substantial investment in the African American community. Funding for the construction was gathered in many different ways. Captain Henry Blun donated the property, which was empty except for a vacant old building. In January 1888, Father J. H. McNally, who was stationed in Augusta, Georgia, but who had previously served in Savannah, donated a diamond ring to the building fund. The ring was an "old style setting with a cluster of twenty-four diamonds." The church raffled off five hundred chances to win at 25 cents a chance, potentially netting $125. At this point, their fund was at $3,000 of their $10,000 goal.[148] Quite a few fundraising fairs and concerts were hosted to raise money, plus Bishop Becker and Abbot Haid contributed funds.[149]

The second St. Benedict's Church was built at East Broad and Gordon Streets, only blocks from the first (see map 6). The cornerstone for this gothic-style church was laid July 14, 1889, and the structure was complete days before its dedication

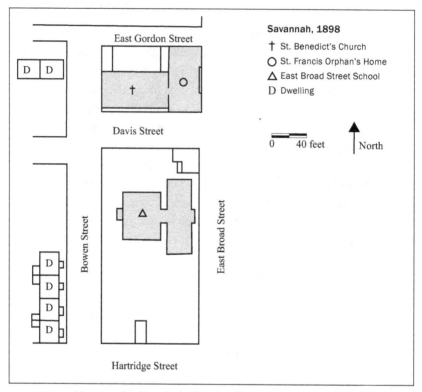

MAP 6. Map of the second St. Benedict's Church in Savannah, Georgia, only blocks from the original on the city's east side. This map is based on the 1898 Sanborn Fire Insurance Map.

on December 8, which is the Feast of the Immaculate Conception. Although the church was originally dedicated to St. Benedict, founder of the Benedictine order, Bishop Keiley later changed the name to St. Benedict the Moor at the request of the pastor and congregation.[150] The dedication was a great event with standing room only despite the church's four-hundred-seat capacity. All of the local clergy attended. Abbot Haid was expected but had to telegraph his regrets when he missed a train. The church was elegantly decorated with evergreens and flowers, and music was prominently featured.[151] The gothic church with its exterior of stuccoed brick was described as "one of the tastiest in the city." The main entrance originally faced East Broad Street, but when the building was altered and expanded to accommodate St. Francis Home, the orphanage took the portion of the lot along East Broad Street. A later priest thought this quite ruined the aesthetics: "St. Benedict was in the beginning quite a handsome building, having two pretty towers facing East Broad street. The improvements made later on for the purpose of having an Orphan Home for colored girls, spoiled the whole architectural beauty of the church."[152]

The interior had archways of "highly polished yellow pine" and stained glass windows.[153] In addition to the nave, the building had a reception room with an adjacent pastor's room and five schoolrooms in the basement. The Sacred Heart parish school for African American children, with its enrollment of approximately 150 students, was transferred here. The church and school were located across Gaston Street from the public East Broad Street School. The Sisters of St. Francis operated the renamed St. Benedict parish school, teaching up to 175 students.[154]

Reichert stayed only until 1891, when he moved permanently to Mary Help Abbey. At this time, St. Benedict's had 350 members.[155] Reichert remained in North Carolina except for a few temporary assignments in Richmond and Savannah in 1916 and 1917. Father Lester, who had served as the Skidaway school's director since 1887, became St. Benedict's parish priest and ministered to both congregations until 1895. Lester was a Mobile, Alabama, native and taught at Saint Mary's College in Belmont, North Carolina, for two years prior to his initial Skidaway assignment. Between 1888 and 1890, Lester also took temporary assignments in Richmond and San Antonio, Florida, because of overly dramatic staffing issues. Rev. Gregory Windschiegel was stationed at St. Benedict's next, until he was transferred to Richmond in the summer of 1898. Rev. Andrew Plecher replaced him for two years after which Father Windschiegel returned.[156]

Staff moved fairly frequently between the southern missions because positions needed to be filled and because individuals were unhappy in their positions. Abbot Haid's letters are filled with discussions about personnel problems and transfers. Such staff problems led Haid to write, "I find it easier to labor & fast & preach in the wilds of N.C. [North Carolina] than to govern *Monks*."[157] Compounding Haid's problems was racism among the white monks. In 1889, Haid accepted an African American "cook-candidate," but he knew that the candidate "will not be rec'd by the Chapter as the feeling among southerners is very strong against 'social' equality." Haid did not see a way to "swim against the storm."[158] While no one today would describe Leo Haid as anti-racist, he was a Pennsylvania native born to German immigrants and had more northern, patronizing, structural racist attitudes rather than individual racist beliefs. He wrote: "In the South, priests and people think all work done for these poor people *is thrown* away. Even our Brothers . . . have no use for negroes."[159] Even after delivering this criticism, Haid hesitated to hire local African Americans, writing he would feel "safer" if he had German Catholic lay brothers, ones who do not like beer and are "quiet and *not growlers*," to work the kitchen and stables.[160]

MOTHER MATHILDA BEASLEY

St. Benedict's most famous resident is Mother Mathilda Beasley, who was born enslaved in New Orleans on November 14, 1832. Mathilda Taylor Beasley's early life is mostly unknown. Her mother Caroline was a Creole of color and was owned by James C. Taylor, whose last name Mathilda used until her marriage. Her father was Indigenous, French, or possibly both. She was baptized into the Catholic faith at five months old. She arrived in Savannah sometime in the 1850s, an educated, free person of color, who was skilled as a seamstress. She taught a clandestine school in her home prior to the Civil War and likely met her future husband, Abraham Beasley, while working in his Johnson Square restaurant. Newspaper advertisements for the restaurant bearing her name, rather than his, appeared as early as September 1863. Later advertisements from 1866 listed Taylor and Beasley, with her name in greater prominence. He was listed as the "Superintendent."[161] She was clearly an integral part of the business and its public face. The advertisements used language that is forthright, gracious, and not at all reticent, describing the restaurant as "one of the best in the city."[162] Taylor and Beasley were married February 9, 1869. Abraham Beasley was a relatively wealthy man, owning several businesses besides the restaurant, including a grocery store and a saloon. Prior to the Civil War, he even sold enslaved people. He owned extensive land in Savannah, Isle of Hope, and Skidaway Island. Upon his death in 1877, his funeral was held at St. Joseph's Church, and he was buried in the Catholic Cemetery on Wheaton Street. He left his estate to Mathilda.[163]

After her husband's passing, Mathilda began to divest herself of her husband's property and money, making donations to the Catholic Church. She gave some land to Savannah churches, including the lot containing Abraham Beasley's house, and she donated $350 toward the construction of Sacred Heart Church.[164] At some point, she decided to devote herself to the church. Several researchers have noted the correlation between the presence of Poor Clares at Sacred Heart Church and Mathilda's going to a Poor Clare Convent in York, England, for her novitiate from at least May through July 1885. No evidence has been found of her official admittance to a religious order or a record of her vows. Although Mathilda was on Skidaway Island at some point, it is unclear exactly when and for how long, but it was likely later than 1885, so she probably encountered the Poor Clares first at Sacred Heart.[165]

Mother Mathilda Beasley founded her St. Francis orphanage in 1887. Moosmüller recalled it was March or April 1887 when they received the first African American girls.[166] The orphanage, which was first known as the Saint Francis Industrial and Boarding School for Girls, was initially located on the Sacred Heart campus, at the southwest corner of St. James Street (today's 31st Street) and Price Street.[167] The orphanage was housed within the schoolhouse.[168] Beasley's obituary writer speculated, "She, remembering a kindness that had been done her when an orphan child by some negroes, resolved to follow the commands of her Master and gave her entire property to the poor stipulating only that an orphan home for negro children be established."[169] No explicit evidence has been found that Mother Beasley was an orphan or that this was her motivation in founding an orphanage, but several historians have suspected this account is true.

As the Sacred Heart priest, Moosmüller was involved in the orphanage's organization and management. At the outset, he attempted to organize an Orphan Society "of white gentlemen with the Bishop at the head," which would raise money and provide oversight as well as unnecessary control. Once the Orphan Society was formed, it would provide a monthly stipend for each child. Until then, Moosmüller proposed enlarging the garden so the girls could grow their own vegetables and buying a knitting machine for them to make items for sale. He finished the schoolhouse attic to house up to twenty girls there. The girls would, of course, attend the Sacred Heart school. Boys he would send to Skidaway. Moosmüller insisted the orphans be "legally bound over" to the orphan society until they were eighteen years of age.[170] The girls' orphanage sounded both very Dickensian and very much like Skidaway. With the new St. Francis Home established and St. Mary's orphanage for white girls located across St. Paul Street in its own dedicated building with a detached kitchen, Father Moosmüller was "pleased to learn that we find a chance of snatching poor children out of the hands of the evil spirits," and by evil spirits, he meant Protestants, or at least the Protestant faith.[171]

In March 1889, Mother Beasley wrote that they enjoyed "a very great degree [of] support."[172] She had received a $500 check from Miss Elizabeth Drexel and $2,500 over two years from a special church collection for "the Indians and Negroes."[173] By October 1889, Mother Beasley had also established a Black Franciscan nun community, Sisters of the Third Order of St. Francis, which had five nuns in the later 1890s. These women managed the orphanage with Mother Beasley as superior. The orphanage was never large, serving about nineteen or twenty girls in the late 1890s and early 1900s. These numbers are modest when compared with the white St. Mary's Home for Female Orphans that had sixty girls at the same time.[174]

Despite their initial success, the St. Francis Home for Colored Female Orphans, as it was known starting in 1892, and Mother Beasley's religious community had many challenges. Financially, the institution frequently struggled, despite Mother Beasley's previous generous donations to the Catholic Church. She also had difficulty recruiting novices. Bishop Becker asked Katharine Drexel, found-ress of the Sisters of the Blessed Sacrament (SBS) to incorporate Mother Beasley's Order into the SBS. Mother Beasley and a companion traveled to St. Elizabeth's, the Philadelphia home of the Sisters of the Blessed Sacrament, in 1893 to "plead their case directly."[175] Her mission was both spiritual and economic, and the sis-ters initially developed a plan to bring Savannah nuns to St. Elizabeth's for further training and novitiate. The idea was never launched, however, because of racism within the St. Elizabeth's community. According to SBS annals, "It was felt that social prejudice would make it impossible to get recruits among white people; for whilst many would be perfectly willing to work for both races, and to give them-selves unstintingly, yet on the other hand owing to that strong domination of the so-called inferiority complex, they would be unwilling to live in the close contact engendered by community life."[176] The sisters formally voted against admittance of African American or Indigenous American candidates, further justifying their decision that two Black and Catholic convent communities already existed where novitiates could train.[177] Mother Beasley did, however, form a lasting relationship with the Sisters of the Blessed Sacrament founder, Mother Katharine Drexel, who supported the St. Francis Home financially (including a $4,000 donation in 1895) and advised Mother Beasley through their correspondence.[178]

Shortly after this trip, Mother Beasley asked Cardinal Gibbons in Baltimore for help as well; specifically, she needed more staff and wanted nuns. She and the nuns worked to support themselves, but once the school opened, they could not teach and work, hence the need for more staff.[179] She also wrote to Rev. J. R. Slattery at St. Joseph's Seminary in Baltimore requesting more religious staff. A handwritten note at the top of her letter ("tell her I'll do what I can for her") seems to instruct an assistant to respond positively to Mother Beasley's request.[180] Neither these re-quests nor her own recruitment efforts led to more than a few candidates, however.

The Josephites, who specialized in missionary work among Indigenous Ameri-cans and African Americans, sent checks over the years, sometimes in amounts as small as $25 in 1897 to as large as $500 in 1910.[181] Dr. James Read and Savannah's bishop were the orphanage's primary supporters.[182] Although Dr. Read and his wife ("Mrs. Dr. Read") continued to support the orphanage, they were not extremely wealthy, and multiple benefactors were needed. Mother Beasley was further ham-pered by the simple fact that she was a Black woman and therefore had limited rights. For example, she did not sign her own contracts, as she wrote to Mother Drexel, "any agreement that you want signed please send it to us and we will have it signed by good, honest, and responsible men."[183] Apparently, this was something else Dr. Read and the bishop were good for.

Other problems were internal to the orphanage. In mid-February 1895, two fourteen-year-old girls attempted to burn down the orphanage several times. Fortunately, no one was hurt. The *Savannah Morning News* detailed the girls' attempt. They "put a fire coal in a stocking and threw it under the floor and then thrust a lighted splinter into a [school]book cabinet. The other threw a hot iron into a pile of clothes."[184] This was the girls' fourth attempt at arson, and the police, who had been first notified a few days prior, were again called. Both girls, Georgiana Frizzle and Meta Douglass, confessed immediately, explaining they just wanted to leave. Frizzle was still at the orphanage where she had lived for over a year, but Douglass had run away to her mother's house at 105 Jones Street. When questioned, Douglass said she did not get enough to eat while living at the orphanage and wanted to care for her ailing mother. "Neither seemed to have the least comprehension of the enormity of the crime attempted."[185] The charges were reduced from arson, which was punishable by death or life imprisonment, to malicious mischief, a misdemeanor. The girls were sentenced to six months in prison.[186]

A few weeks later, three more girls attempted to set fire to the orphanage. One morning Mother Beasley found the ironing room on fire, where some girls had been working. She and several girls put out the fire themselves. Much clothing was destroyed, but the building and its inhabitants were largely unharmed. The police were notified, and the chief and two detectives arrived. Carrie Wilkerson, Susanne Sturtevant, and Anna Briner were arrested and taken to the police barracks.[187]

Orphanages were part of the nineteenth-century reform movements. Reformers generally focused on education, citizenship training, and laws against child labor. Orphanages were one tool to achieve reformers' goals; they acted as surrogate families to teach white, Protestant Christian values, basic education, and the "values" of capitalism—"industry, competition, and the sanctity of property."[188] The idea of "orphan" can be misleading. As Jane Eva Baxter indicates, "The majority of children in nineteenth century orphanages had at least one living parent or extended family member, but orphanages tried to estrange children from these family members."[189] Some orphanages restricted or stopped family visits and censored mail. The idea behind this was to reeducate and resettle children in a new environment to break the cycle of poverty. Typically, orphanages took young, white, urban children who lived in the orphanage until eighteen to twenty-one years of age. The institutions were usually single sex or heavily segregated and were women-operated because women were perceived as better caregivers.[190]

So although orphans were not necessarily lacking parents, social reformers had deemed they lacked a "proper" home or adequate support network. The orphanage removed the child from the supposedly inappropriate situation and molded the child into an idealized middle-class citizen "who embodied traditional American values of hard work, industry, and discipline."[191] Mother Beasley's orphanage had some of these characteristics, including taking children who still had living parents, but most orphanages were for European immigrants or first-generation immigrants and working-class white Americans. African Americans were not allowed in most orphanages.[192]

Especially if her own childhood experiences led to her creating the St. Francis Home, Mother Beasley should have been more sensitive to the needs and desires of her "inmates," as Frizzle and Douglass were described, but the girls' behavior and statements about not getting enough food are disturbing. Mother Beasley's constant struggle to get enough resources for the orphanage despite her generous donations to the church reveals the deep racism and priorities of the Savannah Diocese. The only known documentation of Mother Beasley's financial transactions with the church is an 1891 letter from Moosmüller detailing donations toward Sacred Heart's construction, including Beasley's $350 given in two installments. Moosmüller helped her administer her bank accounts especially during her absences from Savannah, sending her $50 money orders during her novitiate in England. Mother Beasley received a $20 monthly allowance from her accounts that carried her through the end of 1889.[193] How she disposed of multiple properties in Savannah plus those on Isle of Hope and Skidaway Island remains a mystery. As she took religious vows in some form, it can be safely assumed the Catholic Church financially benefited from her wealth. Her obituaries suggest as much, simplifying the situation into a property donation for an orphanage exchange.[194] The reality was likely much slower and less overtly transactional. Without knowing exactly what happened to her wealth, it is hard to accuse the Savannah diocese of taking her money, then leaving her and the orphans destitute. Between her husband's 1877 death and the orphanage's 1887 founding, Beasley had ten years to evolve and develop her plans. She may have donated her money without stipulations, then decided to build the orphanage, leaving her without control over funding.

As early as 1894, Mother Beasley began planning for a new building to house the orphanage. For reasons that she does not detail in her letters, she was desperate for a new place, writing to Mother Katharine Drexel: "The Present and Future success of our Mission depends entirely on you. . . . So dear kind Mother for the love of God and for the souls of these poor little ones who daily raise hands [and] voices to Him in heaven for a home. Good Mother we are all homeless. Our hopes are cast on your noble generous charity."[195] Over the next several months, her letters become increasingly desperate, graciously beseeching, and bordering on obsequious. In mid-March 1895, Beasley received word from Mother Drexel

that she would help fund a new orphanage. Bishop Becker, who had also promised a contribution, was out of the country until the summer, so it was not until
November 1895 that an agreement was drafted and signed. Mother Drexel's Sisters
of the Blessed Sacrament for Indian and Colored People donated $4,000 "to be
used by Mother M: Matilda [*sic*] Beasley and her successors, for the benefit of the
Colored People of the Diocese of Savannah," although the title was vested with
the diocese, not the Sisters of the Third Order of St. Francis.[196] Between then and
1898, the orphanage transferred from its original location to St. Benedict's. The
new, two-story building fronted East Broad Street and shared its western wall
with St. Benedict's Church.[197]

Although the building was constructed according to the original contract,
the Sisters of Blessed Sacrament felt the need to amend their agreement in 1904
shortly after Mother Beasley's death. "It has recently been brought to our attention that this agreement should have been more specific in defining the objects to
which the fund should be applied on the contingency of Mother Beasley's school
being discontinued, and we have, therefore, to ask if it meets with your approval, as
we trust it will, that the enclosed supplementary agreement sent to you in duplicate
be executed and returned to us." While the original agreement carried stipulations
about how the money was spent and what should happen if the building's function
should change over time, this agreement sharpened up the stipulations, insisting
that the buildings "shall at all times be used for the education of colored people in
the diocese of Savannah." If not, the diocese must spend $4,000 elsewhere on Af-
rican American education or return the full amount to the donor.[198] This amended
agreement hints, not at outright fraud or theft, but at a fear of reappropriating
funds away from African American students and parishioners. Mother Beasley
held a certain amount of social capital; although this was much less power than
that held by white priests such as Moosmüller, her influence somewhat protected
the St. Francis Home while she was alive. After her death, the home was vulnerable, so the Sisters of Blessed Sacrament acted to protect their investment and the
people dependent on the orphanage.

Mother Beasley also turned for help to the white Missionary Franciscans of
Immaculate Conception, who had established an African American school in
Augusta, Georgia, the same year the Skidaway Island mission opened. In October
1897, three white Franciscan nuns arrived from their Motherhouse in Rome to take
over administration of the St. Francis Home. Mother Beasley was not well, and
she was making provisions for her succession. She admitted in May 1898 that her
"health has failed," and she was no longer able to carry out her duties.[199] She regretted not being able to build a local religious community to continue her work and,

therefore, needed to invite other Franciscans to carry on her work. With Bishop
Becker's blessing, the nuns began to manage the new location on East Broad Street.
At this point, most of Mother Beasley's order "had dispersed." One nun died, and
another joined an African American convent up north. The third took the habit
of an auxiliary sister, remaining at the St. Francis Home.[200] The sisters were able to
care for about twenty girls, all living together until they built a convent across Gordon Street in 1909.[201] Mother Mathilda lived and worked with this new group of
Franciscans briefly but was not impressed with the first few nuns. "I am going out
in the cold world to be alone until I pass for I see plane [*sic*] that I can't stay with
them . . . it is sad to give up the mission, but better give up then let them make me
do it as I see they will."[202] In 1901, she moved into a cottage at 1511 Price Street. The
house, which was on the same block as Sacred Heart, may have been part of her
husband's estate. From here, she continued to support the orphanage and took in
sewing projects, giving away her earnings to those in need. Congregation members
in the diocese helped care for her in her last years.[203]

On December 20, 1903, Mother Beasley was found dead in the private chapel of
her home. She had been kneeling at prayer when she died, and her burial clothes,
instructions, and will were neatly placed nearby. Mother Beasley was well loved
and admired for her life's work. A newspaper obituary stated, "Her extreme height
and her commanding figure marked her among those with whom she labored."[204]
Her orphanage operated until the late 1930s or early 1940s when the last few orphans were transferred to Augusta, Georgia.[205]

THE MIRAULT FAMILY

While Mother Beasley shepherded her orphanage, the Catholic leadership was
debating whether the Skidaway Island mission should continue and in what capacity. Despite the success with baptisms, rumors persisted over closing the Skidaway
mission. In early 1886, Rev. Cafferty, a diocesan priest, addressed such rumors after hearing that Abbot Haid told Father Reichert he might give up or move the
Skidaway "Industrial School for Colored boys."[206] Cafferty cited the 1880 Federal
Census, which counted 725,000 African Americans in Georgia, as the reason
that "the institution on the Island must be regarded as of greater importance than
your parish in this City," although he noted both institutions were important and
should support each other.[207] At the very least, Cafferty requested six months' no-
tice before the school was closed, as required by the Second Plenary Council of
Baltimore's decree 407, which he quoted in Latin.[208]

Ultimately, Haid chose a middle road. In February 1889, he declared, "In Savah all are well and everything looks promising. I settled the Sidaway difficulty to the satisfaction of parties concerned [sic]."[209] He neither closed the school entirely in 1889, nor did the Benedictines continue the day-to-day operations on Skidaway Island. His compromise was to hire an African American Catholic school teacher and property manager. In October 1890, the Benedictines entered into a formal contract with a caretaker for the Skidaway Island facility. Josephine Mirault was to live in the monastery and teach at the school. Mrs. Mirault (and possibly her husband Simon along with their children) would live rent free in exchange for maintaining the property and protecting it from vandalism. Mrs. Mirault would teach the school and clean the church rooms and library for the priests' continued, occasional use. Additionally, Mirault and a subagent, Sam "Proy," were authorized to rent the Poor Clare houses and "the building known as College" and would collect rent as well as evict any tenants who were not properly maintaining the properties. Stephen Dupon, once again, acted as an agent for the priests in establishing this agreement.[210] The Skidaway property was income generating, so having a manager made financial sense, but it was not critical to the financial health of the parish or the Benedictine Order in Georgia. In the first half of 1894, $57 was collected. This was a small percent of the parish income ($973.05), but considering the $858.63 in expenses, the fathers needed every dollar. Between January and October of 1895, $75 was collected. Sacred Heart Parish's income was higher that year at $2,619.38.[211]

"Sub agent Sam Proy" was actually Samuel Pray, the sixty-year-old African American patriarch of the Pray family who farmed near the monastery. Sam's wife Hagar gave birth to fourteen children, eight of whom were still alive in 1900. Sam and Hagar, born well before the Civil War, were illiterate farmers who ensured their children got at least a basic education. The Pray family can illustrate some of the larger social and economic changes on the island. In the roughly twenty years that the mission school operated, the economy shifted from farming to fishing and oystering. In 1880, farmers and farmhands greatly outnumbered the fishermen on Skidaway and the surrounding islands. In 1900, as the mission closed, fishermen and oystermen outnumbered farmers on Skidaway almost six to one.[212] For example, Emanuel Pray (Sam and Hagar's son) had attended school, but as a fifteen-year-old in 1880, he was living with his parents and working on their farm. Emanuel married Sarah Jane Bacon in 1889. By 1900, the couple, both literate, were living with their two young children on the island. Though they rented their house, Emanuel was no longer farming, but working as a fisherman. Sarah Jane's relatives also lived on Skidaway. Three generations of the Bacon family lived and farmed near the monastery in the 1880s, but most had left Skidaway by 1900.[213] Much like the Pray family, the oldest generation, Joseph and Maria Bacon, each born around 1830, were illiterate farmers, working cooperatively with their older children. Younger members of the Bacon family received an education, either at the island's county school or the mission school.

Formal education and these shifts in occupations were moves toward more self-determination and away from tenant farming and sharecropping with their dependence on white landlords. Fishermen and oystermen, unlike farmers, do not need to rent large areas of land, so islanders could more easily disentangle themselves from white landowners while still maintaining a homeplace and roots in their cultural landscape. During the plantation era, fishermen were almost exclusively African Americans. These small-scale fishing and oystering practices continued largely unchanged until the late nineteenth century and were among the very few options for independent means open to African Americans post-emancipation. As Savannah held the predominant seafood market on the Georgia coast, selling the catch was reasonably easy. Starting in the 1890s with the expansion of oyster canneries, African Americans would eventually become marginalized within the industry as white-owned capital was used to expand and commercialize the industry.[214] However, while the Skidaway mission was active, fishing and oystering remained a way to maintain an independent occupation.

Even Mrs. Mirault's employment represents a move toward Black empowerment, as Black teachers were more effective than white teachers in African American schools.[215] Mrs. Mirault was a compromise; Skidaway residents would finally get rid of the white Catholics and gain an African American teacher, albeit a Catholic one. The Miraults were both born into free Black families who had the means to educate their children, and the extended Mirault family owned property for generations. Miraults, including Peter Michael Joseph Mirault, who stood as a godfather in a 1798 baptism, are among the first Black Catholics listed in the Cathedral registers.[216] Later, the Miraults embraced the segregated African American Catholic congregations. Simon's father (Simon Sr.) was buried from the original St. Benedict's Church on December 5, 1875, and Simon Jr.'s funeral was at the new St. Benedict's in February 1901.[217]

Josephine married Simon Mirault Jr., a bricklayer by trade, in 1876, and the family lived on Jones Street in Troup Ward through the later 1870s to 1885 or 1886, when they bought a house at Duffy and Price Streets. When she agreed to administer the monastery buildings and teach at the school, Josephine Mirault (née Black) was thirty-eight years old and mother to six children, although she had lost

Simon III to diphtheria in 1881 at only four years old. How she got her education is a mystery, including whether she was formally trained to teach; however, her mother and all of her siblings were literate, which indicates a family commitment to education. Josephine, in turn, was committed to her children's education. Her youngest, William, was six years old when the family moved to Skidaway, and ten years later he remained in school. Although this is unremarkable by today's standards, Savannah did not have a public high school for African Americans until the twentieth century. Private schools such as the Beach Institute were the only option for higher grade levels.[218]

BUTTONS AND BAUBLES

Unlike the early years under Moosmüller, when the monks lacked beer, wine, fresh beef, and "other luxuries of that kind," the artifacts found suggest the Miraults brought some creature comforts and a different standard of living with them. These minor luxuries extended to the Mirault's clothing and style choices, which contrast sharply with the monastery-era clothing artifacts. Three of the five buttons dating to the monastery era are cheap Prosser buttons (including a rare, bizarre "whistle" button with a single hole on the front that splits into two holes at the back).[219] Prosser buttons, called "small chinas" by modern collectors, were named after their inventor, Richard Prosser. Before the Prosser process was patented in 1840, buttons were handmade and expensive. Once the Prosser method pumped out five hundred buttons at once, the price dropped radically, and most everyone could afford these buttons.[220] The small buttons found at the school are likely from students' shirts.[221] In the historic photograph of the school (see figure 3), the boys wore pants (many appearing short and ill-fitting), a shirt, and a jacket, all of which would have had buttons.[222]

The other two monastery-era buttons were sew-throughs (one made of iron and the other shell), which could have been used by either the monks or students. As Brother Tim Brown explains, "The monks' habit consists of a tunic (cassock) which buttons up the front, and a button [was] used to attach the cowl (hood) to another piece called the scapular. I'm not sure if the tunic of the 19th century had buttons on it, but I am sure that a button was used to attach the cowl."[223]

Most of the buttons (fifteen of the twenty-two total) found on site dated to the Miraults' occupation, and these were found exclusively at the church. These fifteen buttons, which were quite diverse in their types, sizes, and material, appear in two distinct soil layers and therefore seem to be the result of two incidents of loss or discard. The later deposit had two Prosser buttons, one shell button, one button with brass and iron, and three iron buttons. The iron and shell materials were rather corroded, making analysis difficult. The second, slightly older deposit had six shell buttons and two brass buttons, all of varying sizes and styles, and all in good condition with the exception of iron backing on the brass buttons.

It is useful to compare the monastery's buttons to the archaeological assemblage from the Third New City Cemetery in the Freedmen's Town neighborhood of Houston, Texas. Although burial clothing was often a person's "best" and might differ slightly from everyday clothing, this site can give some insight into buttons that freedpeople typically wore. African Americans were buried at this cemetery from 1880 to 1904, making this site contemporary with the monastery within a few years. A few observations are pertinent. First, at the cemetery, a little over half of the buttons recovered were Prosser buttons. Prosser buttons are 37 percent of the monastery's entire button assemblage and a mere 13 percent of the 1890s Mirault subassemblage. Metal buttons are 37 percent of both sites' collections. Metal buttons are most frequently advertised for men in mail-order catalogs, a finding supported by the cemetery's assemblage. Metal buttons with two or four holes were commonly used on men's trousers. Where the assemblages really diverge is in shell buttons. Although the cemetery contained only 2 shell buttons out of 306 total buttons found in 97 graves, the monastery had 8 shell buttons that comprised 42 percent of the assemblage, all but one from the 1890s deposits.[224] Before the McKinley tariff in 1890, shell buttons were handmade, imported, and expensive at ten to twenty-five cents per dozen. In 1895, the domestic shell button industry expanded greatly for the first time.[225] The large percentage of shell buttons shows the Miraults' interest in fashion and the ability to purchase these small frills. More expensive clothing items may have been a way to self-represent themselves as middle class and demand respect in a country that was already deep into the Jim Crow era.

These concentrations of buttons may also represent an expression of African American style and ethnicity. Laurie Wilkie has shown that personal adornment artifacts comprise large portions of the African American assemblage at Oakley Plantation, Louisiana, peaking at 27.9 percent in the late nineteenth century. Buttons were the most common personal adornment item. In contrast, only 2.8 percent of the postbellum white planters' assemblage were items of personal adornment. Wilkie sees this as a "direct continuity of African personal aesthetic traditions," although some forms of personal adornment such as body modifications, jewelry, and African hairstyles were suppressed by slave owners who saw these as threatening.[226] Beads and buttons were strung into jewelry or sewed onto clothing as an affordable way to enliven plain clothing.

The Miraults' tablewares and meals were also less ascetic than the monastery's table. The Miraults consumed more bottled beverages and bottled foods such as con-diments and pickles, resulting in almost four times as many bottle glass sherds de-posited during the Miraults' occupation than the monks'. Most ceramic types were found in numbers too small to be statistically conclusive; however, there were some areas of divergence between the monastery and Mirault occupations. The Miraults' table had more white granite ceramics and glass tableware, both important indica-tors of respectability according to the white, middle- and upper-class cult of domes-ticity.[227] Because they were white in color, white granite ceramics symbolized purity and domesticity, while the glassware held nonalcoholic drinks. However, as a Black woman who sometimes worked outside the home, Mrs. Mirault was excluded from the cult of domesticity. Instead as an educator, she may have felt more allied with reform movements.[228] The use of white granite may have been another assertion of middle-class status and a demand for the accompanying respect.

The Miraults had decorative items as well, as shown by three decorative cast iron elements (otherwise unidentified) and sherds of Japanese hard paste porce-lain. These sherds are decorated with the circa 1890s Geisha Girl design, and their size differences indicate two vessels were present. It must be noted that the "Geisha Girl design" is a term used by modern collectors, showing their Western bias to use the term "geisha" for any kimono-swathed Japanese woman. The design typi-cally depicts premodern Japanese scenes, including women in traditional dress. The wares were available in common dining and household forms.[229]

Porcelain has long been a desired, high-status marker in European and North American countries. From the 1600s, the Dutch East India Company made masses of money importing porcelain to the European markets; however, Japanese iso-lation between 1700 and 1850 made their porcelain nearly impossible to obtain. In 1853, American naval commodore Matthew Perry sailed his fleet into Tokyo's harbor with an official letter from the U.S. president to the Japanese emperor and orders to negotiate a trade agreement. An unsettled political situation in Japan, new mass production methods, and the Industrial Revolution feeding Western consumerism meant that starting around 1860 large amounts of porcelain were purchased in American markets.

The Japanese were savvy in taking advantage of the American markets. Jap-anese diplomats sent abroad to get Western educations learned that Americans were immensely interested in consuming new goods, but the middle and lower classes could not afford high-quality, imported porcelain. So mass production for export ramped up, starting with family businesses. This was gendered labor: men mixed clay, women filled larger molds, and children filled smaller molds and com-pleted the decorations.[230] Japanese businessmen used their new understanding of

Western culture to appeal to their Western clientele. The forms and designs catered to Western audiences and their stereotypes of Asia, whereas Japanese wares for Japanese customers were "less flamboyant and deferred to more naturalized forms." The irony has not been lost on the observant—Americans and Europeans looking for authenticity in this Westernized porcelain.[231] World exhibitions and fairs helped turn porcelain and other imported Asian objects into a fad. After World War I, Western tastes shifted from Japan to China, and Japanese porcelain sales declined after 1915.[232]

There were more than 135 Geisha Girl producers and therefore much diversity in the designs, which were mostly executed via stencil method, similar to European transfer print. Colored enamels were also painted over the underlying design, and gilding was done last, because the gold had to be fired at a lower temperature. Early border colors include red, maroon, cobalt blue, pale green, and nile green. More colors were added over the years. Pine green, blue green, and turquoise were added in the late 1910s. Pale cobalt blue was introduced in the late 1920s into the 1930s, and black in the 1940s. Both sherds found at the monastery were stencil designed with red enamel. Few dinner plates were made because knives easily damaged the stencil decoration's raised lines. Small plates for lunch, tea wares, and serving vessels were more common. Jars, small containers, and trays were also produced.[233] Geisha Girl porcelains were distributed in expensive and cheaper shops, sold in sets or individually. They were also given away as promotions. Salt and pepper shakers and mustard jars were common advertising premiums. These items would have the company name, slogan, address, or other promotional information. Montgomery Ward and Company gave away a teacup and saucer for every five pounds of tea purchased. Children's tea sets with store names were also popular.[234]

Geisha Girl wares were part of Victorian (over)consumption. After 1850, white middle-class Americans could afford these "exotic" goods, but whereas customers were attempting to showcase their taste and sophistication, these items were inauthentic and had little to do with the original culture. Influenced by expositions and world fairs, white Americans purchased these items and felt they were knowledgeable, even curious about other cultures, while simultaneously distancing themselves from the actual cultures and colonial violence that made these purchases possible.[235] It was not only white Americans who were attracted to these colorful, textured pieces. Geisha wares have been found on Japanese American, African American, Chinese American, European American, and Mexican American sites in small amounts. In the Chinese community at Sandpoint, Idaho, Japanese ceramics were found in a much greater percentage (15.4 percent) than other Chinese communities in the United States. More commonly, Japanese ceramics are totally absent or are less than 1 percent of Chinese American ceramic assemblages. The archaeologists noted the continuing irony of this Westernized-Asian porcelain. As stated in *The Other Side of Sandpoint*, "Geisha Girl wares thus played into a primarily white Western audience's fantasies about the East, but was marketed to a specific lower class demographic."[236] Like white American collectors, the Chinese immigrants were sending messages with their material consumption, albeit different messages. Researchers concluded that the Chinese immigrants used Geisha wares and other "exotics" as a "marketing ploy by the business' owners to demonstrate their acceptance of Euro-American cultures and gain favor with their Euro-American patrons."[237] Essentially, Chinese immigrants were using this irony as a tool for blending into American culture (at least on the surface) and as an anti-racism tool. By "fitting in," immigrants were more likely to get business and be perceived as more American, while they distanced themselves from racial stereotypes including poverty.[238]

Were the Miraults sending similar messages declaring their social position? Paul Mullins analyzed bric-a-brac and display items found on sites inhabited by people of color. Mullins argues that contrary to contemporary white observers' opinions, people of color were not imitating the more affluent or dominant culture in an attempt to appear more wealthy. Similar to the Chinese Americans in Idaho, African Americans used this ceramic as window dressing. He offers a nuanced exploration of multiple and not mutually exclusive meanings from inspirational affluence to social commentary to a protective veneer of bland middle-class conformity. He states: "There is, indeed, a genuine measure of self-imposed oppression that is reproduced by consumption and its reproduction of wage labor. Yet it might just as well be argued that when consumers transform the meaning of mass-produced goods, they are using those goods as vehicles of social critique as much as self-inflicted oppression."[239] Erika Martin Seibert came to a similar conclusion about the African American Robinson family living in Manassas, Virginia, from 1850 to 1936, when the area became a National Battlefield. Martin Seibert suggested the Geisha Girl porcelain objects found in a trash pit were display items indicating social aspirations that included "rights of citizenship that are associated with social positions in society" as well as negotiating their place in larger American society and within their community.[240]

Both the Robinsons and the Miraults had plenty of older ceramics and bought at least a few of the newest patterns. The Mirault family, as modest property owners and free people of color before the Civil War, were among Savannah's African American elite. They had long navigated the color line successfully, and their material culture on display would have been part of that strategy, whether seeming to conform to middle-class standards or showing their wealth as a means of asserting social power.

THE SKIDAWAY MISSION CLOSES

It is unclear how long the Miraults lived on Skidaway. The family was still living and working on Skidaway Island in February 1894 when both Simon and Josephine witnessed a receipt acknowledging a priest's payment to Emanuel Pray for a house on Skidaway.[241] However, by 1900 when the mission closed, the Miraults were living on Gaston Street in Savannah's Berien Ward with three of their children, Sarah, John, and William N., along with Josephine's mother, Sarah Ann Black. Simon died in 1901, and by 1905, most of the immediate family had moved to New Jersey, including Josephine and three of her sons (William, John, and Matthew), as well as William's wife Susan and their two young children. Josephine continued to live with William's growing family, but her other sons moved out after several years.[242]

The mission and school closed forever at the turn of the century. Catholic directories list the mission for the last time in 1900. The Benedictine Order in Georgia sold the monastery tract in January 1906 to A. G. Guerard Jr. for $2,500. Guerard then sold the property to the Floyd family, who remodeled the seventeen-room monastery as a vacation home.[243] The last African American families probably left the island in the 1930s.[244] In 1941, Union Bag and Paper Company (later Union Camp and today International Paper) bought the property along with most of the island in order to log the trees. At that time, only the wooden monastery was standing, although uncertainly. Union Camp staff dismantled the decrepit building in 1949.[245]

The last known picture of the monastery appeared in a 1945 newspaper article. The picture was a reprint from former mayor Thomas Gamble's collection, so it may have been taken earlier than 1945. The photographer was standing on the opposite side of the building from the 1880s photographer. Most of the ell, including the building's lighter-colored end, is visible on the left, but it is unclear whether the church is still present, as that end of the building is completely lost in the trees and shrubbery, which had grown significantly since the 1880s. Elements are recognizable from the earlier photograph—clapboard siding throughout, window size and placement, the chimney, and the gabled dormer window protruding from the roof.[246] After the property was logged, it was used intermittently as a hunting and fishing retreat and for camping trips into the early 1970s, when Skidaway Island State Park, Skidaway Institute of Oceanography, and the Landings residential

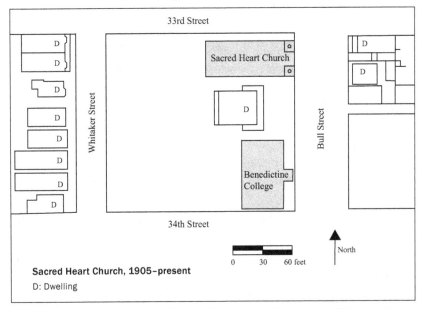

MAP 7. Map of Sacred Heart Church's second (and current) location on Bull Street in Savannah, Georgia. The parsonage is between the church and the former location of Benedictine College, today called Benedictine Military School. This map is based on the 1916 Sanborn Fire Insurance Map.

community were developed.[247] These three institutions remain the major uses of the island today.

EVOLUTION INTO THE TWENTIETH CENTURY

Although the Skidaway mission had closed, the Benedictines' work continued in Savannah. Sacred Heart had become an entirely segregated, white church by the twentieth century. All African American Catholic institutions had been transferred to East Broad Street, including St. Benedict's Church and Parish School as well as the St. Francis Home. In October 1901, the Benedictine Order in Georgia approved the purchase of land along Bull Street between 33rd and 34th Streets for a new Sacred Heart Church. Simultaneously, they mortgaged Sacred Heart's Habersham Street property to fund the purchase.[248] Hyman Witcover, who designed several Savannah landmarks including City Hall and the Bull Street Library, was contracted as the architect for the new Sacred Heart Church (see map 7). In 1905, the new church was dedicated.

Meanwhile, Benedictine College (BC) was started on September 29, 1902, at Sacred Heart's Habersham Street campus, moving to Bull and 34th Streets in 1905, thus completing development of the block's eastern half with the rectory between BC and Sacred Heart Church. The first year, 21 students attended, and by 1927, enrollment reached 225.[249] Benedictine colleges were not like today's universities. These institutions typically accepted white male students between ages ten and twenty, who were taught trade school courses and a liberal arts curriculum or studied to be priests.[250] Benedictine Military School (renamed, but still locally referred to as "BC") and the Sacred Heart Priory moved to the current campus on Seawright Drive in 1963. In 1967, both institutions returned to the Saint Vincent umbrella. Today, Benedictine Military School is a highly regarded boys' high school. Sacred Heart Church continues to flourish on Bull Street, renting the former Benedictine College space to Susie King Taylor Community School, a public charter school.

Meanwhile downtown, the Catholic Church's influence within Savannah's African American community increased significantly in the twentieth century by educating more African American children and subsequently converting more Savannahians. Once the students were enrolled in Catholic schools, they were more likely to be baptized in the Catholic Church, and their parents would sometimes follow. This increased influence coincides with the arrival of the Society for African Missions (SMA).[251] Their directive came from Rome. The Propaganda Fide, a department in the Vatican that wanted white priests from the SMA to take over all of the southern African American missions, applied to Bishop Keiley for permission to manage St. Benedict's, and Keiley consented. Keiley reassured Abbot Haid the transition was not because of "dissatisfaction with your fathers."[252] The SMA priests took over St. Benedict's Parish on January 1, 1907, and rapidly grew the number of churches and schools, creating a "statewide framework for education and ministry" based on their experience with African missions.[253]

When the SMA took over, St. Benedict's was the only remaining Black parish in Savannah. Father Ignatius Lissner, using St. Benedict's as his "home base," began expanding and creating new Black parishes in Black neighborhoods, unlike the Benedictines' approach with Sacred Heart. He founded St. Anthony of Padua in West Savannah in 1908, opening a parish school in October 1909 with 225 students in the overcrowded basement. This area was rural, turning urban in the early 1900s. By the time Most Pure Heart of Mary was founded in the Cuyler-Brownsville neighborhood in 1911, the three existing Catholic schools had almost 300 students. Tuition was five cents per week for kindergarten and ten cents per week for other grades.[254] Father Lissner was dedicated to educating African American children because he was a firm believer in many harmful stereotypes including the "bad working mother" stereotype and the supposed Black tendency to be lazy and immoral without proper instruction.[255] The SMA fathers continued to minister on

Skidaway Island as necessary. For example, in early 1910, John Tyson died on the island "and was interred in the graveyard near the old church."[256] Father Obrecht, accompanied by members of the Mutual Aid Society, went to the island to assist the family.[257]

Throughout Georgia, the SMA fathers went from one priest baptizing five adults and nine children in 1907 to seven priests baptizing fifty-two adults and fifty-eight children in 1909 while maintaining six schools throughout the state. The SMA fathers were much more successful in recruiting students and converts than the Benedictines. One important difference was that the SMA fathers were committed to an academic program, rather than an industrial school. These schools had Black lay teachers whose level of dedication and involvement far surpassed that of white teachers. Savannah's twentieth-century Black and Catholic schools had two other important differences from their white Catholic counterparts that contributed to their success. First, non-Catholic students comprised the majority in Black Catholic schools, so any student had access to education. Second, the schools somewhat reflected their neighborhoods but also became "urban centers for dispersed black populations" that helped create a Black and Catholic community in the same way as their Black Protestant counterparts.[258] The SMA fathers assisted community building by hiring from within the parish, employing women who were members of the parish to cook and clean. As Gary W. McDonogh states, the "housekeeper's role extended to scheduling and errands in which she, too, became an extension of rectorial authority."[259] This is in contrast to white Catholic parishes, which hired both white and African American workers, but they were not necessarily parish members and were given less responsibility.

The idea to gain converts by educating children was used throughout the centuries. This pattern was seen in the Catholic Spanish mission system in Southern California, where records show the children were baptized before their parents.[260] In 1886, Abbot Haid proposed building a school near North Carolina's Belmont Abbey for African American children. "Now many negroes come to church, but it is hard to get these old fellows; we must take the children first," Haid wrote using rather possessive language.[261] In general, once the children were baptized, sometimes the parents followed. More women converted as adults than men, which suggests women were converting at marriage. Since the 1970s, infant baptism has been most common.[262]

After 1922, there was steady growth in the schools and parishes, interrupted by a big drop in the mid-1930s because of migration north. One drawback was that the highest grade available was ninth grade at St. Benedict's until 1952, when St. Pius X High School opened. Before this, students had to transfer to the public high school. Savannah's Catholic and public schools were first desegregated in the fall of 1963; however, at this time, only Catholic Black children could attend formerly white Catholic schools, which limited the policy's effectiveness.[263]

A May 1969 diocese-commissioned study recommended closing St. Pius X High School and building a new coed, integrated high school. Instead, the diocese closed St. Pius X in September 1971, directing the boys to Benedictine Military School and sending the girls to St. Vincent's Academy. This decision was made despite the opposition of the vast majority of St. Pius X faculty, board, students, and parents. Objections included higher tuition, farther commutes from home to school, single-sex schools, and the fact that religious orders ran the schools, which meant they were out of the diocese's control. Finally, the community loved their school, took pride in St. Pius X, and wanted to continue their school traditions. Unfortunately, this story was repeated as desegregation resulted in the closure of nearly every Black Catholic school in the Savannah diocese.[264] The other Black Catholic schools closed between 1968 and 1977, due to the larger integration movement and the Catholic hierarchy's desire to create one Catholic community. Savannah's African American community members, who were not consulted about the decision to close schools and were not listened to when they objected to the closings, were angry and unhappy about the decision.[265] As Mark Newman states, "Implemented overwhelmingly at the cost of black Catholic institutions, diocesan desegregation was one-sided and ignored the wishes of many African Americans for desegregation based on reciprocity that would maintain at least some histori- cally black churches and schools."[266]

Despite Father Lissner's belief that "the war cry here should be: 'Convert the Negroes by the Negro,'" the SMA fathers and twentieth-century Catholic Church leaders were much less successful at encouraging and recruiting Black priests and lay brothers than congregational converts. Robert Eugene Chaney, baptized at St. Benedict the Moor and ordained at St. John the Baptist in 1988, was the first Black Savannahian to become a priest, 110 years after the Skidaway mission began to train African American lay brothers. He was only the second African American ordained in the Savannah diocese, following his contemporary Father Bruce Greening from Columbus, Georgia.[267] Nationwide, only 74 Black priests were ordained between 1854 and 1954, most of whom entered the clergy after the 1930s. By the mid-1980s, there were approximately 300 Black priests, 265 Black deacons, and about 700 Black nuns, or one African American priest for every 40,000 African American Catholics. Why so few? McDonogh explains: "Prejudice clearly holds primacy as an explanation."[268] There were (and are) few role models and little encouragement, either during childhood or during seminary. Until the 1970s, Catholic education included both Latin and "rudimentary" religious instruction, but not enough for students to gain more than "limited participation" in Roman Catholic life.[269] This practice was not encouraging toward potential future priests, let alone congregation members who sought to understand the church and its teachings.

Abbot Wimmer was often questioned about his devotion to the Georgia missions and his commitment to Black education. He responded, "One must be a martyr for so noble a goal, one must be capable of working for an idea, of which the fruit will certainly not be in the present, one must attribute it to his honor to be allowed to assist in such apostolic work."[270] Wimmer's patience was rewarded, but it was not until the twentieth century that the Catholic Church gained more trust within the African American community and, consequently, began to build larger, more significant parishes with a generational following and develop "a coherent institutional framework vis-à-vis blacks."[271]

The Skidaway Island mission took on two iterations during its existence, first as a monastery and boarding school for boys and then as a Black Catholic-managed private school before its closure in 1900. Most of the baptisms and conversions were short-term, ephemeral gains, with the notable exception of Sister Rosa. The effects of educating youth were surely longer lasting but more difficult to quantify. Although the Skidaway mission was an important entrance into African American education, unfortunately it was not as much of a learning experience for the Benedictines as it was for the school's children. However, it was from this Benedictine platform that the SMA fathers were able to dive in and rapidly expand educational opportunities. The SMA fathers were more successful because they supported greater African American agency in Savannah schools and parishes, giving the community what it wanted: quality schools that challenged African American students in the best way. Ultimately, although the Benedictines did not continue teaching African American schools, their Benedictine Military School (BC), now desegregated for over fifty years, is the last man standing of Savannah's earliest Catholic schools.

CHAPTER 5
Mission Accomplished?

"From the very beginning, Skidaway, and everything attached to it, was a curse," Rev. William Mayer grumbled to Rev. Patrick Donlon in 1893.[1] This statement was certainly an exaggeration born of administrative frustration; however, the Skidaway mission was not without its flaws. Although eventually Savannah's Catholic schools became an important option for African American children, the Skidaway school had many challenges: lack of consistent teachers, staff with racist beliefs of varying magnitudes, a Catholic curriculum on a Protestant island, few academic instructional hours per day, a lack of parental oversight and involvement, cultural misconceptions, and few African American teachers. The archaeological record suggests the school lacked adequate educational supplies and materials. These factors all led to high student turnover despite the school's primary advantage: free education.

KEY PROBLEMS

For Skidaway Island's African American parents, the mission school was an undesirable option for many of the above reasons, including the Catholic faith and manual labor elements of the school. The Catholic teachings were the lesser of these concerns. Other contemporary African American Catholic schools had high enrollments, including the Sacred Heart Parish School, which averaged 150 children, and then St. Benedict's Parish School, which varied between 100 and 175 students. Earlier, the cathedral school was initially well attended, and Father Bergier's first school started well with 50 students in East Savannah. However, the mission was a more intense religious education, with the students more deeply immersed in Catholicism. The mission environment meant that the students' lives revolved around school and Catholicism, rather than family life.

Students objected to the rigorous daily schedule, which closely matched novitiates' schedules, so "the regime imposed upon the students was more monastic than scholastic."[2] This framework followed the traditional European, religion-based schools that provided a classical education on a monastic schedule. According to Jane Eva Baxter, "The origins of American institutions lie in the early monastic communities of medieval Europe where confinement and regimented living were seen as important toils for cultivating moral and spiritual uplift for the residents."[3] When the Benedictines and other religious orders immigrated to the United States, they found the European model did not quite fit. It had to be adapted to an American schedule, and the course content changed.[4] Father Moosmüller, a native of Germany, was raised in the European tradition and was only partially willing to adapt. Father Reichert was also born in Germany; however, he immigrated as a toddler and was more culturally American than Moosmüller and more willing to adopt an American style of education.[5]

More concerning than the religious instruction was the fact that the school was a manual school, or industrial school, which was incompatible with many parents' desires for their children's future. Students were required to work the farm daily, which left fewer hours for academic instruction. Most parents wanted their children to get an education so they could leave the fields for better jobs and opportunities. Parents had, in Moosmüller's words, "a horror against working in the field . . . they want their boys to get such an education that they would not need to do manual labor, they would rather be clerks, bookkeepers, or anything else than a farmer."[6] In response, Moosmüller nominally modified his plans to have an agricultural school, creating two educational tracks, one for business and one for farming.[7] However, for all practical purposes, the school was an industrial school. Parents' objections to a manual labor school, discussed in detail in chapter 3, were part of the larger debate in African American education about the benefits of industrial schools versus academic schools. In the early twentieth century, this would be embodied in the discourse between Booker T. Washington and W. E. B. Du Bois. The Benedictines chose to build a manual school not necessarily because of any philosophical position, but because of the location and personnel available to them. Unfortunately, any benefits derived from the curriculum's manual labor components were severely compromised by the teachers' lack of farming skills.

Sister Mary Anthony Rosa Lucas, an African American Third Order Franciscan nun who lived on Skidaway as a very young child, recalled that the conflict between the Benedictines and island residents was at least partly caused by islanders' resentment and anger over the fathers trying to teach farming to a group of farmers, while simultaneously lacking agricultural skills. The clash culminated in fires and property destruction. Sister Rose's story reinforces the understanding that the Benedictines stepped far outside their expertise on Skidaway Island. Once they focused on Savannah and taught traditional schools, their positive impact increased because they were better serving their students and relying on their educational strengths.[8]

To varying degrees, all of the white priests and brothers held racist beliefs that hindered their ability to teach and treat the students and lay brothers as equals.

Brother Rhabanus Canonge and Father Siricius Palmer both described a toxic, racist environment that eventually caused them to leave. If they experienced this as fellow religious, the students certainly experienced the same. Most white teachers throughout the South incorrectly assumed that African Americans did not truly understand the importance of education, although some teachers had vaguely positive ideas about what schools and education meant to African American students and their parents. Ultimately, the Benedictines' general attitude toward African Americans was similar to their understanding of Indigenous Americans: people "who came from an alien culture that had little or no religion and needed to be evangelized."[9] The priests believed schools were the best means of evangelization and conversion. The majority of white teachers (priests and lay people) were primarily interested in doing God's work, because it fulfilled themselves and their religious aims. Applicants to northern aid societies used words and phrases such as "benevolence," "mission," "do good," and "be useful," while failing to mention emancipation or the students. Most white teachers failed to even attempt to understand the students' or parents' perspectives, likely because it did not occur to the teachers that African Americans had perspectives or theories on the importance of education. The same can be said of the monks. Worse, by Reconstruction's end, more than half of the teachers were white southerners, who were often more motivated to continue white supremacist policies or to get a paycheck than to educate students.[10] For these reasons, Skidaway Islanders specifically requested a Black Protestant teacher for their public school.[11]

We know very little about what academic subjects the monks were teaching, other than vague references to broad topics such as reading, writing, basic mathematics, and Catholicism. Nor do we know what books and other materials were used. On their corporate charter, the Benedictine Order in Georgia stated their purpose was education, but the mission lacked focus on education and did not create an academically challenging program at the Skidaway school. Even Moosmüller's curriculum prospectus indicated the education provided was quotidian. In the Benedictines' voluminous correspondence, some topics received much attention (personnel issues, finances, farming, and illnesses) while others did not. Most notably, there was almost no discussion of books, curriculum, subject matter, or students' educational progress, and what little there was, was not positive. Teaching specifics did not warrant a detailed discussion, while the newer, more challenging issues of building an institution received attention. When students and local residents were mentioned, it was often in reference to numbers of people baptized and confirmed. Conversion of souls, running a farm, saying mass in several churches, and continued scholarship (such as Moosmüller's *Der Geschichtsfreund*) all vied for the monks' time and attention, but, ultimately, the educational mission was secondary and received a lower priority to the mission of conversion.

Cultural differences on many levels inhibited the monks' success in educating students and converting islanders. There were obvious cultural differences in language and dialect, food, religion, and so on, but these were superficial. The deeper cultural differences were unconscious or unacknowledged by the priests and brothers. Their internalized white privilege and racism meant they believed their knowledge and experience was superior to African Americans' knowledge. It did not occur to the priests to learn about the culture they were entering. It did not occur to them to consult the local leaders and parents to understand their needs and wants for their children's future. On the other hand, the African American community, long used to this naivete and ignorance, was prepared to block the fathers' unwanted advances. Moosmüller encountered this early on when he met with "about a dozen" African American fathers and told them about his new, free school. He wrote to Father Zilliox:

> One of them answered that they had to give their word to their preacher (a Baptist) not to send their children to any School except a Baptist school; afterwards I learned that there was one amongst them here (but who did not utter a word in this house) who is a Deacon and who told them at church that he would excommunicate any one who would send his children to the 'Fathers' School; at the same time he always flattered me, pretending to be my best friend, he is also the foreman on our place, collects the rents, etc., etc., and has his land free of rent from us.[12]

Moosmüller's reaction to this discovery was not self-reflection, learning from the experience, or even adjusting his approach to better suit his audience. Rather, he was insulted at the locals' ingratitude. The ability to charge forward without concern for how your actions affect people of color, women, and other historically marginalized groups and to do so without consequences is part of white privilege and male privilege. This situation, where the privileged are willfully ignorant of their actions' effects on others who are constantly dodging and blocking those ramifications, continues today both in education and other areas of society. Granted, Fathers Moosmüller, Reichert, and others were typical of their time and culture. However, today's parents, teachers, administrators, and children live with the system established by these past educators. Our school system still bears the scars of segregation, underfunding, white flight, and white privilege. Skidaway Island parents were making choices at the beginning of this system, navigating the best options for their children with a lot fewer choices than we have today.[13]

Finally, for African American parents, the biggest problem was that the Skidaway mission school was a boarding school. African Americans strongly resisted allowing their children to leave their households for many reasons, including practical ones. The children's labor was needed, as it was in many lower socioeconomic households regardless of race. Children's labor could mean the difference between being a financially independent household or not. More importantly, African Americans were adamant about the simple human right to raise your own children. After centuries of enslaved families being ripped apart on a whim or financial quirk, Black parents were simply unwilling to relinquish their children. Abbot Haid observed rather obtusely: "It is remarkable how negroes cling together. I am sure I could not induce anyone to leave her parents, or the parents to surrender the child."[14] The white Catholic priests, especially foreign-born priests such as Moosmüller, were less likely to understand the details of African American lives and culture (especially in historic context), but this statement still exposed their unwillingness to inquire into the needs of African American parents.

Despite their shortcomings, the Skidaway school and the Benedictine schools in Savannah helped fill an important gap between the initial excited rush to form schools during Reconstruction and the time when enough schools were established for all students to attend, which was many, many decades later. As Ronald E. Butchart states, "Before Reconstruction had run half its course, the Freedmen's Bureau had ceased operations, northern aid societies had retrenched or withdrawn entirely, and most of the northern white teachers had quit teaching in the black schools."[15] The Benedictines went against this tide, supporting this critical need by building more schools and providing more teachers. The Benedictines laid some of the groundwork that the public school board should have done.

THE PENN SCHOOL

The Penn School on St. Helena's Island, South Carolina, offers a revealing contrast to the Benedictine's Skidaway school. Freedpeople were the majority population on St. Helena's Island after the United States Navy took the island in 1862. White Pennsylvanians Laura Matilda Towne and Ellen Murray founded the Penn School with support from the Port Royal Relief Committee of Philadelphia, which appointed Towne, a graduate of the Female Medical College of Pennsylvania (later called the Woman's Medical College of Pennsylvania). In addition to teaching, Towne initially continued her medical practice as the only qualified person on the island. Towne and Murray came to St. Helena's as young women and would spend the rest of their lives dedicated to the school.[16]

Classes started in June 1862, and in late September, the brick church was offered as a space to house the school, which had 80 students to start. By October, the school had grown to 110 students, and Charlotte Forten, an African American teacher from Philadelphia, was hired. By December 15, 1862, the school had 147 students registered. However, the distance between students' homes and the school could be several miles, and the students' labor was often needed at home or working the fields; therefore, daily attendance varied widely. The school was open seven days a week, including Sunday school. The curriculum was a New England model with a rigorous curriculum that included reading, writing, spelling, grammar, diction, history, geography, math, and music. The new school was not without challenges. There was no "school culture" on the island, and the expectations of the teachers, students, and parents could be very different. There was also a dialect barrier between the northern teachers and Gullah-speaking students.[17] In the early years, the newly arrived teachers and the local residents had a lot to learn about each other.

During the Civil War, island residents faced many hardships including violence, illness, heat, lack of food, and a shifting population. Many displaced people arrived on St. Helena's Island during the Civil War. The Union Army sometimes kidnapped freedmen for unpaid labor. But the students persisted. In 1864, the school had 194 students. Union General Saxton, whose experiences serving at Port Royal made him a Black ally, arranged to have a new schoolhouse built, which was ready in January 1865 with monetary help from the Freedman's Aid Society of Pennsylvania. The frame building had three rooms and was one of the first prefabricated buildings in America. It was "put into service as the first real schoolhouse in the South designed for the instruction of former slaves."[18] In December 1868, the school began normal practice, or training teachers. As there were no clocks on the island, Towne's family donated a school bell that could be heard three miles away, although some students walked as far as five or six miles to school.[19]

During Reconstruction, the American Missionary Association supplied volunteer teachers. Charities also funded the school, which meant constantly searching for support, but the lack of government funding also allowed for independence. For example, South Carolina public schools did not have African American teachers, but the Penn School did. After Laura Towne's death on February 22, 1901, the school passed to new leadership. The Penn School, now the Penn Center, a museum and community center, was radically successful in educating many students and maintaining its independence despite many challenges.[20]

A number of key differences separate the Penn School and the Skidaway Island mission. Starting in 1862, Laura Towne, an abolitionist who studied at the Woman's Medical College of Pennsylvania, set the tone for the school and for many of the other assistance programs on St. Helena's Island. She was not immune to racist and patronizing ideas, occasionally expressing them herself, but she was emphatic that she arrived in South Carolina to do antislavery work. She understood the need for holistic help; early on, she distributed clothes, maintained a medical practice, and taught school. Her writing reveals that she grasped the perspective of her African American neighbors, and she was interested in understanding the local culture. Towne, along with her partner Ellen Murray, formed genuine, lifelong relationships within the community, discussing people by name and including rich details about islanders' lives in her letters home and in her diary. Towne truly loved teaching, and the curriculum at her school was academic and challenging. Students learned United States history, physiology, math, geography, and complex English lessons including spelling, parts of speech, sentence structure, and composition.[21] The women were effective because they were committed to helping as the community wished them to help—by offering an academic education, employing and training African American teachers, and providing desperately needed medical services.

SKIDAWAY SCHOOLS' EFFECTIVENESS

Were Skidaway Island schools effective at educating the island's population despite their problems? In 1880, 14 percent of the Black children ages five to twenty throughout Chatham County's coastal islands can be identified as having attended school. While Black boys and girls were educated at the same dismal rate, 51 percent of white boys but only 42 percent of white girls attended school in the same geographic area. For the Black population age ten or older, 8 percent of the women could read and 21 percent of the men could read.[22] It is possible, even likely, that education rates were actually slightly higher but simply not recorded on the census and other sources. Even considering this, only 14 percent of Black children attending school fifteen years after the war's end is abysmal but not surprising due to the lack of schools.

The situation improved by 1900, when 44 percent of Skidaway Island's African American population 10 years of age or older could read, and, importantly, men and women were equally literate. Those able to read and write were typically between the ages of 10 and 35 (born after 1865), with only three individuals older than 35 able to read (they were ages 40, 42, and 50). Of those who could not read, 56 percent were older than 35, still leaving a large percentage of younger individuals who did not get an education. By this time, the total Black population of Skidaway Island had dropped to 201 individuals, and the white population was 16, of whom 7 were illiterate.[23]

In the twenty years that the public county school and the mission school operated on Skidaway Island, the literacy rates grew significantly, especially for Black women and girls. Attendance numbers and the fact that girls and boys were educated at nearly identical rates suggests that the county school had a greater impact on island residents than the mission school, which only taught boys. These statistics also suggest the mission school students were more likely outsiders, with only a few island residents attending. Nothing is known of Mrs. Mirault's students. Was she teaching only boys? And did the school continue as a boarding school? The public school continued to educate an average of nineteen boys and twenty-two girls from the mid-1890s until at least 1920. The daily attendance rates were typically between 75 and 85 percent, except for the 1910s when the attendance rate dropped to 55 percent. While each year showed a fair amount of fluctuation, it is unclear what events during the 1910s caused a drastic drop in the average daily attendance rate.

IMPLICATIONS FOR ARCHAEOLOGY, HERITAGE, AND PRESERVATION

With so many questions still to be researched, where is there potential for further research and interpretation? Some school buildings remain, while others have been razed. Due to the urban environment, most of the schools' former locations have little physical space that could be excavated. In other cases, the exact location of the school is not currently known, especially for schools in private homes and the public county schools. An enormous amount of further research is required to pinpoint these locations before they can be assessed for archaeological potential.

West Broad Street School, now the Ships of the Sea Museum, and the Massie School, currently the Massie Heritage Center, hold the best potential for further archaeological research. Both are museums with preservation and education missions, so they are more likely to be receptive to archaeological research. Both locations also have some greenspace for excavations. Ships of the Sea Museum has more physical space, but renovations to the garden and the creation of a performing and event space on the property's northern section mean that the back courtyard is likely the best preserved. Massie Heritage Center does not have much open space for excavations, but the space present is likely well preserved, as the building has maintained its function as a school and education center since its construction.

The public East Broad Street School (Fair Lawn School) is no longer standing; on its site now is St. John's Villa apartments. However, significant amounts of greenspace remain, leaving the possibility of archaeological resources. The northwest corner of Harris and East Broad Streets was the location of the first St. Benedict's church and later the Georgia Military Cadet School. The lot is currently empty and therefore has archaeological potential. The same is true of the former Anderson Street School at the northeast corner of Anderson and East Broad Streets. The two blocks bounded by Habersham and Price Streets and 31st and 33rd Streets, which originally housed Sacred Heart and St. Mary's Home, are now residential, containing a mix of homes, yards, and a parking lot. Although much of the archaeological resources were likely disturbed when the houses were built, there is still enough greenspace for testing. A similar situation is present on the western end of Anderson Street. Haven Home Industrial School was razed, but the adjacent Cuyler Street School is still present and now houses the Economic Opportunity Authority for Savannah-Chatham County, Inc. (EOA). Some of the surrounding area is paved, but other space is grass. The EOA is an excellent opportunity for more interpretation, if not archaeology. An exhibit on the Cuyler School is already present in the building's lobby.

The Beach Institute has remained an educational institution to the present day. After the American Missionary Association closed the school in 1919, it was operated briefly as a nautical school and then reopened as a continuation school from 1922 to 1928. The building stood vacant for several years; then the Savannah Board of Education bought the property for $5,000 and opened the Harris Street School, which operated from 1939 until 1960. Later several education groups worked from the building, including Harris Vocational Trade School, Harris Reading Center, Harris Adult Education Center, and Beach Institute Alternative High School, and the building operated as the board of education central office annex in the 1970s.[24] Today, the Beach Institute is a cultural center and museum open to the public. On the east side of the building is a lovely garden where the original teachers' housing was. However, necessary renovations during the first decade of the 2000s seriously disturbed the soils in this area, greatly reducing the possibility for archaeological research.

The Oglethorpe Free School was located in Yamacraw Village on the western side of downtown Savannah. The U.S. Department of Housing and Urban Development (HUD) owns Yamacraw Village. There is greenspace surrounding the school's general location, but modern development has somewhat disturbed the area. Ground-penetrating radar during a previous, unrelated archaeological project showed many buried utilities but also found anomalies that had archaeological potential. These specific anomalies were not ground-truthed; however, a utility pipe installation gave archaeologists a peek at the deeper stratigraphy, revealing mid-nineteenth-century artifacts two meters below surface. In fact, modern fill may have helped preserve deeper archaeological resources.[25]

The rest of the known school locations lack adequate space to do archaeological excavations. The Cathedral of St. John the Baptist, which housed the Sisters of St. Joseph school, as well as First Bryan Baptist Church and First African Baptist Church, have potential for interpretation such as signage and programming. St. Stephen's Episcopal Church, now a Unitarian Universalist Church, is in the same position. The Montmollin Building, which housed the Bryan Free School, is still standing in City Market and currently hosts businesses. There is no space for excavations; however, this would be an excellent opportunity for interpretive signs.

Modern development has completely eliminated other school locations. Renovations at the old Candler Hospital to transform it into Savannah College of Art & Design's Ruskin Hall likely eliminated most if not all archaeological resources. Conversations with construction workers employed on the project revealed the destruction of archaeological resources including artifacts, soils, and human remains.[26] Any traces of St. Joseph's Academy at the original cathedral were completely eliminated with the construction of the Perry Lane Hotel.

Finally, although the Skidaway Island mission school was destroyed, the church site is still preserved on the Landings' property. When we completed the fieldwork for this project, we intended to leave the church site for future archaeologists. Leaving part of a site preserved for future research is standard ethical practice. However, in subsequent years, I have questioned how long this site will truly be preserved as the climate crisis advances and sea level rise encroaches on the barrier island. This site and many others will be inaccessible to future archaeologists without drastic reductions in greenhouse gas emissions. A one-meter rise in sea level (a conservative estimate) will result in over thirteen thousand archaeological sites being lost in the southeastern United States alone.[27]

CONCLUSION

What is the legacy of the Skidaway Island mission? Institutionally, the Savannah Diocese gained two churches that are still active congregations today: the predominately white Sacred Heart Church and the traditionally African American St. Benedict's.[28] Both churches are still in their same locations since the early 1900s, but St. Benedict's built a new brick church and changed the name to St. Benedict the Moor in the mid-1900s. The other major contribution is Benedictine Military School ("BC"), a well-regarded boys' high school with an extensive roster of powerful, connected alums.

The story of the Skidaway Island mission captures the origins and trajectory of Savannah's school systems. After the Civil War came the desperate rush to create schools for African American children. The public school system, in its infancy, struggled to create any quality schools and deliberately dragged its feet in creating African American schools. Then legal segregation stunted the schools' growth, forcing Black schools into the cycle of school poverty with underfunded, overcrowded schools staffed by underpaid, underappreciated teachers. Savannah's African American Catholic schools, while not perfect, were vital, alternative options in the twentieth century when the segregated public schools were separate and unequal. Taught by white Irish or English priests and nuns or African American lay teachers, the schools had high standards and lofty expectations of the students.

The most recent decades of the civil rights movement have vastly improved the educational options for African American children, but the inequities have not been entirely erased. Cultural attitudes allow for complacency and ongoing white flight to private schools, and there is a deep lack of political will to make real changes. In Savannah, our public education system bears the scars of low funding, white flight, and class and racial inequities. We are living with the results of these past educational mistakes and structural inequities. The right to quality, free public education is the backbone of our democracy. Education remains one of the most critical components of our society. As more factions seek to control our culture for their personal gain, education should provide not only basic skills but also accurate and inclusive histories, critical thinking practice, and competence in information literacy. These skills will be the difference between America the democracy and America the autocracy.

Abbot Boniface Wimmer's motto was "forward, always forward." Wimmer's many missions paralleled contemporary white American's cultural attitudes and policies including manifest destiny and Western colonization. In the same mindset, the Benedictine leadership believed that building schools and churches and converting people to Catholicism was the right, and righteous, action. But our past is much more complicated than a few powerful people with hegemonic ideas controlling the rest of society. Nor is the resistance and persistence of less powerful people a monolithic presence. Hopefully, this book illustrates the many shades of action and counteraction, learning and dogmatic ignorance that occurred over the first twenty-five years of Benedictine education in Savannah.

Notes

AUTHOR'S NOTE

1. Murphy, "Archives of Removal"; Wagner, "In Final Report."

CHAPTER 1. A BRIEF SKETCH OF SKIDAWAY ISLAND

1. When the original developer designed the Landings, lots were set aside for natural and cultural preservation. This property and several others are dedicated as common properties of the Landings Association and subject to the Landings Association covenants. The Landings is committed to their preservation, because these reserved lots increase quality of life and raise property values. Although the property could theoretically be transferred out of the Landings Association control and therefore no longer preserved, the process is long, is extremely complicated, and involves a vote of the Landings Association membership, and then the property can only be transferred to a public agency, authority, or utility. Sean Burgess, elec. comm.

2. Babits, "Report on Preliminary Investigations."

3. In the middle of this project, the University System of Georgia Board of Regents announced they were merging Armstrong State University with Georgia Southern University. Although the former Armstrong State University is now the Armstrong Campus of Georgia Southern University, I continue to use Armstrong State University (or just Armstrong) here because most of the fieldwork was done while Armstrong was still independent and because the faculty, staff, and students were nearly unanimously against the merger.

4. Seifert, "Horror of Farm Work."

5. Emily Jones, "Student Archaeologists Dig Up History."

6. Jones.

7. Agabe-Davies and Fay, *2013 Archaeology Report*; Agabe-Davies, "Archaeology of the Old Elliot School"; Landon et al., "Investigating the Heart"; Vance, Jones, and Landon, "Persistence of Equality." The Manassas Industrial School in Manassas, Virginia, has also been subject to archaeological excavations. Dedicated in September 1894, it was technically around in the nineteenth century, but the bulk of its existence and its curriculum and philosophy really make it a twentieth-century school.

8. Monica L. Smith, "Archaeology of a 'Destroyed' Site," 36.

9. Gibb and Beisaw, "Learning Cast Up," 107.

10. Gibb and Beisaw, 107; Rotman, "Rural Education," 71–73.

11. Struchtemeyer, "Separate but Equal?"; Betti, "Gloucester's Public School Past"; Betti, "Archaeology Is Revealing."

12. Gibb and Beisaw, "Learning Cast Up," 122–26.

13. Rotman, "Rural Education," 71–73; Baxter, *Archaeology of American Childhood*, 108. This was generally true at the Benedictines' school as well. Although over eleven thousand artifacts were found, most were architectural, and few were small finds or other highly diagnostic artifacts.

14. Baxter, *Archaeology of American Childhood*, 109–11.

15. Agbe-Davies and Fay, *2013 Archaeology Report*, 1.

16. Agbe-Davies and Fay, 1–18; Agbe-Davies and Martin, "'Demanding a Share,'" 109–14.

17. Agbe-Davies, "Archaeology of the Old Elliot School," 129–50.

18. Agbe-Davies, 144–45.

19. Landon et al, "Investigating the Heart," ii-14.

20. "Parker Academy"; Vance, Jones, and Landon, "Persistence of Equality."

21. Kelly, *Short History of Skidaway Island*, 12.

22. Marvin T. Smith and Elliott, *Archaeological Survey for the Landings*, 39–40.

23. Piechocinski, *Once upon an Island*, 105; Kelly, *Short History of Skidaway Island*; Elliott and Holland, *Archaeological Survey of Priests Landing*, 15–16.

24. Marvin T. Smith and Elliott, *Archaeological Survey for the Landings*, 40; Elliott and Holland, *Archaeological Survey of Priests Landing*, 16–17.

25. Georgia Historical Society (GHS), Georgia Writers' Project, Savannah Unit research materials, MS 1355, Folder 184.

26. GHS, MS 1355, Folder 184.

27. GHS, MS 1355, Folder 184.

28. GHS, MS 1355, Folder 182–86.

29. Kelly, *Short History of Skidaway Island*, 80; "Right Reverend John Barry D.D."

30. Elliott and Holland, *Archaeological Survey of Priests Landing*, 17–22. Priest's Landing is a modern place-name and references the monastery.

31. Kurtz, "War Diary of Cornelius," 44–45.

32. Kurtz, "Hanleiter War Diary II," 57.

33. Fort Pulaski National Monument Archives (FOPU), L. W. Landershine Diary, March 25, 1862.

34. Parden, "'Somewhere toward Freedom,'" 138–39; Fraser, *Savannah in the New South*, 13–15.

35. Sherman, *Memoirs*, 250.

36. "The Bryan Schoolhouse," *Savannah Daily Herald*, March 20, 1865.

37. Cimbala, *Under the Guardianship*, 3.

38. Parden, "Somewhere toward Freedom," 139; Oubre, *Forty Acres and a Mule*, 47.

39. Records of the Assistant Commissioner for the State of Georgia, Bureau of Refugees, Freedmen and Abandoned Lands, 1865–1869, National Archives Publication M798 Roll 36, "Register of Land Titles Issued to Freedmen," s.v. "Skidaway Island," Freedmen's Bureau Online, Freedmensbureau.com/georgia/landtitles/index.htm.

40. Quoted in Kelly, *Short History of Skidaway Island*, 60; Elliott and Holland, *Archaeological Survey of Priests Landing*, 22–23.

41. Simms, *First Colored Baptist Church*, 135.

42. Jacqueline Jones, *Saving Savannah*, 225; Hoskins, *Trouble They Seen*, 28; Fraser, *Savannah in the New South*, 15; Bryant, "'We Defy You!,'" 161; Coffin, *Four Years of Fighting*, 425.

43. Perdue, *Negro in Savannah*, 38; Jacqueline Jones, *Saving Savannah*, 216; *Savannah Tribune*, October 5, 1889.

44. Coffin, *Four Years of Fighting*, 423.

45. Bryant, "'We Defy You!,'" 161.

46. Cimbala, *Under the Guardianship*, 175.

47. Parden, "Somewhere toward Freedom," 138; Beard, "Promise Betrayed," 46–50.

48. Cimbala, *Under the Guardianship*, 168–71.

49. Cimbala, 189; GHS, MS, 1355, Series III, Box 16.

50. GHS, Joseph Frederick Waring II papers, MS 1275, Box 13, Folder 125.

51. Dorsey, "Great Cry,'" 247.

52. Elliott and Holland, *Archaeological Survey of Priests Landing*, 23.

53. "The Skidaway Shell Road," *Savannah Morning News*, December 15, 1868, Digital Library of Georgia.

54. "The Skidaway Island Trouble," *Savannah Morning News*, December 21, 1868, Digital Library of Georgia.

55. "Trouble on Skidaway Island," *Savannah Morning News*, December 18, 1868, Digital Library of Georgia.

56. "Another Affidavit in Relation to the Lawless Conduct of Negroes on the Islands below This City," *Savannah Morning News*, December 22, 1868, Digital Library of Georgia.

57. *Savannah Morning News*, July 21, 1884.

58. "Bishop Gross Visits Our Coast," *Savannah Daily Advertiser*, June 14, 1873, Genealogy Bank; *Macon Weekly Telegraph*, April 5, 1867, Genealogy Bank.

59. The bridge debate would continue until 1898 when the Supreme Court of Georgia ruled in favor of the Chatham County Commissioners. *Savannah Morning News*, July 3, 1873; "The Skidaway Island: The Proposed New Road," *Savannah Morning News*, July 4, 1873, Digital Library of Georgia; *Southeastern Reporter*, 167–69.

60. Elliott and Holland, *Archaeological Survey of Priests Landing*, 23–25.

CHAPTER 2. THE RADICAL ACT OF EDUCATION

1. Whittington B. Johnson, *Black Savannah*, 70; Litwack, *Trouble in Mind*, 53–55.

2. Green, *Educational Reconstruction*, 15.

3. Blassingame, "Before the Ghetto," 473; Burton, *Penn Center*, 29–30; Williams, *Self-Taught*, 41, 43, 52–53, 147.

4. Williams, *Self-Taught*, 87–89; Hoskins, *Yet with a Steady Beat*, 171; Jacqueline Jones, *Saving Savannah*, 218.

5. Williams, *Self-Taught*, 14–15, 19.

6. "Contraband school" is a term commonly used for schools that secretly taught en-

slaved people or free people of color when laws forbade their education. Contraband here refers to forbidden education, not to the people. This is different from the Civil War–era definition of formerly enslaved people who escaped behind Union lines prior to the Thirteenth Amendment.

7. Williams, *Self-Taught*, 104; Hoskins, *Yet with a Steady Beat*, 163–68.

8. Federal Writers' Project, *Georgia*, part 3, 231.

9. Kytle and Roberts, *Denmark Vesey's Garden*, 235–44. An accidental experiment was conducted in Charleston when ex-bondperson Susan Hamilton was interviewed by Augustus Ladson, a Black writer, and then Jessie Butler, a white writer, after the South Carolina director Mabel Montgomery did not believe Ladson's original report because the details were so harsh. Indeed, the two accounts are very different, but not necessarily contradictory. Ladson's report has details of sexual violence, harsh punishments, and families permanently separated by slave auctions. Butler's contains entirely different details and a different focus, while using neutral, cautious terms. Fortunately, all of the interviews were included in the final volume.

10. Williams, *Self-Taught*, 28.

11. Harden, *History of Savannah*, 415.

12. Otto, "Public School System," vol. 2, 157–64; Harden, *History of Savannah*, 415–17.

13. Williams, *Self-Taught*, 69.

14. James D. Anderson, *Education of Blacks*, 4.

15. Williams, *Self-Taught*, 40.

16. James D. Anderson, *Education of Blacks*, 6.

17. Bonner, Shearouse, and Smith, *History of Public Education*, xi, xii; Williams, *Self-Taught*, 50, 172.

18. Federal Writers' Project, *Georgia*, part 2, 191.

19. Federal Writers' Project, *Georgia*, parts 1–4.

20. Williams, *Self-Taught*; Butchart, *Schooling the Freed People*.

21. Federal Writers' Project, *Georgia*, parts 1–4.

22. Prothero, *American Bible*, 99.

23. Prothero, 99.

24. Prothero, 98–102.

25. Williams, *Self-Taught*, 129–30; WPA narratives and other archival sources have many reminiscences of using this book.

26. Washington, quoted in Prothero, *American Bible*, 104–5.

27. Federal Writers' Project, *Georgia*, part 4, 112.

28. Otto, "Public School System," vol. 1, 22; Penny Clarke Johnson, "Second Class Students," 6, 14; Butchart, *Schooling the Freed People*, 3, 21–22.

29. William, *Self-Taught*, 112, 129.

30. Williams, 19.

31. King Taylor, *Reminiscences*, 5–6, 11, 54–55.

32. Williams, *Self-Taught*, 106–10, 127.

33. Hoskins, *Yet with a Steady Beat*, 171.

34. There were other northern aid societies supporting schools in Savannah, including the New York Society of Friends, the National Freedmen's Aid Society, and the New England Freedmen's Aid Society, but they funded fewer schools and were all gone by 1871. Blassingame, "Before the Ghetto," 471.

35. Jacqueline Jones, *Soldiers of Light and Love*, 74.

36. Jones, 73–74.

37. Butchart, *Schooling the Freed People*; Taylor, "Mary S. Peake," 125.

38. Mitchell, *Raising Freedom's Child*; Green, *Educational Reconstruction*, 146.

39. *The Colored Tribune*, April 22, 1876, Digital Library of Georgia.

40. Hoskins, *Yet with a Steady Beat*, 58–60, 169. There has been some debate as to exactly where the Bryan Free School was located.

41. "The Bryan School House," *Savannah Daily Herald*, March 20, 1865. Digital Library of Georgia.

42. "Bryan School House."

43. Coffin, *Four Years of Fighting*, 433.

44. Coffin, 433.

45. Coffin, 433.

46. Penny Clarke Johnson, "Second Class Students," 14; Hoskins, *Yet with a Steady Beat*, 169–70; Otto, "Public School System," vol. 1, 404–6. The entirely African American staff included Principal Louis B. Toomer (who was originally from Charleston), A. De La Motta (the assistant principal from Macon), Eugene Truchelut, William Rose, Mrs. Flora Jones, Mrs. Catherine Dasler, Mrs. Mary Ann Deas, Mrs. E. Burke, and Mrs. H. Gunn.

47. Cimbala, *Under the Guardianship*, 115.

48. Cimbala, 115, 122–23.

49. Jacqueline Jones, *Soldiers of Light and Love*, 73–75; Hoskins, *Yet with a Steady Beat*, 171–72.

50. Otto, "Public School System," vol. 1, 406.

51. Jacqueline Jones, *Soldiers of Light and Love*, 75.

52. Hoskins, *Yet with a Steady Beat*, 172.

53. Jacqueline Jones, *Soldiers of Light and Love*, 75–76; Williams, *Self-Taught*, 87–89; Hoskins, *Yet with a Steady Beat*, 171; Jacqueline Jones, *Saving Savannah*, 218.

54. Green, *Educational Reconstruction*, 45.

55. Mitchell, *Raising Freedom's Child*, 95.

56. Mitchell, 103.

57. Jacqueline Jones, *Soldiers of Light and Love*, 76.

58. Jones, 76.

59. Mann, "Benedictine Missionaries."

60. Albert Jackson, William Pollard, Alexander Harris, Reverend Robert Carter, and

Charles E. Middleton formed the negotiating committee that brought the Beach Institute under the public schools' purview.

61. James D. Anderson, *Education of Blacks*, 4–13; Bryant, "'We Defy You!,'" 169; Butchart, *Schooling the Freed People*, 166; Hoskins, *Yet with a Steady Beat*, 172–73; Penny Clarke Johnson, "Second Class Students," 37–39; Jacqueline Jones, "Wartime Workers, Moneymakers," 154–57; Otto, "Public School System," vol. 1, 407 vol. 4, 408; *Savannah Morning News*, November 13, 1878, Digital Library of Georgia; Williams, *Self-Taught*, 121–25.

62. James D. Anderson, *Education of Blacks*, 19; Tyack and Lowe, "Constitutional Moment," 243.

63. Blassingame, "Before the Ghetto," 472.

64. Otto, "Public School System," vol. 4, 411.

65. Penny Clarke Johnson, "Second Class Students," 3–27. Hoskins reported that male teachers were paid $750 per year, while the female teachers were paid only $450 per year. Hoskins, *Yet with a Steady Beat*, 178. This is much higher than other reports of Savannah's public school salaries.

66. DeRenne was a descendant of Noble Jones, one of the earliest white colonists in Georgia. Part of the family's plantation, Wormsloe, is now a Georgia State Historic Site. DeRenne was in a very privileged position and able to influence public policy and afford building donations.

67. Hoskins, *Yet with a Steady Beat*, 188–190.

68. Penny Clarke Johnson, "Second Class Students," 26–32, 39–40; Hoskins, *Yet with a Steady Beat*, 190.

69. Penny Clarke Johnson, "Second Class Students," 32–33; Hoskins, *Yet with a Steady Beat*, 190.

70. GHS, Eleanor Knorr Strain genealogical research materials, MS 1519.

71. Otto, "Public School System," vol. 4, 22–23.

72. BRFAL Records, M799 (United States, Freedmen's Bureau, "Records of the Superintendent of Education and of the Division of Education, 1865–1872" [database with images], FamilySearch, accessed July 20, 2023, http://FamilySearch.org [citing multiple microfilm publications of the National Archives and Records Administration, 1969–78; Georgia is M799]). Charles Smith, teacher at the Wormslow Day School and Wormslow Night School, dutifully sent his monthly teacher reports to the Freedmen's Bureau in 1866. His March and April reports have odd, probably incorrect locations written on them including "Wormslow, Ga Skidaway Island" and "Wormslow Island." Starting in May 1866, he consistently writes Isle of Hope, the actual location of Wormsloe Plantation, which dates to the earliest days of colonial Georgia. It is most likely that Smith was simply confused on his location. It is also possible, but unlikely, that some Skidaway Island children commuted by boat to the Wormsloe school, as the two islands are adjacent, separated by the Skidaway River.

73. Massie Heritage Center Archives (MHCA), "Thirteenth Annual Report," 14.

74. Oetgen, "Oswald Moosmüller," 15.

75. Benedictine Military School Archives (BMSA), Moosmüller to Wimmer, October 12, 1878.

76. *Savannah Daily Advertiser*, October 7 and 13, 1871, Genealogy Bank.

77. Mann, "Benedictine Missionaries," 44–46.

78. Sources disagree whether Palmer was a priest. Moosmüller refers to him as "Father Siricius" in his writings, but Oetgen writes that he was only a priest candidate, was never ordained, and left the order after several years. Oetgen, *Mission to America*, 566. Given the Catholic Church's policies, it is unlikely Palmer would have been allowed to be ordained because he was African American. I follow Moosmüller in referring to him as Father.

79. "Saint Vincent College, School Catalogs: 1876, 1877," s.v. "Charles Siricius Palmer," Ancestry, https://www.ancestry.com/search/; BMSA, Moosmüller to Wimmer, October 12, 1878; Oetgen, *Mission to America*, 56; Saint Vincent Archabbey Archives (SVAA), Moosmüller to Zilliox, September 15, 1878.

80. BMSA, Moosmüller to Wimmer, October 12, 1878.

81. SVAA, Moosmüller to Zilliox, September 15, 1878.

82. BMSA, Moosmüller to Wimmer, November 27, 1878.

83. BMSA, Moosmüller to Wimmer, December 9, 1878; Oetgen, "Origins of the Benedictine Order," 175; BMSA, Moosmüller to Wimmer, January 17, 1879; Barnum, "In Female-Dominated Education Field."

84. BMSA, Moosmüller to Wimmer, January 17, 1879.

85. BMSA, Moosmüller to Wimmer, January 17, 1879.

86. BMSA, Moosmüller to Wimmer, February 7, 1879.

87. MHCA, "Annual Reports," 1878–1920.

88. BMSA, Moosmüller to Wimmer, April 18, 1884.

89. BMSA, Moosmüller to Wimmer, April 18, 1884.

90. BMSA, Moosmüller to Wimmer, April 18, 1884; Moosmüller, *Ersabt Bonifaz Wimmer*, 198.

91. Oetgen, "Origins of the Benedectine Order," 178.

92. MHCA, "Annual Reports," 1878–1920.

93. MHCA, "Thirteenth Annual Report," 18.

94. Williams, *Self-Taught*, 149.

95. MHCA, "Thirteenth Annual Report," 19, 23. For these early years, the demographics for the county "colored" schools were lumped together, making it difficult to directly compare the Skidaway county school to the monks' school.

96. MHCA, "Twenty-Fourth Annual Report," 19.

97. MHCA, "Twenty-Fourth Annual Report," 13.

98. MHCA, "Twenty-Seventh Annual Report," 14.

99. Butchart, *Schooling the Freed People*, 175; Williams, *Self-Taught*, 195.

100. MHCA, "Twenty-Seventh Annual Report," 14.

101. MHCA, "Twenty-Sixth Annual Report," 16; MHCA, "Twenty-Eighth Annual Report."

102. MHCA, County Schools Inspection Records, 1892–1916.

103. MHCA, County Schools Inspection Records, 1892–1916.

104. It is unknown if the public school teachers were Black or white. MHCA, County Schools Inspection Records, 1892–1916.

105. *Savannah Tribune*, April 11, 1903, NewsBank.

106. Green, *Educational Reconstruction*, 145; Butchart, *Schooling the Freed People*, 70, 76, 106–7; Savannah Chatham County Public School System, Board of Education Archives (SCCPSS), annual reports state that they had trouble getting teachers at all.

107. MHCA, County Schools Inspection Records, 1892–1916.

108. Penny Clarke Johnson, "Second Class Students," 20–23; Hoskins, *Yet with a Steady Beat*, 177.

109. Mann, "Benedictine Missionaries," 13.

110. Penny Clarke Johnson, "Second Class Students," 35, 41.

111. Otto, "Public School System," vol. 1, 417–18.

112. James D. Anderson, *Education of Blacks*, 4–13; Jacqueline Jones, "Wartime Workers, Moneymakers," 154–57; Bryant, "'We Defy You!,'"169.

CHAPTER 3. THE BENEDICTINES BEGIN

1. Cheney, "Diocese of Savannah." The Diocese of Savannah consists of the southern half of Georgia. The Archdiocese of Atlanta covers the northern half of the state.

2. Hoskins, *Yet with a Steady Beat*, 61.

3. Davis, *History of Black Catholics*, 81.

4. Hoskins, *Yet with a Steady Beat*, 61–62; Brown, "People of Faith," 22; McDonogh, *Black and Catholic*, 100. The school may have actually been postbellum; the historical record is scant.

5. Buttimer, "New South, New Church," 49.

6. Davis, *History of Black Catholics*, 118.

7. Gannon, *Rebel Bishop*, 128; Davis, *History of Black Catholics*, 116, 119.

8. Alvord, *Letters from the South*, 1870.

9. Gannon, *Rebel Bishop*, 128–142.

10. "Board Commissioners: An Interesting Meeting," *Savannah Morning News*, July 3, 1873, Digital Library of Georgia; "The Skidaway Island," *Savannah Morning News*, July 4, 1873; "The County Commissioners: The Road to Skidaway Island," *Savannah Morning News*, July 22, 1873, Digital Library of Georgia.

11. *Savannah Daily News and Herald*, February 20, 1867; *Savannah Morning News*, April 27, 1870, Digital Library of Georgia; *Savannah Morning News*, February 12, 1873, Digital Library of Georgia; *Savannah Morning News*, April 25, 1870, Digital Library of Georgia; *Savannah Morning News*, April 25, 1870, Digital Library of Georgia.

12. "Letter from South Georgia," *Augusta Chronicle*, June 14, 1874, Genealogy Bank.

13. Diocese of Savannah, Archives and Records Department (DSA), Moosmüller to Wimmer, May 24, 1887, original at SVAA.

14. Oetgen, "Origins of the Benedictine Order," 166–67; Hoskins, *Yet with a Steady Beat*, 63.

15. Oetgen, "Origins of the Benedictine Order," 168.

16. BMSA, Moosmüller to Innocent Wolf, October 28, 1877.

17. Fellner, *Abbot Boniface and His Monks*, 557.

18. Fellner, 558.

19. Oetgen, "Origins of the Benedictine Order," 168.

20. BMSA, Moosmüller to Wimmer, March 20, 1877.

21. BMSA, Moosmüller to Wimmer, April 13, 1877; GHS, Walter Charlton Hartridge Jr. collection, MS 1349, Box 27, Folder 400, Gross to Moosmüller, November 17, 1877.

22. "U.S. Passport Applications, 1795–1925," s.v. "Raphael Wissel," Ancestry.

23. "New South Wales, Australia," s.v. "Raphael Wissel," Ancestry; "New Zealand, Officiating Ministers," s.v. "Raphael Wissel," Ancestry.

24. "Trouble in Samoa," *Baltimore Sun*, March 14, 1889, Genealogy Bank; "Mission at St. James' Church," *Baltimore Sun*, October 24, 1898, Genealogy Bank.

25. These young Benedictines included Bernard Murphy and John Shea. Murphy, who caught yellow fever in 1876 but recovered, would eventually become the abbot in Oklahoma (BMSA, Box VGS, BC, DO). Moosmüller referred to Shea as "ex-Benedictine Dom Benedict Joseph Shea" when announcing Shea's death and funeral at Savannah's Cathedral in August 1886 (BMSA, Moosmüller to Wimmer, August 11, 1886).

26. BMSA, Moosmüller to Innocent Wolf, October 28, 1877; "The Catholic Church," *Savannah Tribune*, October 3, 1914, NewsBank.

27. McDonogh, *Black and Catholic*, 149; Hoskins, *Yet with a Steady Beat*, 63; GHS, MS 1349, Box 27, Folder 400, William Mayer to Patrick Donlon, October 25, 1893.

28. DSA, Moosmüller to Wimmer, May 24, 1887, original at SVAA.

29. DSA, Moosmüller to Wimmer, May 24, 1887.

30. McDonogh, *Black and Catholic*, 148–152.

31. *Hoffman's Catholic Directory*, 1886; Fridolin Eckert, grave marker, Saint Joseph Cemetery, Cabery, Ford County, Illinois, digital image, s.v. "Fridolin Eckert," Find a Grave, https://findagrave.com; "New York, Passenger," digital image, s.v. Fridolin Eckert, Ancestry. com.; DSA, Moosmüller to Wimmer, May 24, 1887, original at SVAA.

32. Belmont Abbey Archive (BAA), Gross to Wimmer, January 4, 1877.

33. Oetgen, "Origins of the Benedictine Order," 167–69.

34. Fellner, *Abbot Boniface and His Monks*, 557.

35. Neuhofer, *In the Benedictine Tradition*, 11–12.

36. Fellner, *Abbot Boniface and His Monks*, 558; Oetgen, "Origins of the Benedictine Order," 170; BMSA, Moosmüller to Wimmer, March 3, 1877.

37. BMSA, Moosmüller to Wimmer, March 20, 1877.

38. GHS, MS 1355, Folder 182–86; BMSA, SIO-BO Collection, Folder 2.

39. BAA, A 1.0 Folder 1, Benedictine Society of Georgia.

40. BAA, A 1.0 Folder 1, Benedictine Society of Georgia.

41. SVAA, Wimmer to Archbishop, August 27, 1877.

42. BAA, Gross to Wimmer, March 14, 1877.

43. BMSA, Moosmüller to Wimmer, March 3, 1877.

44. BMSA, Moosmüller to Wimmer, March 3, 1877.

45. BMSA, Moosmüller to Wimmer, March 9, 1877.

46. BMSA, Moosmüller to Wimmer, March 9, 1877.

47. BMSA, Anderson to Dupon, June 20, 1877.

48. BMSA, Moosmüller to Wimmer, November 28, 1879.

49. Fellner, *Abbot Boniface and His Monks*, 560.

50. BAA, Gross to Wimmer, March 14, 1877; Fellner, *Abbot Boniface and His Monks*, 560.

51. BMSA, Moosmüller to Wimmer, March 20, 1877.

52. Rippinger, *Benedictine Order*, 147, 161.

53. *Savannah Morning News*, July 24, 1875, Digital Library of Georgia.

54. "The Crops on Skidaway," *Savannah Morning News*, July 28, 1875, Digital Library of Georgia.

55. "Is It Black Tongue?," *Savannah Morning News*, November 6, 1876. Digital Library of Georgia.

56. Dr. Lisa Hesse, in-person discussion, Mount Pleasant, South Carolina, October 6, 2019.

57. SVAA, Wimmer to Abbot, May 23, 1883.

58. BMSA, Moosmüller to Wimmer, April 13, 1877.

59. BMSA, Moosmüller to Wimmer, April 27, 1877; BMSA, Moosmüller to Wimmer, April 13, 1877.

60. BMSA, Moosmüller to Wimmer, June 14, 1877.

61. BMSA, Moosmüller to Wimmer, April 27, 1877.

62. BMSA, Moosmüller to Wimmer, April 29, 1877.

63. BMSA, Moosmüller to Wimmer, April 29, 1877.

64. BMSA, Moosmüller to Wimmer, June 14, 1877.

65. BMSA, Moosmüller to Wimmer, June 2, 1877. A well made of Savannah Gray bricks approximately twenty feet from the southwest corner of the golf course comfort station was archaeologically recorded in 1990 but is no longer visible on the surface. The bricks were standard size, not well bricks, with extra mortar filling the gaps to create a circle. Babits, "Report on Preliminary Investigations," 19.

66. BMSA, Moosmüller to Wimmer, July 1, 1877 (English translation in archives).

67. BMSA, Moosmüller to Wimmer, July 1, 1877.

68. BMSA, Moosmüller to Wimmer, July 1, 1877.

69. BMSA, Moosmüller to Wimmer, July 1, 1877.

70. BMSA, Moosmüller to Wimmer, July 1, 1877.

71. BMSA, Moosmüller to Wimmer, August 17, 1877.

72. Swanson, *Remaking Wormsloe Plantation*, 117–19.

73. "The Rights of Fishermen," *Savannah Daily Advertiser*, June 26, 1873, Genealogy Bank.

74. "The Georgia Press," *Macon Weekly Telegraph*, May 12, 1874, Genealogy Bank.

75. SVAA, Moosmüller to Zilliox, September 15, 1878.

76. Fraser, *Lowcountry Hurricanes*, 142–43.

77. SVAA, Wimmer to Amberger, January 15, 1886.

78. BMSA, Moosmüller to Wimmer, August 17, 1877.

79. BMSA, Moosmüller to Wimmer, August 17, 1877.

80. BMSA, Anderson to Dupon, June 20, 1877.

81. BMSA, Moosmüller to Wimmer, September 19, 1877.

82. BMSA, Moosmüller to Innocent Wolf, October 28, 1877.

83. BMSA, Moosmüller to Wimmer, October 30, 1877.

84. BMSA, Moosmüller to Wimmer, October 30, 1877.

85. BMSA, Moosmüller to Wimmer, October 30, 1877.

86. BMSA, Moosmüller to Wimmer, October 30, 1877.

87. BMSA, Moosmüller to Innocent Wolf, October 28, 1877.

88. BMSA, Moosmüller to Wimmer, December 8, 1877.

89. BMSA, Moosmüller to Innocent Wolf, December 21, 1877.

90. BMSA, Moosmüller to Wimmer, December 8, 1877.

91. BMSA, Moosmüller to Innocent Wolf, December 21, 1877.

92. BMSA, Moosmüller to Innocent Wolf, December 21, 1877.

93. BMSA, Moosmüller to Innocent Wolf, December 21, 1877.

94. BAA, Gross to Wimmer, March 14, 1877.

95. BMSA, Moosmüller to Wimmer, December 18, 1877.

96. Wimmer, quoted in Oetgen, *American Abbot*, 372–73.

97. BMSA, Moosmüller to Wimmer, December 18, 1877.

98. BMSA, Moosmüller to Innocent Wolf, March 12, 1878.

99. BMSA, Moosmüller to Innocent Wolf, March 12, 1878.

100. BMSA, Moosmüller to Innocent Wolf, March 12, 1878.

101. "Dedication of the Benedictine Monastery on Skidaway Island," *Savannah Morning News*, May 16, 1878, Digital Library of Georgia.

102. BMSA, SIH Collection.

103. "Vespers at the Monastery," *Savannah Morning News*, July 21, 1884, Digital Library of Georgia.

104. BMSA, SIH Collection.

105. Babits, "Report on Preliminary Investigations," 9.

106. Babits, 4.

107. Babits, 17.

108. Babits, 18.

109. Adams, "Machine Cut Nails," 70.

110. Lindsey, "Bottle Finishes & Closures"; Lindsey, "Bottle Bases."

111. BMSA, SIH Collection. Babits suggested that the middle section of the church/monastery building is the same building as the school pictured in the second photograph. However, careful analysis shows enough differences between the buildings to discard this theory.

112. Baxter, *Archaeology of American Childhood*, 112.

113. Rotman, "Rural Education," 71–73; Baxter, *Archaeology of American Childhood*, 108.

114. MHCA, "Supplies"; MHCA, "Record of Supplies."

115. "Grand Excursion to Skidaway Island," *Savannah Morning News*, June 8, 1878, Digital Library of Georgia.

116. Oetgen, "Origins of the Benedictine Order," 172; SVAA, Moosmüller to Andrew Hintenach, July 8, 1878.

117. SVAA, Moosmüller to Hintenach, July 8, 1878.

118. Mann, "Benedictine Missionaries," 29. Isabel Mann notes this positive tone in her 2018 thesis and attributes it to the importance of Catholics to Savannah's health care and education.

119. BMSA, Moosmüller to Wimmer, August 18, 1878.

120. SVAA, Moosmüller to Hintenach, July 8, 1878. Anderson's first name was originally Francis. Joseph was the religious name he took.

121. BMSA, Moosmüller to Innocent Wolf, March 12, 1878.

122. Clark et al., "1873 Irwin's Code," 789.

123. Rosenfeld, *Age of Independence*, 156, 165.

124. SVAA, Moosmüller to Hintenach, July 8, 1878; Golden, "Through the Muck and Mire," 26.

125. SVAA, Moosmüller to Hintenach, July 8, 1878.

126. BMSA, Moosmüller to Wimmer, April 21, 1877.

127. SVAA, Moosmüller to Hintenach, July 8, 1878.

128. BMSA, Moosmüller to Wimmer, April 21, 1877.

129. BMSA, Moosmüller to Wimmer, June 2, 1877.

130. Kryder-Reid, "'With Manly Courage,'" 102.

131. BMSA, Moosmüller to Wimmer, February 15, 1879; Rhabanus Canonge, grave marker, Saint Peters Abbey Cemetery, Muenster, Prince Albert Census Division, Saskatchewan, Canada, digital image s.v. "Rhabanus Canonge," Find a Grave.

132. BMSA, Moosmüller to Wimmer, February 15, 1879; Davis, *History of Black Catholics*, 123, 292; SVAA, Moosmüller to Andrew Hintenach, July 8, 1878.

133. BMSA, Moosmüller to Wimmer, February 15, 1879.

134. BMSA, Moosmüller to Wimmer, February 15, 1879.

135. BMSA, Moosmüller to Wimmer, February 15, 1879.

136. 1880 United States Census, Savannah, Chatham County, Georgia, digital image, Ancestry.com; SVAA, Moosmüller to Wimmer, November 10, 1880.

137. SVAA, Palmer to Wimmer, September 20, 1882.

138. SVAA, Fridolin and Reichert to Wimmer, November 28, 1880.

139. SVAA, Palmer to Wimmer, September 20, 1882.

140. SVAA, Canonge to Wimmer, November 28, 1880.

141. And, in doing so, Rhabanus would be joining some of the original religious from Bergier's Isle of Hope mission. SVAA, Rhabanus to Wimmer, November 28, 1880.

142. Oetgen, "Oswald Moosmüller," 26–35.

143. 1900 United States Census, Savannah, Chatham County, Georgia, digital image, Ancestry.com.

144. 1911 Census of Canada, digital image, s.v. "Rhabanus Canonge," Ancestry; Rhabanus Canonge, grave marker, Saint Peters Abbey Cemetery, Muenster, Prince Albert Census Division, Saskatchewan, Canada, digital image, s.v. "Rhabanus Canonge" Find a Grave; Davis, *History of Black Catholics*, 124.

145. SVAA, Moosmüller to Andrew Hintenach, July 8, 1878.

146. BMSA, Moosmüller to Wimmer, February 20, 1879.

147. SVAA, Mason to Wimmer, October 31, 1880.

148. SVAA, Mason to Wimmer, November 9, 1880.

149. SVAA, Mason to Wimmer, November 9, 1880.

150. SVAA, Mason to Wimmer, November 9, 1880.

151. SVAA, Mason to Wimmer, November 9, 1880.

152. Davis, *History of Black Catholics*, 292.

153. SVAA, Mason to Wimmer, November 9, 1880.

154. SVAA, Mason to Wimmer, November 9, 1880.

155. SVAA, Mason to Wimmer, November 9, 1880.

156. BMSA, Moosmüller to Wimmer, May 15, 1884.

157. Davis, *History of Black Catholics*, 124.

158. SVAA, Reichert to Wimmer, October 31, 1880.

159. Wimmer, *Boniface Wimmer*, 518.

160. Adams, "Dating Historical Sites," 59. The monastery-era ceramics have a mean ceramic date of 1828.7, leaving a fifty-year time lag, which is more than double what is considered typical.

161. A mean ceramic date of 1853.8 was calculated for the 1890s layers, but clearly a longer than expected time lag remains.

162. Adams, "Dating Historical Sites," 59.

163. BMSA, Moosmüller to Wimmer, November 22, 1878.

164. Oetgen, "Oswald Moosmüller," 16.

165. In the 1880s layers, shells numbered 567 compared to 58 fragments of bone. In the 1890s layers, shell numbered 198 to 26 fragments of bone. A full artifact catalog is available at Savannah Archaeological Alliance, Benedictine Monastery and Freedmen's School, https://savarchaeoalliance.files.wordpress.com/2018/06/appendix-b_monastery_final.pdf.

166. BMSA, Reichert to Wimmer, September 2, 1879.

167. SVAA, Moosmüller to Wimmer, January 12, 1881.

168. BMSA, Moosmüller to Wimmer, November 22, 1878.

169. BMSA, Moosmüller to Wimmer, October 12, 1878.

170. Mann, "Benedictine Missionaries," 41.

171. BMSA, Moosmüller to Wimmer, December 8, 1877.

172. BMSA, Moosmüller to Wimmer, July 9, 1879.

173. BMSA, Moosmüller to Wimmer, August 18, 1878.

174. BMSA, Moosmüller to Wimmer, August 18, 1878.

175. Moosmüller, *Ersabt*, 198.

176. BMSA, Moosmüller to Wimmer, August 18, 1878.

177. BMSA, Moosmüller to Wimmer, August 18, 1878.

178. BAA, Gross to Wimmer, March 14, 1877.

179. BMSA, Moosmüller to Wimmer, August 18, 1878.

180. BMSA, Moosmüller to Wimmer, August 18, 1878.

181. BMSA, Moosmüller to Wimmer, August 18, 1878.

182. BMSA, Moosmüller to Wimmer, August 18, 1878.

183. BMSA, Moosmüller to Wimmer, August 18, 1878.

184. BMSA, Moosmüller to Wimmer, November 22, 1878.

185. BMSA, Moosmüller to Wimmer, August 23, 1878.

186. SVAA, Moosmüller to Andrew Hintenach, July 8, 1878. A July 3, 1873, *Savannah Morning News* article stated the population was "nearly 1000 persons," but the estimator, Judge O'Byrne, was promoting a new road to the island and therefore would be inclined to overestimate in order to over-emphasize the need. By the time the Benedictines arrived, the island's population had decreased significantly from its post–Civil War height when Reverend Houston helped people settle the island and take advantage of Special Field Order No. 15.

187. Oetgen, "Oswald Moosmüller," 15. See chapter 1 for a discussion of Sherman's Field Order No. 15 and the postbellum occupation of Skidaway Island.

188. BMSA, Moosmüller to Wimmer, April 18, 1884; Moosmüller, *Ersabt Bonifaz Wimmer*, 197–98.

189. BMSA, Moosmüller to Wimmer, September 30, 1878, Digital Library of Georgia, original spellings retained. At the bottom of the list, Father Moosmüller added, "Dan Sullivan, Scholastic at St. Vincents is to be considered as belonging to this house also."

190. 1880 United States Census, Savannah, Chatham County, Georgia, digital image, Ancestry.

191. "Savannah, Georgia Vital Records, 1803–1966," s.v. "Abraham Jackson," Ancestry, 1870 United States Census, Savannah, Chatham County, Georgia, digital image, Ancestry.com.

192. 1880 United States Census, Savannah, Chatham County, Georgia, digital image, Ancestry.com.

193. Williams, *Self-Taught*, 142–43.

194. Moosmüller, *Ersabt Bonifaz Wimmer*, 197–200.

195. Oetgen, "Oswald Moosmüller," 16; SVAA, Moosmüller to Zilliox, September 15, 1878.

196. Gibb and Beisaw, "Learning Cast Up."

197. Baxter, *Archaeology of American Childhood*, 102.

198. Rotman, "Rural Education," 80.

199. Agbe-Davies, "Archaeology of the Old Elliot School," 137.

200. Baxter, *Archaeology of American Childhood*, 109.

201. Oetgen, "Origins of the Benedictine Order," 173–75.

202. BMSA, Moosmüller to Wimmer, November 22, 1878.

203. BMSA, Moosmüller to Wimmer, November 22, 1878.

204. Butchart, *Schooling the Freed People*, 130–131.

205. Oetgen, "Origins of the Benedictine Order," 175.

206. Williams, *Self-Taught*, 162.

207. BMSA, Moosmüller to Wimmer, November 22, 1878.

208. BMSA, Moosmüller to Wimmer, January 17, 1879.

209. Williams, *Self-Taught*, 152.

210. Joseph Opala, email to author, June 14, 2023.

211. BMSA, Moosmüller to Wimmer, September 6, 1878.

212. BMSA, Moosmüller to Wimmer, December 31, 1878.

213. Oetgen, "Origins of the Benedictine Order," 172–74; Oetgen, *American Abbott*, 348; Oetgen, *Mission to America*, 163–64; BMSA, Moosmüller to Wimmer, January 17, 1879.

214. BMSA, Moosmüller to Wimmer, February 15, 1879.

215. BMSA, Moosmüller to Wimmer, November 27, 1878.

216. BMSA, Reichert to Wimmer, September 2, 1879.

217. BMSA, Moosmüller to Wimmer, November 28, 1879.

218. BMSA, Moosmüller to Wimmer, November 28, 1879.

219. BMSA, Moosmüller to Wimmer, February 7, 1879.

220. BMSA, Moosmüller to Wimmer, February 15, 1879.

221. BMSA, Moosmüller to Wimmer, February 15, 1879.

222. BMSA, Moosmüller to Wimmer, July 12, 1879.

223. BMSA, Moosmüller to Wimmer, July 12, 1879.

224. BMSA, Moosmüller to Innocent Wolf, December 21, 1877.

225. BMSA, Moosmüller to Wimmer, July 12, 1879.

226. BMSA, Moosmüller to Wimmer, July 12, 1879.

227. Wimmer, *Boniface Wimmer*, 486–87.

228. Moosmüller, *Ersabt Bonifaz Wimmer*, 198.

229. BMSA, Moosmüller to Wimmer, July 12, 1879.

230. BMSA, Moosmüller to Wimmer, July 12, 1879.

231. GHS, MS 1349, Box 27, Folder 400.

232. BMSA, Moosmüller to Wimmer, February 7, 1879.

233. BMSA, Moosmüller to Wimmer, December 9, 1878.

234. Oetgen, "Oswald Moosmüller," 18.

235. BMSA, Moosmüller to Wimmer, December 9, 1878.

236. Father Andrew Campbell O.S.B., in-person communication, Savannah, Georgia, January 2017.

237. Murray and Howland, "Improved Argand-Lamp."

238. Sandwell, "Coal-Oil Lamp," 193.

239. Weisbuch, "Historical Perspective."

240. SVAA, Mason to Wimmer, November 9, 1880.

241. Sandwell, "Coal-Oil Lamp," 191, 200–201; Thuro, *Oil Lamps*, 4–5.

242. Moosmüller, *Ersabt Bonifaz Wimmer*, 197–98.

243. BMSA, SIH-BO Collection, Warranty Deed Folder 2.

244. BMSA, SIH-HI Collection, Moosmüller to Beasley, August 21, 1891.

245. "A New Church," *Savannah Morning News*, December 13, 1880, Digital Library of Georgia.

246. SVAA, Wimmer to Abbot, May 23, 1883.

247. SVAA, Wimmer to Utto Lang, June 8, 1883.

248. BMSA, SIH-HI Collection, Moosmüller to Beasley, August 21, 1891.

249. SVAA, "Centennial Committee of Sacred Heart Parish," 3–4.

250. *Sadliers' Catholic Directory*, 1884; *Hoffman's Catholic Directory*, 1897.

251. Wimmer, *Boniface Wimmer*, 518; BMSA, Moosmüller to Wimmer, June 5, 1883.

252. Oetgen, "Origins of the Benedictine Order," 177.

253. SVAA, Moosmüller to Wimmer, September 29, 1885.

254. BMSA, Moosmüller to Wimmer, November 29, 1886.

255. BMSA, Moosmüller to Wimmer, November 29, 1886.

CHAPTER 4. EXPANDING THE BENEDICTINE MISSION

1. BMSA, Reichert to Wimmer, September 2, 1879.

2. Gamble, *Georgia Miscellany*, 84.

3. BMSA, Moosmüller to Wimmer, November 28, 1879.

4. Costello et al., "Luck of Third Street"; Delaunay, "Disarticulation of Aónikenk Hunter-Gatherer Lifeways."

5. Wettstaed, "Perspectives"; Brandon, "Reversing the Narrative"; Monica L. Smith, "Archaeology of a 'Destroyed' Site."

6. Gindick, *Harmonica Americana*, 17; Krampert, *Encyclopedia of the Harmonica*, 231.

7. Field, *Harmonicas, Harps, and Heavy Breathers*, 24–25; Krampert, *Encyclopedia of the Harmonica*, 215, 253.

8. Krampert, *Encyclopedia of the Harmonica*, 9–11, 123–24; Field, *Harmonicas, Harps, and Heavy Breathers*, 23–34; Gindick, *Harmonica Americana*, 22–23.

9. Krampert, *Encyclopedia of the Harmonica*, 95.

10. BMSA, Moosmüller to Wimmer, December 31, 1878.

11. BMSA, Moosmüller to Wimmer, January 17, 1879.

12. SVAA, Skidaway boys to Wimmer, December 27, 1880.

13. Cimbala, "Black Musicians," 15.

14. Cimbala, "Black Musicians," 15–20.

15. Cimbala, "Black Musicians," 20.

16. Cimbala, "Black Musicians," 21.

17. Cimbala, "Black Musicians," 22–25.

18. SVAA, Moosmüller to Hintenach, October 7, 1878.

19. SVAA, Moosmüller to Wimmer, January 12, 1881.

20. SVAA, Reichert to Wimmer, February 27, 1884; Reichert to Wimmer, March 26, 1884.

21. SVAA, Reichert to Wimmer, November 11, 1883.

22. SVAA, Reichert to Wimmer, August 12, 1885; SVAA, Moosmüller to Wimmer, August 22, 1885.

23. SVAA, oral history; BAA B5 #1 Reminiscences; GHS, MS 1349, Box 27, Folder 400, Mayer to Donlon, October 25, 1893.

24. BMSA, Moosmüller to Wimmer, August 18, 1878.

25. SVAA, Moosmüller to Wimmer, September 15, 1878.

26. BMSA, Moosmüller to Wimmer, November 27, 1878.

27. SVAA, Reichert to Wimmer, n.d.; 1880 United States Census, Savannah, Chatham County, Georgia, digital image, Ancestry.

28. SVAA, Moosmüller to Wimmer, September 15, 1878; SVAA, Reichert to Wimmer, n.d.; SVAA, Haid to Wimmer, August 5, 1887.

29. BAA, Drawer 18, Folder 4, Haid to Wimmer, October 17, 1887.

30. SVAA, oral history; Belmont Abbey Cemetery, in-person visit, July 26, 2021.

31. Oetgen, "Origins of the Benedictine Order," 176; Oetgen, "Oswald Moosmüller," 17.

32. Oetgen, "Origins of the Benedictine Order," 176.

33. Lockhart, Serr, et al., "Dating Game," 2, 9.

34. Meyer, "Solomon's Strengthening & Invigorating Bitters."

35. SVAA, Boys at Skidaway School and Reichert to Wimmer, December 27, 1880.

36. SVAA, Boys at Skidaway School and Reichert to Wimmer.

37. Moosmüller, *Ersabt Bonifaz Wimmer*, 197–198; *Sadliers' Catholic Directory*, 1879–81, 1883–91, 1893–95; *Hoffman's Catholic Directory, Almanac and Clergy List*, 1892, 1896–1897, 1899, 1900.

38. Oetgen, "Origins of the Benedictine Order," 177–78; Kelly, *Short History of Skidaway Island*, 85.

39. SVAA, Wimmer to Lang, June 8, 1883.

40. SVAA, Wimmer to Abbot, May 23, 1883.

41. SVAA, Reichert to Wimmer, September 8 and 11, 1883.

42. As of January 1968, the cross was at Saint Vincent Archabbey in the possession of Abbot Egbert, at which time it was photographed. SVAA, Skidaway File.

43. BAA, Drawer 18, Folder 5, Haid to Wimmer, September 15, 1885.

44. BAA, Drawer 18, Folder 5, Haid to Wimmer, October 1, 1885.

45. BAA, Drawer 18, Folder 4, Haid to Wimmer, February 11, 1886.

46. BAA, Drawer 18, Folder 4, Haid to Wimmer, January 13, 1886; BAA, Drawer 18, Folder 4, Haid to Wimmer, February 26, 1886.

47. SVAA, Skidaway File, oral history.

48. 1870 United States Census, Savannah, Chatham County, Georgia, digital image, Ancestry.com; 1880 United States Census, Savannah, Chatham County, Georgia, digital image, Ancestry.com; 1900 United States Census, Savannah, Chatham County, Georgia, digital image, Ancestry.com; 1910 United States Census, Savannah, Chatham County, Georgia, digital image, Ancestry.com; 1920 United States Census, Savannah, Chatham County, Georgia, digital image, Ancestry.com; 1930 United States Census, Savannah, Chatham County, Georgia, digital image, Ancestry.com.

49. BAA, B5, Folder 1, Archival Materials.

50. BAA, "Chronological Data of Belmont Abbey" (unpublished manuscript).

51. BAA, Irwin to Bernard, March 8, 1928; BAA, F.I.R to Father Bernard, March 24, 1928.

52. BAA, Irwin to Bernard, March 8, 1928; BAA, "Chronological Data of Belmont Abbey."

53. "New York, Passenger and Crew Lists (Including Castle Garden and Ellis Island), 1820–1957," s.v. "Daniel Hefti," Ancestry; SVAA, Reichert to Wimmer, December 7, 1883.

54. "U.S., School Catalogs, 1765–1935," s.v. "Daniel Hefti," Ancestry.

55. SVAA, Reichert to Wimmer, October 7, 1883.

56. Quoted in Oetgen, "Origins of the Benedictine Order," 178.

57. Daniel Hefte, grave marker, Belmont Abbey Cemetery, Belmont, Gaston County, North Carolina, digital image, s.v. "Daniel Hefti," Find a Grave. A 1938 letter from Joseph D. Mitchell to Thomas Gamble also mentions an "old cemetery at Skidaway alongside the ruins of the old monastery" (Gamble, "Georgia Miscellany," 80). No associated cemetery has been found archaeologically.

58. SVAA, Wimmer to Kecarnik, December 16, 1883.

59. BMSA, Moosmüller to Wimmer, June 2, 1877.

60. BMSA, Moosmüller to Wimmer, August 17, 1877.

61. BMSA, Moosmüller to Wimmer, November 28, 1879.

62. Cimbala, *Under the Guardianship*, 207.

63. Cimbala, 204, 207–8.

64. Morris, "Materialities of Homeplace," 34–35.

65. Morris, 36.

66. BMSA, Moosmüller to Wimmer, January 4, 1884.

67. BMSA, Moosmüller to Wimmer, January 4, 1884.

68. SVAA, Reichert to Wimmer, December 8, 1883.

69. SVAA, Reichert to Wimmer, February 17, 1886.

70. SVAA, Reichert to Wimmer, January 2, 1884.

71. BMSA, Moosmüller to Wimmer, January 15, 1884.

72. BMSA, Moosmüller to Wimmer, February 25, 1884.

73. BMSA, Moosmüller to Wimmer, February 25, 1884.

74. SVAA, Reichert to Wimmer, April 6, 1884.

75. BMSA, Moosmüller to Wimmer, May 15, 1884.

76. BMSA, Moosmüller to Wimmer, May 15, 1884.

77. BMSA, Moosmüller to Wimmer, May 15, 1884.

78. BMSA, Moosmüller to Wimmer, May 27, 1884.

79. BMSA, Moosmüller to Wimmer, May 27, 1884.

80. BMSA, Moosmüller to Wimmer, May 27, 1884.

81. Oetgen, "Origins of the Benedictine Order," 178.

82. 1860 United States Census, Savannah, Chatham County, Georgia, digital image, Ancestry.com; 1870 United States Census, Savannah, Chatham County, Georgia, digital image, Ancestry.com; 1880 United States Census, Savannah, Chatham County, Georgia, digital image, Ancestry.com; 1900 United States Census, Savannah, Chatham County, Georgia, digital image, Ancestry.

83. "Chinamen Happy after Long Wait: American Widow Marries Baltimore Celestial Who Persists," *Baltimore Evening Post*, July 27, 1912; "Abbot Gasquet a Guest, Noted Benedictine Pays Visit to Rev. Alexius Grass," *Baltimore Sun*, September 12, 1913; "New Rector of Holy Martyrs," *Baltimore American*, September 14, 1909, Genealogy Bank; Oetgen, *Mission to America*, 240.

84. Pennsylvania (State) Death certificates, 1906–1968, Series 11.90, Records of the Pennsylvania Department of Health, Record Group 11, Pennsylvania Historical and Museum Commission, Harrisburg, Pennsylvania, digital image, s.v. "Alexius Grass," Ancestry; Alexius Grass, grave marker, Saint Vincent Cemetery, Unity Township, Westmoreland County, Pennsylvania, digital image, s.v. "Alexius Grass," Find a Grave; Oetgen, *Mission to America*, 277.

85. Wimmer, "Letters of Boniface Wimmer," 518; SVAA, Wimmer to Braunmüller, October 9, 1884.

86. SVAA, Reichert to Wimmer, August 12, 1885.

87. SVAA, Moosmüller to Wimmer, August 22, 1885.

88. 1900 United States Census, Savannah, Chatham County, Georgia, digital image, Ancestry.com.

89. "Vespers at the Monastery," *Savannah Morning News*, July 21, 1884, Digital Library of Georgia.

90. SVAA, Reichert to Wimmer, March 26, 1884.

91. Mensing, "Rise and Fall," 319–20; BMSA, Moosmüller to Wimmer, May 13, 1887.

92. SVAA, Dominick to Wimmer, December 1, 1884; SVAA, Dominick to Wimmer, January 31, 1885.

93. There are multiple sources describing the women's begging attempts, all of which are relatively similar. These sources are all white men; the abbess never wrote about their financial adventures (or the letters have not survived). The men were outraged and emotional over the women's behavior, and therefore I suspect some or all of the authors exaggerated their accounts.

94. Mensing, "Rise and Fall," 321–24.

95. BAA, Haid to Wimmer, July 29, 1887.

96. BMSA, Moosmüller to Wimmer, May 13, 1887.

97. BAA, A 1.0 Folder 1.

98. BAA, Haid to Wimmer, August 5, 1887.

99. Mensing, "Rise and Fall," 324–25; Davis, *History of Black Catholics*, 124–125; DSA, Gibbons to Becker, July 3, 1890.

100. Davis, *History of Black Catholics*, 292; BMSA, Moosmüller to Wimmer, May 13, 1887.

101. Gibbons and Griffin, *Mission Work among the Negroes*, 29.

102. DSA, Becker to Gibbons, n.d.

103. DSA, Becker to Gibbons, n.d.

104. DSA, Becker to Gibbons, n.d.

105. BAA, Haid to Wimmer, August 5, 1887.

106. BAA, B5 Reminiscences #1, Oral Histories.

107. Oetgen, "Oswald Moosmüller," 19–21.

108. BAA, Wimmer to Lang, March 22, 1885.

109. BAA, Doris, "Belmont Abbey" (unpublished manuscript); BAA, B5, Folder 1.

110. BAA, Wimmer to Innocent Wolf, April 11, 1885.

111. Rippinger, *Benedictine Order*, 39–40.

112. BAA, Drawer 18, Folder 5, Haid to Wimmer, October 13, 1885; BAA, Drawer 18, Folder 5, Haid to Wimmer, September 7, 1885.

113. BMSA, Moosmüller to Wimmer, July 15, 1885.

114. BAA, Creagh to Wimmer, April 15, 1884.

115. BAA, B5, Folder 1, Creagh to Herman Wolf, February 6, 1878.

116. BMSA, Moosmüller to Wimmer, August 22, 1885.

117. BMSA, Moosmüller to Wimmer, August 22, 1885.

118. BMSA, Moosmüller to Wimmer, August 22, 1885.

119. BMSA, Moosmüller to Wimmer, August 22, 1885.

120. Rippinger, *Benedictine Order*, 40.

121. BMSA, Moosmüller to Wimmer, September 23, 1885.

122. BMSA, Moosmüller to Wimmer, September 23, 1885.

123. BMSA, Moosmüller to Wimmer, September 29, 1885.

124. Baumstein, *My Lord of Belmont*, 59–60.

125. BAA, Drawer 18, Folder 4, Haid to Wimmer, July 18, 1886.

126. BAA, Drawer 18, Folder 4, Haid to Wimmer, August 25, 1886.

127. BAA, Drawer 18, Folder 4, Haid to Wimmer, July 23, 1887.

128. BAA, Drawer 18, Folder 4, Haid to Wimmer, July 23, 1887.

129. BAA, Drawer 18, Folder 4, Haid to Wimmer, July 23, 1887; BAA, Drawer 18, Folder 4, Haid to Wimmer, January 6, 1887; BAA, Drawer 18, Folder 4, Haid to Wimmer, October 17, 1887. Despite Abbot Haid having full control of the Savannah missions after Moosmüller left, he still received help, including staff, from Saint Vincent. Brother Matthias, who had been assigned as Skidaway's cook, stopped at Mary Help Abbey on his way to Skidaway Island in January 1887. Haid traveled with Brother Matthias to Skidaway.

130. BAA, Drawer 18, Folder 4, Haid to Wimmer, August 5, 1887.

131. BAA, Drawer 18, Folder 4, Haid to Wimmer, July 29, 1887.

132. Oetgen, "Oswald Moosmuller," 21.

133. SVAA, Wimmer to Archbishop, August 27, 1877.

134. SVAA, Wimmer to Lang, June 8, 1883.

135. Wimmer, "Letters of Boniface Wimmer," 518; SVAA, Wimmer to Smith, April 1885.

136. SVAA, Wimmer to Amberger, January 15, 1886.

137. "Board Commissioners: An Interesting Meeting," *Savannah Morning News*, July 3, 1873; SVAA, Moosmüller to Hintenach, July 8, 1878.

138. Dietler, Gibson, and Vargas, "'Mourning Dirge Was Sung,'" 62.

139. BMSA, Moosmüller to Wimmer, May 24, 1887.

140. BMSA, Moosmüller to Wimmer, May 13, 1887.

141. BMSA, Box VGS PR4, HI, VA.

142. BAA, Moosmüller to Wimmer, July 27, 1886.

143. DSA, Moosmüller to Wimmer, May 24, 1887, original at SVAA.

144. BMSA, Box CBS/DC12–20/HII–3/PRII–4.

145. BAA, B5, Folder 1, Archival Materials.

146. "For St. Benedict's Chapel," *Savannah Morning News*, January 24, 1888, Digital Library of Georgia.

147. "Bishop Becker and the Colored Catholics," *Savannah Tribune*, July 13, 1889.

148. "For St. Benedict's Chapel," *Savannah Morning News*, January 24, 1888.

149. "Orphan's Concert," *Savannah Tribune*, June 2, 1888, Digital Library of Georgia; "The St. Benedict's Church: The Edifice Completed and to Be Dedicated," *Savannah Tribune*, November 30, 1889, NewsBank.

150. Hoskins, *Yet with a Steady*, 64; "Dedicated to God," *Savannah Morning News*,

December 9, 1889, Digital Library of Georgia; "St. Benedict's Church," *Savannah Tribune*, November 30, 1889.

151. "The St. Benedict's Church Dedicated," *Savannah Tribune*, December 14, 1889, NewsBank.

152. "The Catholic Church," *Savannah Tribune*, October 3, 1914, NewsBank.

153. "St. Benedict's Church," *Savannah Tribune*, November 30, 1889.

154. *Sadliers' Catholic Directory*, 1889; *Hoffman's Catholic Directory*, 1890; Sanborn Map & Publishing Co., *Insurance Maps of Savannah, Georgia, 1888*, Digital Library of Georgia, https://dlg.usg.edu/record/dlg_sanb_savannah-1888#item.

155. McDonogh, *Black and Catholic*, 153.

156. BAA, Box A1.0, Folder 1, Board Meeting Minutes, January 5, 1891; BAA, Drawer B18, Folder 16; BAA, Drawer B18, Folder 9; *Sadliers' Catholic Directory*, 1890–91, 1893; *Hoffman's Catholic Directory*, 1897, 1899, 1905.

157. BAA, Drawer B18, Folder 9, Haid to Wimmer, November 6, 1888.

158. BAA, Drawer 18, Folder 9, Haid to Wimmer, April 8, 1889.

159. BAA, Drawer 18, Folder 4, Haid to Wimmer, September 6, 1886; Baumstein, *My Lord*, 43.

160. BAA, Drawer 18, Folder 4, Haid to Wimmer, September 6, 1886.

161. *Savannah Morning News*, September 30, 1863; *Savannah Daily Herald*, January 5, 1866, Digital Library of Georgia.

162. *Savannah Republican*, March 21, 1865, Digital Library of Georgia.

163. "Educator of Slave Children," Georgia Historical Society, https://georgiahistory .com/education-outreach/online-exhibits/featured-historical-figures/mother-mathilda -beasley/educator-of-slave-children (no longer a working link); Jung, "Mother Mathilda Beasley"; Wells-Bacon, "Life of Mathilda Beasley," 1–3; *Savannah Morning News*, September 4, 1877, GHS, MS1349, Box 27, Folder 400.

164. Davis, *History of Black Catholics*, 110.

165. BMSA, SIH-HI, Moosmüller to Beasley, August 21, 1891; Jung, "Mother Mathilda Beasley"; Wells-Bacon, "Life of Mathilda Beasley," 3–4.

166. BMSA, SIH-HI, Moosmüller to Beasley, August 21, 1891. Mother Dominick, the Poor Clares Abbess, addressed her January 31, 1885, letter from "The Colored Orphanage near the Church of the Sacred Heart, Savannah Georgia." So apparently, an orphanage in some form was in existence prior to 1887. SVAA, O'Neill to Wimmer, January 31, 1885.

167. McDonogh, *Black and Catholic*, 106.

168. DSA, hand-drawn map; Sanborn Map & Publishing Co., *Insurance Maps of Savannah, Georgia, 1888*; Sanborn-Perris Map Co., *Insurance Maps of Savannah, Georgia, 1898*, Digital Library of Georgia, https://dlg.usg.edu/recorddlg_sanb_savannah-1898#item.

169. "Died at the Altar," *Savannah Morning News*, December 21, 1903, Digital Library of Georgia.

170. DSA, Moosmüller to Wimmer, May 24, 1887, original at SVAA.

171. DSA, Moosmüller to Wimmer, May 24, 1887; Sanborn Map & Publishing Co., *Insurance Maps of Savannah, Georgia, 1888.*

172. DSA, Beasley to Elizabeth Drexel, March 26, 1889, original at Catholic Historical Research Center of the Archdiocese of Philadelphia.

173. DSA, Beasley to Drexel, March 26, 1889.

174. Davis, *History of Black Catholics*, 111; *Sadliers' Catholic Directory*, 1890–91, 1893; *Hoffman's Catholic Directory*, 1897, 1899; Sanborn Map & Publishing Co., *Insurance Maps of Savannah, Georgia, 1888.*

175. Williams, *Subversive Habits*, 54.

176. DSA, "Annals of the Sisters of the Blessed Sacrament," 1893.

177. Williams, *Subversive Habits*, 53–55.

178. "Georgia Catholics Rejoice," *Southern Cross*, November 17, 1988.

179. DSA, Beasley to Gibbons, August 24, 1893.

180. DSA, Beasley to Slattery, July 16, 1897.

181. DSA, Slattery to Harty, April 9, 1897; DSA, "Missionary Work 1910," 15–31.

182. Wells-Bacon, "Life of Mathilda Beasley," 4–5.

183. DSA, Beasley to Katharine Drexel, December 18, 1894, original at Catholic Historical Research Center of the Archdiocese of Philadelphia.

184. "Set Fire," *Savannah Morning News*, February 13, 1895, Digital Library of Georgia.

185. "Set Fire," *Savannah Morning News*, February 13, 1895, Digital Library of Georgia.

186. *Savannah Morning News*, March 17, 1895.

187. "Set on Fire Again," *Savannah Morning News*, March 3, 1895.

188. Baxter, *Archaeology of American Childhood*, 47–49.

189. Baxter, 49.

190. Baxter, 49–50.

191. Baxter, 117–18.

192. Baxter, , 117–18.

193. BMSA, Moosmüller to Beasley, August 21, 1891.

194. "Died at the Altar," *Savannah Morning News*, December 21, 1903, Digital Library of Georgia; "Clasped Virgin," *Atlanta Constitution*, December 21, 1903.

195. DSA, Beasley to Katharine Drexel, December 18, 1894.

196. DSA, Agreement, November 16, 1895, original in Catholic Historical Research Center of the Archdiocese of Philadelphia.

197. Sanborn-Perris Map Co., *Insurance Maps of Savannah, Georgia, 1898*, Digital Library of Georgia, *https://dlg.usg.edu/record/dlg_sanb_savannah-1898#item.*

198. DSA, Agreement, April 1904, original in Catholic Historical Research Center of the Archdiocese of Philadelphia.

199. DSA, Beasley to Slattery, May 24, 1898.

200. The last of Mother Beasley's order, Sister Francis, died in 1910. "St. Benedict's," *Savannah Tribune*, April 9, 1910, Newsbank.

201. DSA, Beasley to Slattery, May 24, 1898; DSA, Benignus to Keyes, September 10, 1927.

202. DSA, Beasley to Slattery, May 24, 1898.

203. Wells-Bacon, "Life of Mathilda Beasley," 6–7; Davis, *History of Black Catholics*, 113; Hoskins, *Yet with a Steady Beat*, 167; McDonogh, *Black and Catholic*, 106–107.

204. "Died at the Altar," *Savannah Morning News*, December 21, 1903. Her obituary in the *Atlanta Constitution* stated she was six feet, four inches in height. This extreme height is likely an exaggeration, but she was apparently quite a striking figure ("Clasped Virgin," *Atlanta Constitution*, December 21, 1903).

205. Wells-Bacon, "Life of Mathilda Beasley," 8.

206. BAA, Cafferty to Wimmer, February 26, 1886.

207. BAA, Cafferty to Wimmer, February 26, 1886.

208. BAA, Cafferty to Wimmer, February 26, 1886.

209. BAA, Drawer 18, Folder 9, Haid to Wimmer, February 19, 1889.

210. GHS, MS 1349, Box 27, Folder 400.

211. BAA, Drawer A 1.0, Folder #7, Savannah Apostolate—Financials.

212. 1880 United States Census, Savannah, Chatham County, Georgia, digital image, Ancestry.com; 1900 United States Census, Savannah, Chatham County, Georgia, digital image, Ancestry. These statistics assume the census data is representative of the island's whole population.

213. The Pray family remained on Skidaway Island until the early 1900s but moved to Savannah before 1910 when a widowed Sarah Pray was living with her two surviving children. Sarah was a laundress, and her boys, age seventeen and fifteen, were working as a laborer for a cotton factory and a grocery store porter. All were literate. They lived next door to Sarah's brother Joseph Bacon and his family.

214. Blount, "Coastal Refugees," 293–94, 307.

215. See chapter 2 for a discussion of this topic.

216. Davis, *History of Black Catholics*, 81.

217. "Funeral Invitations," *Savannah Morning News*, December 4, 1875, Digital Library of Georgia; *Savannah Tribune*, February 23, 1901, NewsBank.

218. Penny Clarke Johnson, "Second Class," 19, 39, 41. Cuyler Street School, built in 1913, offered a junior high school and later was a high school. The Florance Street School was built in 1930.

219. Lindbergh, "Buttoning Down Archaeology," 52.

220. Sprague, "China or Prosser Button Identification," 111, 124.

221. Lamm et al., *Guidelines for Collecting China Buttons*.

222. Typically men's clothing had more fasteners overall. Men usually had only Prosser buttons on their shirts; women were more likely to have many Prosser buttons, although hooks and eyes were very common on women's clothing. This period was also a time of great changes in men's and women's clothing. Between 1885 and 1917, the availability of

cheaper women's ready-made clothing greatly increased. Men's shirts were pulled overhead (with one to three buttons at the upper chest) until the late 1890s, when the shirts became fully buttoned-up, "coat front shirts." Prosser buttons were very common as shirt closures. Because of these changes to clothing styles, between 1890 and 1910 there was a big increase in button demand. Franklin, "Gender, Clothing Fasteners," 8, 14–15, 20; Classen, "Freshwater Pearl Buttons," 66.

223. Brother Tim Brown, Benedictine Military School, email message to author, 2017.

224. Franklin, "Gender, Clothing Fasteners," 556–62, 568–71, 575.

225. Classen, "Useful Shellfish," 5; Classen, "Freshwater Pearl Buttons," 67; Lindbergh, "Buttoning Down Archaeology," 51.

226. Wilkie, "Archaeological Evidence."

227. Wall, "Examining Gender, Class, and Ethnicity"; Rotman, "Domestic Ideals and Lived Realities."

228. Spencer-Wood, "Diversity."

229. Litts, *Collector's Encyclopedia*, 8; Ross, "Late-Nineteenth- and Early-Twentieth-Century."

230. Schiffer, *Japanese Export Ceramics*, 9–11; Litts, *Collector's Encyclopedia*, 10.

231. Litts, *Collector's Encyclopedia*, 11.

232. Schiffer, *Japanese Export Ceramics*, 9–11.

233. Litts, *Collector's Encyclopedia*, 11, 16, 28–29.

234. Litts, 41.

235. Schiffer, *Japanese Export Ceramics*, 9–11; Mullins, "Racializing the Parlor," 169–74.

236. Weaver, *Other Side of Sandpoint*, 76.

237. Weaver, 76.

238. Weaver, 74–76.

239. Mullins, "Racializing the Parlor," 175.

240. Martin Seibert, "Hidden in Plain View," 111–32.

241. BAA, A 1.0 Folder 1.

242. 1900 United States Census, Savannah, Chatham County, Georgia, digital image, Ancestry.com; New Jersey State Census, 1905, Jersey City, Hudson County, digital image, Ancestry; New Jersey State Census, 1910, Jersey City, Hudson County, digital image, Ancestry.

243. Kelly, *Short History of Skidaway Island*, 86; Chatham County Deeds 9E 162, Chatham County Courthouse; 1900 Federal Census via Ancestry.

244. Gamble, "Georgia Miscellany."

245. Kelly, *Short History of Skidaway Island*, 86; *Savannah Morning News*, April 25, 1949, GHS, MS1349, Box 27, Folder 400.

246. "Ruins of Benedictines Monastery on Skidaway Recall Venture of 1859," *Savannah Evening Press*, March 29, 1945, GHS, MS 1349, Box 27, Folder 400.

247. Kelly, *Short History of Skidaway Island*, 86; Daniel T. Elliott and Holland, *Archae-

ological Survey of Priests Landing, 23–25; Charles M. Elmer, in-person communication, Chatham County, Georgia, September 2022.

248. BAA, Drawer A 1.0 Folder 1, Benedictine Society of Georgia.

249. Otto, "Public School System," vol. 2, 142.

250. Rippinger, *Benedictine Order*, 118.

251. The acronym SMA comes from the Latin name for the order, Societas Missionum ad Afros.

252. BAA, Drawer A 1.0 Folder 1, Keiley to Haid, December 11, 1906.

253. McDonogh, *Black and Catholic*, 106.

254. McDonogh, 107–9, 156, 158; DSA, "Mission Work," 1909.

255. DSA, "Mission Work," 1908.

256. "The St. Benedict's Church," *Savannah Tribune*, January 1, 1910, NewsBank. I found several isolated references to a graveyard associated with the mission church, but little mention of who was buried there. Father Daniel Hefti, who died on the island, was likely buried there but was later reinterred at Belmont Abbey. No evidence of a graveyard was found during our limited archaeology. Given the development surrounding the site (golf course, houses, roads), it is very likely the graveyard was destroyed.

257. "St. Benedict's Church," *Savannah Tribune*, January 1, 1910.

258. McDonogh, *Black and Catholic*, 97, 111–19.

259. McDonogh, 245.

260. Hull and Douglass, *Forging Communities*, 52.

261. BAA, Drawer 18, Folder 4, Haid to Wimmer, August 30, 1886.

262. McDonogh, *Black and Catholic*, 263.

263. Newman, "Diocese of Savannah," 293, 299.

264. Newman, 307–10.

265. McDonogh, *Black and Catholic*, 97–98, 119.

266. Newman, "Diocese of Savannah," 310.

267. McDonogh, *Black and Catholic*, 185, 188.

268. McDonogh, 204–5.

269. McDonogh, 301.

270. Moosmüller, *Ersabt Bonifaz Wimmer*, 198.

271. McDonogh, *Black and Catholic*, 38–39.

CHAPTER 5. MISSION ACCOMPLISHED?

1. GHS, MS 1349 Box 27, Folder 400, Mayer to Donlon, October 25, 1893. Mayer was complaining about the Benedictines' 104-acre property in Sandfly, Georgia, that was mired in questions over who owned the deed and who controlled the property. Sandfly is a small community on the southeast border of Savannah and only a few miles from Skidaway Island.

2. Davis, *History of Black Catholics*, 123.

3. Baxter, *Archaeology of American Childhood*, 95.

4. Rippinger, *Benedictine Order*, 117.

5. Melchior Reichert, Belmont Abbey Cemetery, Belmont, Gaston County, North Carolina, digital image, s.v. "Melchior Reichert," *FindaGrave.com*.

6. BMSA, Moosmüller to Wimmer, August 23, 1878; Oetgen, "Oswald Moosmüller," 14–15.

7. Oetgen, *Mission to America*, 163–64; BMSA, Moosmüller to Wimmer, August 18, 1878.

8. BMSA, Box VGS PR4, HI, VA.

9. Rippinger, *Benedictine Order*, 141.

10. Butchart, *Schooling the Freed People*, 8, 13, 106–8.

11. SVAA, Moosmüller to Zilliox, September 15, 1878.

12. SVAA, Moosmüller to Zilliox, September 15, 1878; Oetgen, "Oswald Moosmüller," 15.

13. I use the words "our" and "we" deliberately, as I have a child in the Savannah-Chatham County Public School System, and these issues are both personal and academic.

14. BAA, Drawer 18, Folder 9, Haid to Wimmer, February 19, 1889.

15. Butchart, *Schooling the Freed People*, 171.

16. Burton, *Penn Center*, 1–16, 20.

17. Burton, 16–21.

18. Burton, 25.

19. Burton, 24–25.

20. Burton, 26–43.

21. Towne, *Letters and Diary*.

22. 1880 United States Census, Savannah, Chatham County, Georgia, digital image, Ancestry.com.

23. 1900 United States Census, Savannah, Chatham County, Georgia, digital image, Ancestry.com; 18 percent of Black women and 20 percent of Black men on Skidaway Island could read and write; 25 percent of Black women and 23 percent of Black men could read but not write; 56 percent of Black women and men could neither read nor write.

24. Beach Institute African-American Cultural Center, "Timeline."

25. Rita Folse Elliott and Elliott, "Savannah Under Fire," 65–74.

26. These conversations were casual discussions over my years of doing public archaeology in Savannah, not specific research for this book. The descriptions given by different people on different occasions were too similar to dismiss as incorrect or exaggerations.

27. David G. Anderson et al., "Sea-Level Rise," 1.

28. This is in addition to Our Lady of Good Hope on Isle of Hope, which reopened in 1908.

Bibliography

ARCHIVES

Belmont Abbey Archive (BAA)

Benedictine Military School Archives (BMSA)

Diocese of Savannah, Archives and Records Department (DSA)

Fort Pulaski National Monument Archives (FOPU)

Georgia Historical Society (GHS)

    Eleanor Knorr Strain genealogical research materials, MS 1519

    Georgia Writers' Project, Savannah Unit research materials, MS 1355

    Joseph Frederick Waring II papers, MS 1275

    Walter Charlton Hartridge Jr. collection, MS 1349

Massie Heritage Center Archives (MHCA)

Saint Vincent Archabbey Archives (SVAA)

Savannah Chatham County Public School System, Board of Education Archives

    (SCCPSS BOE)

PUBLISHED MATERIALS AND UNPUBLISHED MANUSCRIPTS

Adams, William Hampton. "Dating Historical Sites: The Importance of Time Lag in the Acquisition, Curation, Use, and Disposal of Artifacts." *Historical Archaeology* 37, no. 2 (2003): 38–64.

———. "Machine Cut Nails and Wire Nails: American Production and Use for Dating 19th-Century and Early-20th-Century Sites." *Historical Archaeology* 36, no. 4 (December 2002): 66–88.

Agbe-Davies, Anna S. "Archaeology of the Old Elliot School." *Bermuda Journal of Archaeology and Maritime History* 13 (2002): 129–54.

Agbe-Davies, Anna S., and Kathryn Fay. *2013 Archaeology Report for 2008–2011: New Philadelphia Archaeology Project.* August 20, 2013. http://faculty.las.illinois.edu/cfennell /NP/2013ReportMenu.html.

Agbe-Davies, Anna S., and Claire Fuller Martin. "'Demanding a Share of Public Regard': African American Education at New Philadelphia, Illinois." *Transforming Anthropology* 21, no. 2 (October 2013): 103–21.

Alvord, J. W. *Letters from the South, Relating to the Condition of Freedmen, Addressed to Major General O. O. Howard, Commissioner Bureau R., F., and A. L.* Washington, D.C.: Howard University Press, 1870. https://americanantiquarian.org/Freedmen /Manuscripts/lettersfromsouth.html.

Anderson, David G, Thaddeus G. Bissett, Stephen J. Yerka, Joshua J. Wells, Eric C. Kansa, Sarah W. Kansa, Kelsey Noack Myers, et al. "Sea-Level Rise and Archaeological Site Destruction: An Example from the Southeastern United States Using DINAA (Digital Index of North American Archaeology)." *PLoS ONE* 12, no. 11 (2017). https://doi .org/10.1371/journal.pone.0188142.

Anderson, James D. *The Education of Blacks in the South, 1860–1935*. Chapel Hill: University of North Carolina Press, 1988.

Babits, Lawrence E. "Report on Preliminary Investigations at the Monastery Site (09CHAS901), Skidaway Island, Chatham County, Georgia." Armstrong State College, 1990.

Barnum, Matt. "In Female-Dominated Education Field, Women Still Lag behind in Pay, according to Two New Studies." Chalkbeat, June 15, 2018. https://chalkbeat.org.

Baumstein, Paschal. *My Lord of Belmont: A Biography of Leo Haid*. Belmont, N.C.: Herald House, 1985.

Baxter, Jane Eva. *The Archaeology of American Childhood and Adolescence*. Gainesville: University Press of Florida, 2019.

Beach Institute African-American Cultural Center. "Timeline." https://www .beachinstitute.org/timeline.

Beard, Rick. "A Promise Betrayed: Reconstruction Policies Prevented Freedmen from Realizing the American Dream." *Civil War Times,* June 2017, 44–51.

Beisaw, April. "Below the Boards: The Taphonomy of Subfloor Assemblages." Paper Presented at 2004 Annual Meeting of the Society for American Archaeology, Montreal, Que., 2004.

Berry, Daina Ramey, and Leslie M. Harris. *Slavery and Freedom in Savannah*. Athens: University of Georgia Press, 2014.

Betti, Colleen. "Archaeology Is Revealing Important Clues about Woodville School." Fairfield Foundation, April 7, 2021. https://fairfieldfoundation.org/archaeology-is -revealing-important-clues-about-woodville-school.

———. "Gloucester's Public School Past: Archaeology and Artifact Update!" Fairfield Foundation, December 9, 2020. https://fairfieldfoundation.org/_gloucesters-public -school-past-update.

Blassingame, John W. "Before the Ghetto: The Making of the Black Community in Savannah, Georgia, 1865–1880." *Journal of Social History* 6, no. 4 (Summer 1973): 463–88.

Blount, Ben G. "Coastal Refugees: Marginalization Of African-Americans in Marine Fisheries Of Georgia." *Urban Anthropology and Studies of Cultural Systems and World Economic Development* 29, no. 3 (Fall 2000): 285–313.

Bonner, James C., H. S. Shearouse, and T. E. Smith. *A History of Public Education in Georgia, 1734–1976*. Columbia: R. L. Bryan, 1979.

Brandon, Jamie C. "Reversing the Narrative of Hillbilly History: A Case Study Using Archaeology at Van Winkle's Mill in the Arkansas Ozarks." *Historical Archaeology* 47, no. 3 (September 2013): 36–51.

Brown, Gillian. *A People of Faith: A Brief History of Catholicism in South Georgia*. Savannah: Diocese of Savannah, Department of Christian Formation, 1978.

Bryant, Jonathan M. "'We Defy You!': Politics and Violence in Reconstruction Savannah." In *Slavery and Freedom in Savannah*, edited by Leslie M. Harris and Daina Ramey Berry, 140–60. Athens: University of Georgia Press, 2014.

Burton, Orville Vernon, and Wilbur Cross. *Penn Center: A History Preserved*. Athens: University of Georgia Press, 2014.

Butchart, Ronald E. *Schooling the Freed People: Teaching, Learning, and the Struggle for Black Freedom, 1861–1876*. Chapel Hill: University of North Carolina Press, 2010.

Butler, Cuthbert. *Benedictine Monachism: Studies in Benedictine Life and Rule*. Cambridge: Barnes and Noble, 1924.

Buttimer, Brendan J. "New South, New Church: The Catholic Public Schools of Georgia 1870–1917." Master's thesis, Armstrong Atlantic State University, 2001.

Cardwell, Kirstyn. "St. James Beverage Company." Student paper, Introduction to Archaeology, ANTH 3820. Armstrong Campus, Georgia Southern University, 2018.

Centennial Committee of Sacred Heart Parish. "A Brief History of Sacred Heart Parish, 1880–1980 in the City of Savannah, Georgia." Unpublished manuscript, Saint Vincent Archives, Skidaway Island Collection, 1981.

Cheney, David M. "Diocese of Savannah." The Hierarchy of the Catholic Church, Savannah, May 2, 2023. https://www.catholic-hierarchy.org/diocese/dsava.html.

"Chronological Data of Belmont Abbey." Unpublished manuscript, Belmont Abbey Archive, n.d.

Cimbala, Paul A. "Black Musicians from Slavery to Freedom: An Exploration of an African-American Folk Elite and Cultural Continuity in the Nineteenth-Century Rural South." *Journal of Negro History* 80, no. 1 (Winter 1995): 15–29.

———. *Under the Guardianship of the Nation: The Freedmen's Bureau and the Reconstruction of Georgia, 1865–1870*. Athens: University of Georgia Press, 1997.

Clark, Richard H., Thomas R. R. Cobb, David Irwin, George N. Lester, and Walter B. Hill. "1873 Irwin's Code, 2nd ed." Historical Georgia Digests and Codes, code 16, 1873. Digital Commons, School of Law, University of Georgia. https://digitalcommons.law .uga.edu/ga_code/16.

Classen, Cheryl. "Freshwater Pearl Buttons." *Historical Archaeology* 28, no. 2 (1994): 53–82.

———. "The Useful Shellfish." *Historical Archaeology* 28, no. 2 (1994): 2–8.

Coffin, Charles Carleton. *Four Years of Fighting: A Volume of Personal Observation with the Army and Navy from the First Battle of Bull Run to the Fall of Richmond*. Boston: Ticknor and Fields, 1866.

Costello, Julia G., Kevin Hallaran, Keith Warren, and Margie Akin. "The Luck of Third Street: Archaeology of Chinatown, San Bernardino, California." *Historical Archaeology* 42, no. 3 (September 2008): 136–51.

Davis, Cyprian, O.S.B. *The History of Black Catholics in the United States*. New York: Crossroad, 1990.

Delaunay, Amalia Nuevo. "Disarticulation of Aónikenk Hunter-Gatherer Lifeways during the Late Nineteenth and Early Twentieth Centuries: Two Case Studies from Argentinean Patagonia." *Historical Archaeology* 46, no. 3 (September 2012): 149–64.

DePratter, Chester B. *An Archaeological Survey of P. H. Lewis Property, Skidaway Island, Chatham County, Georgia*. Report no. 5604. Laboratory of Archaeology, University of Georgia, 1975.

Dietler, John, Heather Gibson, and Benjamin Vargas. "'A Mourning Dirge Was Sung': Community and Remembrance at Mission San Gabriel." In Hull and Douglass, *Forging Communities in Colonial Alta California*, 62–87.

Doris, Sebastian. "Belmont Abbey." Unpublished manuscript, Belmont Abbey Archives, n.d.

Dorsey, Allison. "'The Great Cry of Our People Is Land': Black Settlement and Community Development on Ossabaw Island, Georgia, 1865–1900." In *African American Life in the Georgia Lowcountry: The Atlantic World and the Gullah Geechee*, edited by Philip Morgan, 224–52. Athens: University of Georgia Press, 2010.

Douglass, John G., Kathleen L. Hull, and Seetha N. Reddy. "The Creation of Community in the Colonial Era Los Angeles Basin." In Hull and Douglass, *Forging Communities in Colonial Alta California*, 35–61.

Elliott, Daniel T., and Jeffrey L. Holland. *Archaeological Survey of Priests Landing, Skidaway Island, Georgia*. LAMAR Institute publication series report no. 86. Savannah: LAMAR Institute, 2006.

Elliott, Rita Folse, and Daniel T. Elliott. *Savannah under Fire, 1779: Expanding the Boundaries*. Prepared for the National Park Service, Kristen L. McMasters, Archeologist Planner and Grants Manager, Grant Agreement No. 2255-09-004. Savannah: Coastal Heritage Society, November 2011.

Espenshade, Christopher T., and Ramona Grunden. *Contraband, Refugee, Freedman: Archaeological and Historical Investigation of the Western Fringe of Mitchelville, Hilton Head, South Carolina*. Final report. Atlanta: Brockington and Associates, 1991.

Federal Writers' Project: Slave Narrative Project. Vol. 4, *Georgia*, part 1, *Adams-Furr*. Washington, D.C.; Library of Congress. https://loc.gov/item/mesn041.

Federal Writers' Project: Slave Narrative Project. Vol. 4, *Georgia*, part 2, *Garey-Jones*. Washington, D.C.: Library of Congress. https://loc.gov/item/mesn042.

Federal Writers' Project: Slave Narrative Project. Vol. 4, *Georgia*, part 3, *Kendricks-Styles*. Washington, D.C.; Library of Congress. https://loc.gov/item/mesn043.

Federal Writers' Project: Slave Narrative Project. Vol. 4, *Georgia*, part 4, *Telfair-Young (with Combined Interviews of Others)*. Washington, D.C.: Library of Congress. https://loc.gov/item/mesn044.

Fellner, Felix, O.S.B. "Abbot Boniface and His Monks." Vol. 4. Unpublished manuscript, Saint Vincent Archabbey Archives, n.d.

Field, Kim. *Harmonicas, Harps, and Heavy Breathers: The Evolution of the People's Instrument*. New York: Cooper Square Press, 2000.

Franklin, Maria. "Gender, Clothing Fasteners, and Dress Practices in Houston's Freedmen's Town, ca. 1880–1904." *Historical Archaeology* 54 (2020): 556–80.

Fraser, Walter J. *Lowcountry Hurricanes: Three Centuries of Storms at Sea and Ashore.* Wormsloe Foundation Publication. Athens: University of Georgia Press, 2006.

———. *Savannah in the New South: From the Civil War to the Twenty-First Century.* Columbia: University of South Carolina Press, 2018.

Gamble, Thomas. "Georgia Miscellany." Vol. 4. Unpublished manuscript, Bull Street Library, n.d.

Gannon, Michael. *Rebel Bishop: The Life and Era of Augustin Verot.* Milwaukee:

Gibb, James G., and April M. Beisaw. "Learning Cast up from the Mire: Archaeological Investigations of Schoolhouses in the Northeastern United States." *Northeast Historical Archaeology* 29, no. 1 (2000): 107–29.

Gibbons, James, and M. I. J. Griffin. *Mission Work among the Negroes and the Indians: What Is being Accomplished by Means of the Annual Collection Taken Up for Our Missions.* African American Pamphlet Collection. Baltimore: Foley Bros., Printers, 1893. http://loc.gov/item/92838802.

Gindick, Jon. *Harmonica Americana: History, Instruction and Music for 30 Great American Tunes.* Visalia, Calif.: Cross Harp Press, 1995.

Golden, Kathryn Elise Benjamin. "Through the Muck and Mire: Marronage, Representation, and Memory in the Great Dismal Swamp." PhD dissertation, University of California, Berkeley, 2018.

Green, Hilary. *Educational Reconstruction: African American Schools in the Urban South, 1865–1890.* New York: Fordham University Press, 2016.

Harden, William. *A History of Savannah and South Georgia.* Chicago: Lewis, 1913. Internet Archive, https://archive.org/details/historyofsavanna01hard.

Hoffman's Catholic Directory, Almanac and Clergy List. Vol. 1, no. 1. Milwaukee: Hoffman Bros., 1886. Google Books.

Hoffman's Catholic Directory, Almanac and Clergy List. Vol. 7, no. 1. Milwaukee: Hoffman Bros., 1892. Google Books.

Hoffman's Catholic Directory, Almanac and Clergy List. Vol. 11, no. 1. Milwaukee: Hoffman Bros., 1896. Google Books.

Hoffman's Catholic Directory, Almanac and Clergy List. Vol. 12, no. 1. Milwaukee: M. H. Wiltzius, 1897. Google Books.

Hoffman's Catholic Directory, Almanac and Clergy List. Vol. 14, no. 1. Milwaukee: Hoffman Bros., 1899. Google Books.

Hoffman's Catholic Directory, Almanac and Clergy List. Vol. 15, no. 1. Milwaukee: Hoffman Bros., 1900. Google Books.

Hoskins, Charles Lwanga. *The Trouble They Seen: Profiles in the Life of Col. John Deveaux, 1848–1909.* Savannah: Self-published, 1989.

———. *Yet with a Steady Beat: Biographies of Early Black Savannah.* Savannah: Gullah Press, 2001.

Hull, Kathleen L., and John G. Douglass, eds. *Forging Communities in Colonial Alta California*. Tucson: University of Arizona Press, 2018.

———. "Introduction: Community Formation and Integration in Colonial Contexts." In Hull and Douglass, *Forging Communities in Colonial Alta California*, 3–34.

Johnson, Penny Clarke. "Second Class Students: The First Public School Buildings for African Americans in Savannah, 1872–1914." Master's thesis, Savannah College of Art and Design, 2016.

Johnson, Whittington B. *Black Savannah, 1788–1864*. Fayetteville: University of Arkansas Press, 1996.

Jones, Emily. "Student Archaeologists Dig Up History of Skidaway's Freedmen's School." Georgia Public Broadcasting, May 2, 2017; updated August 14, 2020. http://gpb .org/news/2017/05/02/student-archaeologists-dig-history-of-skidaways-freedmens -school.

Jones, Jacqueline. *Saving Savannah: The City and the Civil War*. New York: Alfred A. Knopf, 2008.

———. *Soldiers of Light and Love: Northern Teachers and Georgia Blacks, 1865–1873*. Fred W. Morrison Series in Southern Studies. Athens: Brown Thrasher Books, University of Georgia Press, 1980.

———. "Wartime Workers, Moneymakers: Black Labor in Civil War–Era Savannah." In *Slavery and Freedom in Savannah*, edited by Daina Ramey Berry and Leslie M. Harris, 161–84. Athens: University of Georgia Press, 2014.

Jung, Ellie. "Mother Mathilda Beasley, O.S.F.: Georgia's First Black Nun." Hidden Histories Online Exhibit, Georgia Historical Society, 2018. http://georgiahistory.com /education-outreach/historical-markers/hidden-histories/mother-mathilda-beasley -o-s-f-georgias-first-black-nun.

Kelly, V. E. *A Short History of Skidaway Island*. Savannah: Branigar Organization, 1980.

King, Barbara. "Georgia Catholics Rejoice at Mother Katharine's Beatification." *Southern Cross*, November 17, 1988.

King Taylor, Susie. *Reminiscences of My Life in Camp with the 33rd United States Colored Troops, Late 1st S.C. Volunteers*. Self-published, 1902.

Krampert, Peter. *The Encyclopedia of the Harmonica*. Arlington Heights, Ill.: Tatanka, 1998.

Kryder-Reid, Elizabeth. "'With Manly Courage': Reading the Construction of Gender in a 19th-Century Religious Community." In Scott, *Those of Little Note*, 97–114.

Kurtz, Elma S., Editor. "Hanleiter War Diary II: March 16, 1862–June 4, 1862." *Atlanta Historical Bulletin* 14, no. 4 (December 1969): 52–99.

———. "War Diary of Cornelius R. Hanleiter: Georgia Light Artillery, Army of Tennessee, C.S.A, Jo Thompson Artillery." *Atlanta Historical Bulletin* 14, no. 3 (September 1969): 8–101.

Kytle, Ethan J., and Blain Roberts. *Denmark Vesey's Garden: Slavery and Memory in the Cradle of Confederacy*. New York: New Press, 2018.

Lamm, Ruth, Beatrice and Lester Lorah, Helen W. Schuler, Lillian Smith Albert, and Jane Ford Smith. *Guidelines for Collecting China Buttons*. Hightstown, N.J.: National Button Society, 1970.

Landon, David B., Teresa Dujnic, Kate Descoteaux, Susan Jacobucci, Darios Felix, Marisa Patalano, Ryan Kennedy, et al. "Investigating the Heart of a Community: Archaeological Excavations at the African Meeting House, Boston, Massachusetts." Andrew Fiske Memorial Center for Archaeological Research Publications no. 22, 2007. https://scholarworks.umb.edu/fiskecenter_pubs/2/.

Lindbergh, Jennie. "Buttoning Down Archaeology." *Australasian Historical Archaeology* 17 (1999): 50–57.

Lindsey, Bill, site manager. "Bottle Bases." Updated May 21, 2022. https://sha.org/bottle/bases.htm.

———. "Bottle Finishes & Closures." Updated May 21, 2022. http://sha.org/bottle/finishstyles2.htm#Crown.

———. "Historic Glass Bottle Identification & Information Website." Updated May 21, 2022. https://sha.org/bottle.

Litts, Elyce. *The Collector's Encyclopedia of Geisha Girl Porcelain*. Paducah, Ky.: Collector Books, 1988.

Litwack, Leon F. *Trouble in Mind: Black Southerners in the Age of Jim Crow*. New York: Vintage Books, 1998.

Lockhart, Bill, Beau Schriever, Bill Lindsey, Carol Serr, and Bob Brown. "William Franzen & Son." Updated August 3, 2020. http://sha.org/bottle/pdffiles/WilliamFranzen&Son.pdf.

Lockhart, Bill, Carol Serr, David Whitten, Bill Lindsey, and Pete Schulz. "The Dating Game: Whitall Tatum & Co." *Bottles and Extras*, Summer 2006,: 2–14. http://sha.org/bottle/pdffiles/WTandCo_BLockhart.pdf.

Mann, Isabel. "Benedictine Missionaries and the Intersection of Religion and Race on Skidaway Island, Georgia." Master's thesis, University of Georgia, 2018.

Martin Seibert, Erika Kristine. "Hidden in Plain View: African American Archaeological Landscapes at Manassas National Battlefield Park." PhD dissertation, University of Maryland, College Park, 2010.

McDonogh, Gary W. *Black and Catholic in Savannah, Georgia*. Knoxville: University of Tennessee Press, 1993.

Mensing, Raymond C. "The Rise and Fall of the Pseudo Poor Clare Nuns of Skidaway Island." *Georgia Historical Quarterly* 61, no. 4 (1977): 318–28.

Meyer, Ferdinand. "Solomon's Strengthening & Invigorating Bitters—Savannah, Ga." Updated December 18, 2012. Peachridge Glass. http://peachridgeglass.com/2012/08/solomons-strengthening-bitters-invigorating-bitters-savannah-ga.

Mitchell, Mary Niall. *Raising Freedom's Child: Black Children and Visions of the Future after Slavery*. New York: New York University Press, 2008.

Moosmüller, Oswald, O.S.B. *Ersabt Bonifaz Wimmer, O.S.B.* 1891. Translated by Maria Von Mickwitz and Warren Murrman. Latrobe, Pa.: Archabbey, 2019.

Morris, Annelise. "Materialities of Homeplace." *Historical Archaeology* 51 (2017): 28–42.

Mullins, Paul. "Racializing the Parlor: Race and Victorian Bric-a-Brac Consumption." In *Race and the Archaeology of Identity*, edited by Charles Orser, 158–76. Salt Lake City: University of Utah Press, 2001.

Murphy, Fiona. "Archives of Removal." *Otherwise*, no. 6 (May–July 2022). http://otherwisemag.com/removal.

Murray, A. K., and A. B. Howland. "Improved Argand-Lamp for Burning Petroleum." United States Patent Office, Letters Patent No. 73,455, January 21, 1868. https://patentimages.storage.googleapis.com/f2/1e/97/ffad1d5504dff1/US73455.pdf.

Neuhofer, M. Dorothy, O.S.B. *In the Benedictine Tradition: The Origins and Early Development of Two College Libraries.* Lanham, Md.: University Press of America, 1999.

Newman, Mark. "The Diocese of Savannah and Desegregation, 1935–73." *Catholic Historical Review* 106, no. 2 (Spring 2020): 282–311.

Oetgen, Jerome. *An American Abbot: Boniface Wimmer, O.S.B., 1809–1887.* Rev. ed. Washington, D.C: Catholic University of America Press, 1997.

———. *Mission to America: A History of Saint Vincent Archabbey, the First Benedictine Monastery in the United States.* Washington, D.C: Catholic University of America Press, 2000.

———. "The Origins of the Benedictine Order in Georgia." *Georgia Historical Quarterly* 53, no. 2 (1969): 165–83.

———. "Oswald Moosmüller: Monk and Missionary." *American Benedictine Review* 27, no. 1 (1976): 1–35.

Otto, Albert S. "The Public School System of Savannah and Chatham County." Manuscript, Savannah Chatham County Public School System Board of Education Archives.

Oubre, Claude. *Forty Acres and a Mule.* Baton Rouge: Louisiana State University Press, 1978.

Parden, Bennet. "'Somewhere toward Freedom': Sherman's March and Georgia's Refugee Slaves." *Georgia Historical Quarterly* 101, no. 2 (2017): 115–46.

"Parker Academy: A Place for Freedom, A Space for Resistance." https://parkeracademy-nsfreu.weebly.com.

Perdue, Robert Eugene. *The Negro in Savannah, 1865–1900.* New York: Exposition Press, 1973.

Piechocinski, Elizabeth Carpenter. *Once upon an Island: The Barrier and Marsh Islands of Chatham County, Georgia.* Savannah: Oglethorpe Press, 2003.

Prothero, Stephen. *The American Bible: How Our Words Unite, Divide, and Define a Nation.* New York: Harper One, 2012.

Public Schools of the City of Savannah and County of Chatham. *Thirteenth Annual Report of the Public Schools of the City of Savannah and County of Chatham.* Savannah: Morning News Steam Printing House, 1878. Massie Heritage Center Archives.

———. *Fourteenth Annual Report of the Public Schools of the City of Savannah and County of Chatham*. Savannah: Morning News Steam Printing House, 1879. Massie Heritage Center Archives.

———. *Twenty-Fourth Annual Report of the Public Schools of the City of Savannah and County of Chatham*. Savannah: Morning News Steam Printing House, 1889. Massie Heritage Center Archives.

———. *Twenty-Sixth Annual Report of the Public Schools of the City of Savannah and County of Chatham*. Savannah: Morning News Steam Printing House, 1891. Massie Heritage Center Archives.

———. *Twenty-Seventh Annual Report of the Public Schools of the City of Savannah and County of Chatham*. Savannah: Morning News Steam Printing House, 1892. Massie Heritage Center Archives.

———. *Twenty-Eight Annual Report of the Public Schools of the City of Savannah and County of Chatham*. Savannah: Morning News Steam Printing House, 1893. Massie Heritage Center Archives.

"The Right Reverend John Barry D.D." Former Bishops of the Diocese of Savannah. https://diosav.org/our-bishops/former-bishops.

Rippinger, Joel. "Adapting Benedictine Monasticism to Nineteenth-Century America." *U.S. Catholic Historian* 3, no. 4 (1984): 294–302.

———. *The Benedictine Order in the United States: An Interpretive History*. Collegeville, Minn.: Liturgical Press, 1990.

Rosenfeld, Michael J. *The Age of Independence: Interracial Unions, Same-Sex Unions, and the Changing American Family*. Cambridge, Mass.: Harvard University Press, 2007.

Ross, Douglas E. "Late-Nineteenth- and Early-Twentieth-Century Japanese Domestic Wares from British Columbia." In *Ceramics in America 2012*, edited by Robert Hunter. Milwaukee: Chipstone Foundation, 2012. https://chipstone.org/article.php/515/Ceramics-in-America-2012/Late-Nineteenth—and-Early-Twentieth-Century-Japanese-Domestic-Wares-from-British-Columbia.

Rotman, Deborah L. "Domestic Ideals and Lived Realities: Gendered Social Relations at the Moors House, Deerfield, Massachusetts, 1848–1882." *Historical Archaeology* 53 (2019): 341–53.

———. "Rural Education and Community Social Relations: Historical Archaeology of the Wea View Schoolhouse No. 8, Wabash Township, Tippecanoe County, Indiana." In *The Archaeology of Institutional Life*, edited by April M. Beisaw and James G. Gibb, 69–85. Tuscaloosa: University of Alabama Press, 2009.

Sacred Heart Catholic Church. "About Our Parish." Savannah. https://www.sacredheartsavannah.org/about-our-parish.

Sadliers' Catholic Directory, Almanac, Ordo. Vol. 1879. New York: D & J Sadlier, 1879. Google Books.

Sadliers' Catholic Directory, Almanac, Ordo. Vol. 1880. New York: D & J Sadlier, 1880. Google Books.

Sadliers' Catholic Directory, Almanac, Ordo. Vol. 1881. New York: D & J Sadlier, 1881. Google Books.

Sadliers' Catholic Directory, Almanac, Ordo. Vol. 1883. New York: D & J Sadlier, 1883. Google Books.

Sadliers' Catholic Directory, Almanac, Ordo. Vol. 1884. New York: D & J Sadlier, 1884. Google Books.

Sadliers' Catholic Directory, Almanac, Ordo. Vol. 1885. New York: D & J Sadlier, 1885. Google Books.

Sadliers' Catholic Directory, Almanac, Ordo. Vol. 1886. New York: D & J Sadlier, 1886. Google Books.

Sadliers' Catholic Directory, Almanac, Ordo. Vol. 1887. New York: D & J Sadlier, 1887. Google Books.

Sadliers' Catholic Directory, Almanac, Ordo. Vol. 1888. New York: D & J Sadlier, 1888. Google Books.

Sadliers' Catholic Directory, Almanac, Ordo. Vol. 1889. New York: D & J Sadlier, 1889. Google Books.

Sadliers' Catholic Directory, Almanac, Ordo. Vol. 1890. New York: D & J Sadlier, 1890. Google Books.

Sadliers' Catholic Directory, Almanac, Ordo. Vol. 1891. New York: D & J Sadlier, 1891. Google Books.

Sadliers' Catholic Directory, Almanac, Ordo. Vol. 1893. New York: D & J Sadlier, 1893. Google Books.

Sadliers' Catholic Directory, Almanac, Ordo. Vol. 1894. New York: D & J Sadlier, 1894. Google Books.

Sadliers' Catholic Directory, Almanac, Ordo. Vol. 1895. New York: D & J Sadlier, 1895. Google Books.

Sanborn Map & Publishing Co. *Insurance Maps of Savannah, Georgia, 1888*. Sanborn Fire Insurance Maps for Georgia Towns and Cities, 1884–1941. Digital Library of Georgia. https://dlg.usg.edu/record/dlg_sanb_savannah-1888#item.

———. *Insurance Maps of Savannah, Georgia, 1916*. Sanborn Fire Insurance Maps for Georgia Towns and Cities, 1884–1941. Digital Library of Georgia. https://dlg.usg.edu record/dlg_sanb_savannah-1916#item.

—. *Savannah, Georgia, March 1884*. Sanborn Fire Insurance Maps for Georgia Towns Cities, 1884–1941. Digital Library of Georgia. https://dlg.usg.edu/record sanb_savannah-1884#item.

-Perris Map Co. *Insurance Maps of Savannah, Georgia, 1898*. Sanborn Fire nce Maps for Georgia Towns and Cities, 1884–1941. Digital Library of Georgia. dlg.usg.edu/record/dlg_sanb_savannah-1898?canvas=0&x=2493&y v=9239.

W. "The Coal-Oil Lamp." *Agricultural History: A Special Issue: Artifacts in* no. 2 (Spring 2018): 190–209.

Schiffer, Nancy N. *Japanese Export Ceramics: 1860–1920*. Atglen, Pa.: Schiffer, 2000.

Scott, Elizabeth M., ed. *Those of Little Note: Gender, Race, and Class in Historical Archaeology*. Tucson: University of Arizona Press, 1994.

Seifert, Laura. *"A Horror of Farm Work": Freedmen School Students and Benedictine Monks on Skidaway Island, 9Ch78, Final Report*. Digging Savannah, Armstrong Campus of Georgia Southern University, 2018. https://savarchaeoalliance.files.wordpress.com/2018/06/monastery-and-school-final-report_11june2018.pdf.

Sherman, William T. *Memoirs of General William T. Sherman*. Vol. 2. New York: D. Appleton, 1889.

Simms, James M. *The First Colored Baptist Church in North America. Constituted at Savannah, Georgia, January 20, A.D. 1788. With Biographical Sketches of the Pastors*. Philadelphia: J. B. Lippincott, 1888. Electronic ed., 2000. https://docsouth.unc.edu/church/simms/simms.html.

Smith, Marvin T., and Daniel Elliott. *Archaeological Survey for the Landings Development, Chatham County, Georgia*. Report by Garrow and Associates, 1985. Report no. 721 Laboratory of Archaeology, University of Georgia. https://archaeology.uga.edu/gasf/report/721.

Smith, Monica L. "The Archaeology of a 'Destroyed' Site: Surface Survey and Historical Documents at the Civilian Conservation Corps Camp, Bandelier National Monument, New Mexico." *Historical Archaeology* 35, no. 2 (June 2001): 31–40.

The Southeastern Reporter. Vol. 31. St. Paul: West, 1899.

Spencer-Wood, Suzanne M. "Diversity and Nineteenth Century Domestic Reform: Relationships among Classes and Ethnic Groups." In Scott, *Those of Little Note*, 175–208.

Sprague, Roderick. "China or Prosser Button Identification and Dating." *Historical Archaeology* 36 no. 2 (2002):111–27.

Struchtemeyer, Dena L. "Separate but Equal?: The Archaeology of an Early Twentieth-Century African American School." Master's thesis, Louisiana State University and Agricultural and Mechanical College, 2008.

Swanson, Drew A. *Remaking Wormsloe Plantation: The Environmental History of a Lowcountry Landscape*. Athens: University of Georgia Press, 2012.

Taylor, Kay Ann. "Mary S. Peake and Charlotte L. Forten: Black Teachers during the Civil War and Reconstruction." *Journal of Negro Education* 74, no. 2 (Spring 2005): 124–37.

Thuro, Catherine. *Oil Lamps: The Kerosene Era in North America*. Paducah, Ky.: Collector Books, 1976.

Towne, Laura M. *Letters and Diary of Laura M. Towne: Written from the Sea Islands of South Carolina, 1862–1884*. Edited by Rupert Sargent Holland. Cambridge: Riverside Press, 1912.

Tyack, David, and Robert Lowe. "The Constitutional Moment: Reconstruction and Black Education in the South." *American Journal of Education* 94, no. 2 (February 1986): 236–56.

United States Census Bureau. "Availability of 1890 Census—History—U.S. Census Bu-

reau." https://www.census.gov/history/www/genealogy/decennial_census_records
/availability_of_1890_census.html.

Vance, Liza M., Sharyn Jones, and William Landon. "Persistence of Equality through Daily
Life at the Parker Academy: New Insights from Archaeological and Archival Research."
Paper presented at the Society for Historical Archaeology annual conference, St.
Charles, Mo., January 9–12, 2019.

Wagner, Laura. "In Final Report, Experts Identify Remains at Notorious Reform School."
NPR, Updated January 21, 2016. https://www.npr.org/sections/thetwo-way/2016/01
/21/463846093/in-final-report-experts-identify-remains-at-notorious-reform-school.

Wall, Diana diZerega. "Examining Gender, Class, and Ethnicity in Nineteenth-Century
New York City." *Historical Archaeology* 33, no. 1 (1999): 102–17.

Weaver, Robert M., ed. *The Other Side of Sandpoint: Early History and Archaeology beside
the Tracks.* Vol. 1, *Sandpoint Stories.* Sandpoint Archaeology Project, 2006–2013. Port-
land, Ore.: SWCA Environmental Consultants, January 31, 2014.

Weisbuch, Claude. "Historical Perspective on the Physics of Artificial Lighting." *Comptes
Rendus Physique* 19, no. 3 (March 2018): 89–112.

Wells-Bacon, Mary. "The Life of Mathilda Beasley." Savannah Biographies no. 16. Georgia
Southern University, 1987. http://digitalcommons.georgiasouthern.edu/sav-bios
-lane/16.

Wettstaed, James R. "Perspectives on the Early-Nineteenth-Century Frontier Occupations
of the Missouri Ozarks." *Historical Archaeology* 37, no. 4 (December 2003): 97–114.

Wilkie, Laurie A. "Archaeological Evidence of an African-American Aesthetic." *African
Diaspora Archaeology Newsletter* 1 no. 1 (April 1994). ScholarWorks@UMass Amherst.
https://scholarworks.umass.edu.

Williams, Heather Andrea. *Self-Taught: African American Education in Slavery and Freedom.* Chapel Hill: University of North Carolina Press, 2005.

Williams, Shannen Dee. *Subversive Habits: Black Catholic Nuns in the Long African American Freedom Struggle.* Durham, N.C.: Duke University Press, 2022.

Wimmer, Boniface. *Boniface Wimmer: Letters of an American Abbot.* Edited by Jerome
Oetgen. Latrobe, Pa: Saint Vincent Archabbey Publications, 2008.

———. "The Letters of Boniface Wimmer, O.S.B." Vol. 3, "1872–1887." Edited by Jerome
Oetgen. Draft. Unpublished manuscript, Saint Vincent Archabbey Archives, 2000.

Index

Ackerman, Ignatius, 80–81
American Missionary Association (AMA):
    in Savannah, 19, 22–23, 27–28, 57, 142; in
    South Carolina, 139; teachers, 16, 26, 32
Anderson, Joseph, 44, 48–49, 55, 65, 70
Anderson Street School, 30, 142
archaeology: of schools, 4–7, 145n7, 154n65;
    survey, 2–3, 59–60, 141–43

Bacon, Joseph, 55, 122
Bacon, Sarah Jane, 121, 168n213
baptism: in Savannah, 41, 46, 122, 131; on
    Skidaway, 103, 109–10, 120, 133
Barry, John, 8
Beach Institute, 22, 27–30, 40, 123, 142,
    149–50n60
Beasley, Abraham, 46, 114
Beasley, Mathilda, 17, 85, 114–20
Becker, Thomas, 104–5, 108, 111, 116, 119–20
Belmont Abbey. See St. Mary Help Priory
Benedictine College, 129, 130
Benedictine Military School, 1–2, 130, 132,
    133, 143
Benedictine Order in Georgia, 48, 85, 121,
    128, 129, 136
Bergier, Gabriel, 43–47, 55; recruiting
    brothers, 49, 57, 65–66, 71, 93; Savannah
    school, 97, 111, 134
Black Catholic lay congress, 71
blue-back speller, 20–21
bullets, archaeological, 98–99
buttons, archaeological, 6, 123–24,
    168–69n222

Canonge, Rhabanus, 67–69, 71, 75, 136
Cassidy, Philip, 44, 97

Cedar Grove Plantation (Orangedale
    Plantation), 8
cemetery, 98, 131, 162n57, 170n256
ceramics, archaeological, 71–72, 125–27,
    157nn160–61
Chaney, Robert, 132
climate crisis, 143
confirmation, 103, 136
conversion, 41, 48, 136; on Skidaway, 33, 71,
    79, 109–10, 136–37
Creagh, Cyprian, 97, 106–7
culture shock, 78–80
curriculum, 19, 130, 139–40; Skidaway school,
    39, 74, 134–36

DeRenne, George Wymberley, 15, 29–30, 53,
    150n66
Der Geschichtsfreund, 83, 85–88, 100, 137
desegregation, 132
Deveaux, Catherine, 17
domestic labor, 48, 50–51, 54, 66–70, 101, 131
Donlon, Patrick, 106, 134, 170n1
Dorsey, James, 57, 66
Drexel, Katharine, 116, 118–19
Du Bois, W. E. B., 77, 135
Dupon, Stephen F., 32, 49, 52; helping monks,
    80, 98, 110, 121; property donation, 44, 47

Eckert, Fridolin, 45–46, 80

Fair Lawn Public School, 28, 30, 141
farm labor: African Americans, 13, 15, 101, 110,
    121–22; Catholics, 50–52, 58, 66, 72–74, 85
finances, 54, 85, 88, 92–93, 107, 136
First African Baptist Church, 23, 26, 143
First Bryan Baptist Church, 12, 23, 143

Printed in the USA
CPSIA information can be obtained
at www.ICGtesting.com
CBHW021007260924
14923CB00009B/34